Change in the Amazon Basin
Volume I:

Man's impact on forests and rivers

Symposium held at
the 44th International Congress of
Americanists, Manchester
6–10 September 1982

CHANGE IN THE AMAZON BASIN

VOLUME I:

Man's impact on forests and rivers

Edited by JOHN HEMMING,
Director and Secretary,
Royal Geographical Society, London

Manchester University Press

Published by Manchester University Press
Oxford Road, Manchester M13 9PL
and 51 Washington Street, Dover
New Hampshire 03820, USA

British Library cataloguing in publication data

Change in the Amazon basin.
   Vol. 1: Man's impact on forests and rivers
   1. Amazon valley – Economic conditions
   I. Hemming, John
   330.981'106   HC188.A5

Library of Congress cataloging in publication data

Main entry under title:

Change in the Amazon basin.

   Organized by the Royal Geographical Society.
   Includes bibliographies and indexes.
   Contents: v. 1. Man's impact on forests and rivers –
v. 2. The frontier after a decade of colonisation.
   1. Land settlement – Amazon River Region – Congresses.
2. Agricultural colonies – Amazon River Region – Congresses.   3. Amazon River Region – Population – Congresses.
4. Man – Influence on nature – Amazon River Region – Congresses.   5. Indians of South America – Amazon River Region – Congresses.   6. Deforestation – Amazon River Region – Congresses.   I. Hemming, John, 1935– . II. International Congress of Americanists (44th : 1982 : Manchester, Greater Manchester) III. Royal Geographical Society.
HD499.A45C47   1985   330.981'1   85–873

ISBN 0–7190–0967–7 (v. 1)
ISBN 0–7190–0968–5 (v. 2)

Photoset in Great Britain
by Northern Phototypesetting Co, Bolton
Printed in Great Britain
by Unwin Brothers Ltd
The Gresham Press
Old Woking, Surrey
A member of the Martins Printing Group

Contents

The Plates illustrating chapters 9 and 10 appear between pp. 132 and 133

List of contributors

JANIS B. ALCORN
Department of Botany, University of Texas

EXPEDITO ARNAUD
Museu Paraense Emílio Goeldi, Belém

C. J. BARROW
Centre for Development Studies, University of Wales, Swansea

WILLIAM M. DENEVAN
Department of Geography, University of Wisconsin, Madison

JULIE DENSLOW
Department of Botany, University of Wisconsin, Madison

PHILIP M. FEARNSIDE
National Institute for Amazonian Research (INPA), Manaus

SALVADOR FLORES PAITÁN
Soils Laboratory, National University of Peruvian Amazonia, Iquitos

WOLFRAM FRANKEN
National Institute for Amazonian Research (INPA), Manaus

JOHN GARDNER
Dover, Delaware

ROBERT GOODLAND
The World Bank, Washington DC

PAULO RODOLFO LEOPOLDO
Faculty of Agronomic Sciences, University of the State of São Paulo
(UNESP), Botucatú

THOMAS E. LOVEJOY
World Wildlife Fund, Washington DC

EIICHI MATSUI
Environmental Sciences Division, Centre of Nuclear Energy in
Agriculture (CENA), Piracicaba, São Paulo

ARMANDO DIAS MENDES
ANPEC, Brasília

THOMAS P. MYERS
Division of Anthropology, University of Nebraska, Lincoln

CHRISTINE PADOCH
New York Botanical Garden

DARRELL A. POSEY
Centre of Anthropological and Folklore Research, Federal University of
Maranhão, São Luis

GHILLEAN T. PRANCE
New York Botanical Garden

HARALD SIOLI
Max Planck Institute for Limnology, Plön, Federal Republic of Germany

ROBERT F. SKILLINGS
The World Bank, Washington DC

JOHN M. TREACY
Department of Geography, University of Wisconsin, Madison

BARBARA WEINSTEIN
Department of History, State University of New York, Stony Brook

Acronyms

ABA	Associação Brasileira de Antropologia (Brazilian Association of Anthropologists)
BID	Banco Interamericano de Desarrollo (Interamerican Development Bank)
BNH	Banco Nacional da Habitação
CAPEMI	Caixa de Peculio dos Militares (Military Pension Fund)
CATIE	Centro Agronómico Tropical de Investigación y Enseñanza (Turrialba, Costa Rica)
CIAT	Centro Internacional de Agricultura Tropical (International Centre for Tropical Agriculture, Cali, Colombia)
CIU	Comité de Iglesias Unidas (Bolivia)
CLAG	Conference of Latin American Geographers
CNPq	Conselho Nacional de Desenvolvimento Científico e Tecnológico (National Council for Scientific and Technological Development)
CVRD	Companhia Vale do Rio Doce (Rio Doce Valley Corporation)
DNER	Departamento Nacional de Estradas e Rodagem (National Highways Department)
Eletronorte	Centrais Eletricas do Norte do Brasil (North Brazil Electricity Board)
EMBRAPA	Empresa Brasileira de Pesquisa Agropecuária (Brazilian Agricultural Research Institute, Ministry of Agriculture)
FIBGE	Fundação IBGE (Brazil)
FUNAI	Fundação Nacional do Indio (National Indian Foundation; Ministry of Interior)
GEAMAM	Grupo de Estudos e Assessoramento de Meio Ambiente (Environmental Study and Assessment Group of CVRD)
IBDF	Instituto Brasileiro do Desenvolvimento Florestal (Brazilian Institute for Forest Development; Ministry of Agriculture)
IBGE	Instituto Brasileiro de Geografia e Estatística (Brazilian Institute of Geography and Statistics)
IBRD	International Bank for Reconstruction and Development (World Bank)
IERAC	Instituto Ecuatoriano de Reforma

IFC	International Finance Corporation (World Bank affiliate investing in the private sector)
ILV	Instituto Linguístico del Verano
INC	Instituto Nacional de Colonización (Bolivia)
INCRA	Instituto Nacional de Colonização e Reforma Agrária (National Institute for Colonisation and Agrarian Reform)
INCRAE	Instituto Nacional de Colonización del Región Amazónica del Ecuador
INPA	Instituto Nacional de Pesquisas da Amazônia (National Institute for Amazonian Research; of CNDCT)
INPES	Instituto de Pesquisas (Brazil)
IPEA	Instituto de Planejamento Econômico e Social (Institute of Economic Planning)
IPLAN	Instituto de Planejamento (Brazil)
IVIC	Instituto Venezolano de Investigaciones Cientificas
KfW	Kreditanstalt für Wiederaufbau (West German Reconstruction Bank)
MINTER	Ministério do Interior (Brazil)
NAEA	Núcleo do Altos Estudos Amazónicos (Belém, Brazil)
Polonoroeste	Programa Integrado de Desenvolvimento do Noroeste do Brasil (Northwest Region Integrated Development Programme)
SEMA	Secretaria Especial do Meio Ambiente (Special Environmental Secretariat, Ministry of Interior)
SEPLAN	Secretaria de Planejamento da Presidência da República (Brazil)
SUDAM	Superintendência de Desenvolvimento da Amazônia (Amazonian Development Superintendency)
SUDECO	Superintendência do Desenvolvimento da Região Centro-Oeste (Superintendency for the Development of the Centre-West Region)
SUDENE	Superintendência do Desenvolvimento do Nordeste (Superintendency for the Development of the Northeast)
UFPa	Universidade Federal do Pará (Belém, Brazil)

Introduction

When Professor Emilio Moran chaired the first session of the symposium 'Change in the Amazon Basin' he announced that he was opening the largest conference ever organised about the world's largest river. The symposium was staged by the Royal Geographical Society as its contribution to the 44th International Congress of Americanists in Manchester, 6–10 September 1982. Thirty-five papers were presented at this symposium and they are published in two volumes. Restrictions of space have made it necessary to publish eight of these papers in summary only.

This volume *Man's Impact on Forests and Rivers* deals with giant projects, with physical geographical aspects of change, and with indigenous use of the tropical rainforest environment. There are summaries of papers on historical themes and on Indian acculturation.

The companion volume *The Frontier after a Decade of Colonisation* looks at the results of Brazil's Programme of National Integration, launched with the start of the Transamazon Highway in late 1970, and similar colonisation schemes in other Amazon countries. It has analyses of demographic change, case histories of frontier communities, appraisal of government development agencies, and studies of native societies' problems of acculturation and nutrition.

Giant projects

The symposium opened by considering forces of change in the Amazon at two important levels: giant projects and individual settlers. Professor Emeritus Armando Mendes, speaking in elegant Portuguese, set the theme by discussing the effect of giant projects on human life. He and the two speakers from the World Bank, Robert Goodland and Robert Skillings, described three vast enterprises that will soon transform parts of Amazonia: the huge Tucuruí hydroelectric dam on the lower Tocantins, the biggest dam solely in Brazil, and one that will flood the largest area of rainforest ever destroyed by such a scheme; the Serra dos Carajás iron-ore strip mine, with its attendant 800 km railway to São Luis do Maranhão, all of superlative size by world standards; and the Noroeste colonisation programme for Rondônia, a huge amalgam of settlement schemes, nature reserves and Indian reserves.

These speakers were encounraged by the dramatic change of heart by the Brazilian authorities during the past decade. There has been a '180-degree' change away from Brazil's attitude at the Stockholm Conference when it propounded development progress at all costs regardless of pollution and environmental havoc. Incentives for destroying forest and introducing cattle into Amazonia have ceased.

The new Código Forestal and a network of new nature reserves are attempting to preserve at least part of the precious rainforests and their biome. The planners of the three giant projects under discussion have made strenuous efforts to mitigate their adverse effects on the environment.

This optimistic attitude was strongly questioned during discussion. Professor Feder would not allow the World Bank speakers to describe the continuing destruction of the forests and poverty of the *caboclos* as 'environmental progress'. Dr Townsend feared that the apparent change of heart by the authorities was mere window-dressing. The debate revolved around the validity of the improvements, and whether the Brazilian government should be praised – as in the recent Paul Getty Conservation Prize, to Paulo Nogueira Neto and Dr Maria Tereza Jorge Padua – or kept under international attack for environmental crimes.

The impact of the Tucuruí dam and Carajás mining projects on local Tupi-speaking Indian tribes was the subject of a paper by Expedito Arnaud. He drew on his many years of experience to describe the terrible recent history of contact with the Parakanã, Asurini and other groups living between the lower Xingu and Tocantins. He pressed for the creation of a reserve territory for these threatened tribes.

Environmental destruction

Three important papers, by Sioli, Lovejoy and Fearnside, warned of environmental dangers that could result from unrestrained human occupation of Amazonia. Amazon soils are extremely poor in nutrients because of the nearly closed nutrient cycle in its forests. The living biomass recycles virtually all the nutrients of the forest ecosystem. It does this through its biological diversity, optimum utilisation of nutrients by a large number of species, and rapid and efficient nutrient capture by the dense but shallow root systems.

There was considerable discussion on rainfall and riverine hydrology, notably in a fine paper by Leopoldo, Franken and Matsui. It was stressed that only half Amazon rainfall comes from the Atlantic Ocean: the other half is generated by the forest itself. This transpiration would decline dramatically if rainforest is felled and converted to pasture or secondary forest. The forest canopy was shown to intercept some 19 per cent of rain that fell upon it. Further urgent research is needed into forest hydrology, with resulting protective measures, if an irreversible drying process is to be avoided.

Interruption of the rainforest's closed nutrient cycle leads inevitably to nutrient loss through leaching and erosion. Deforestation will reduce annual rainfall and make rains more seasonal. Increased surface runoff, resulting from exposure of forest soil, will increase river sediment, and lower rivers will also be more liable to sudden flooding. Soil degradation after forest clearing includes leaching of cations, soil compaction, erosion of upper layers and, sometimes, laterisation. There is also acute concern about the loss of genetic diversity by the extinction of species and entire ecosystems.

One urgent response is the identification of centres of endemism and biological refuges, and the creation of a chain of forest reserves to protect the largest possible number of species. This is hampered by the rudimentary state of biological inventories and studies of forest ecosystems. Most species are not yet defined. Little is known about their distribution. There was praise by speakers for the eight million km² of reserves and biological stations decreed by the Brazilian government since 1980. Some of the research programmes of INPA (Instituto Nacional de Pesquisas da Amazônia) were also commended. But an immense amount of additional research is needed rapidly. Various speakers showed that the '50% law' (requiring retention of areas of forest equal to cleared Amazon rainforest land) is not being enforced or observed. It is also often inadequate for the rainforest ecosystem to survive.

Another policy that could save rainforest on Amazonian *terra firme* would be greater use of the *várzea* floodplain. Dr Barrow said that *várzea* covers 64 000 km² and is less than 2 per cent of the area of Amazonia, but its fertility gives it great potential, particularly for growing rice. Its crops are easily accessible to river transport. It also has potential for farming fish, turtles, alligators or rodents such as capybaras. But exploitation of flooded *várzea* demands difficult changes in prejudices and preconceptions among developers and settlers used to farming a dry land. Dr Lovejoy also warned that excessive cultivation of *várzea* would interfere with nutrient and reproductive cycles of plants and fish that depend on annual flooding of riverine forests.

Indigenous agriculture

Three speakers showed convincingly that there are many lessons to be learned from tribal Indians. Professor Darrell Posey's work with the Kayapó of southern Pará showed dramatically that Indians exploit and manipulate their forests far more intensively than would be obvious to an untrained observer. A Kayapó village is located alongside seven different types of ecosystem zones so that the inhabitants enjoy a full range of forest products. The Indians plant species they want and rearrange the forest along thousands of kilometres of hunting trails. It is essential that Amazon planners learn from this ethnoecology, in order to gain the greatest yield from rainforests without destroying them. This theme was echoed by Dr Prance who described a number of underexploited plants that have long been used by Indians. Western man tries to reduce the number of farmed species or to introduce monoculture, with disastrous results to the complex Amazon ecosystems. Native plants such as babassu palms (for oils), guaraná (for medicinal caffeine), a *Ciccus* for carbohydrate and *Caryocar* for cooking oil, are just a few examples of the treasury of Indian plant knowledge that is being lost through acculturation.

Professor Denevan gave a detailed description of forest manipulation by Bora Indians in Peruvian Amazonia. This tribe uses shifting (or swidden) cultivation. A study of its clearings over a 30-year period showed that the transition from field to fallow is gradual, with certain trees and plants continuing to be managed long after the remainder of a clearing appeared to have been abandoned to the returning forest. Once again, these native lessons are important for any possible Amazon agroforestry.

Historical

Three papers dealt with historical change. Dr Myers sought to locate Omagua groups of the upper Amazon that were described by the earliest Spanish explorers. Professor Weinstein sent a fine historical survey of the rubber boom. She described how working conditions of the independent *seringueiros* became far worse after the influx of Cearense workers fleeing from the droughts of northeastern Brazil of the 1870s. She also illustrated changing attitudes to rubber among the traditional Amazon élite, and how nationalist xenophobia combined with foreign companies' own blunders to cause their rapid failure. Professor Gardner ended the symposium with a beautiful display of paintings of Amazon Indians and Andean scenery by the late-nineteenth-century American artists George Catlin and Frederick Church, but he cast doubt on the veracity and authenticity of Catlin's observations.

The Amazon Basin occupies roughly half the South American continent, and the Amazon is easily the world's largest river. Its basin contains over 60 per cent of surviving tropical rainforests. Within this wilderness and the vast network of Amazonian rivers is a richer diversity of species of flora and fauna than in any other region on earth. The Amazon Basin is suffering more violent and lasting change in the present decade than at any time in its history. Change of this magnitude to such an important but sensitive region is of acute concern, not only to the countries of South America, but to all mankind.

The impetus for the present onslaught is to enrich the Amazonian countries. It was hoped that Amazonia could help to feed and house the poor of these Third World countries. The attempt to colonise the Amazon frontiers is one of the most ambitious settlement programmes of recent times. It was launched into a region whose tribal societies are successfully adapted to their difficult environment, but who are very vulnerable to violent acculturation. For these reasons, the Amazonian settlement experiments provide important lessons in both development and ethnographic studies.

John Hemming
Director and Secretary
Royal Geographical Society
London

1   Brazil's environmental progress in Amazonian development

ROBERT GOODLAND

Introduction

At the 1972 Stockholm Conference on the Human Environment, some countries voiced the view that environmental activities are luxuries impeding development, and that pollution was a sign of the industrialisation they desired. Brazil's official attitude has now turned 180 degrees, according to Dr Paulo Nogueira Neto of SEMA.[1]

In 1982, the world's premier recognition of superlative environmental achievement – the Getty Prize – was awarded to the Brazilian Government's leading environmentalists: Dr Maria Tereza Jorge Padua of IBDF and Dr Paulo Nogueira Neto of SEMA.

These Brazilians share the view that since prevention costs less than cure, developing countries would be wise to allocate scarce resources with more environmental prudence than do richer countries. Furthermore, since tropical environments are more fragile and much damage is irreversible, the case can be made that environmental prudence is even more important than in industrial countries. This conviction is shared to such an extent that 102 developing nations now have environmental ministries or similar top-level agencies, up from eleven in 1972. Brazil's Special Environmental Secretariat (SEMA) was created in October 1973 and formalised a comprehensive National Environmental Policy into law in August 1981.

This paper observes Brazil's *environmental* progress in only one region, Amazonia, and in only three development projects there. In chronological order, these are the Tucuruí hydroproject, the Northwest Region land settlement project, and the Carajás iron ore project (Figure 1). The World Bank is involved only in the last two.[2] This paper specifically does not attempt economic assessment of the developments. Furthermore, this paper outlines progress rather than the far better documented destruction (e.g. Bunker 1981; Fearnside 1982; Hecht 1981; Sioli 1980a, b; Smith 1981a).

The Tucuruí hydroproject

Description of the project

Tucuruí will be Brazil's largest hydroproject, and the world's fourth largest when

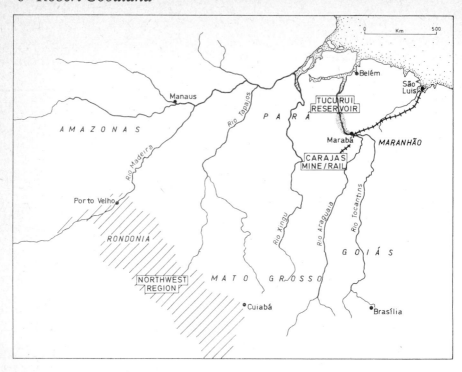

Fig. 1 Map of Amazonia showing location of the three projects

the final installed capacity totals 8000 MW. Itaipu on the Paraná river in southern Brazil will be the world's biggest (12 600 MW), but is half Paraguayan. Tucuruí, the first large hydroproject to be built in Amazonia, is expected to cost US$4 thousand million. The dam will create a 2160 km² reservoir on the Tocantins river 300 km SSW of Belém. The impounded water will back up 200 km almost reaching the town or Marabá (Figure 2). Commercial operation of the first of the twelve 330 MW units is scheduled to start in September 1984.

The first stage will generate almost 4000 MW of power, a base load of 18 500 gigawatt-hours per year. Most of the power will be transmitted at 500 kV to the national grid 385 km east of Imperatriz. A second 500 kV line will power a bauxite alumina smelter under construction at Vila do Conde, 280 km north of the dam. A small 230 kV line will supply the city of Belém, 70 km northeast of the smelter. Some of the power will be consumed by the Carajás iron ore mine in the first stage. The 890 km Carajás iron ore railroad may be electrified in the future. Data on the project are shown in Table 1.

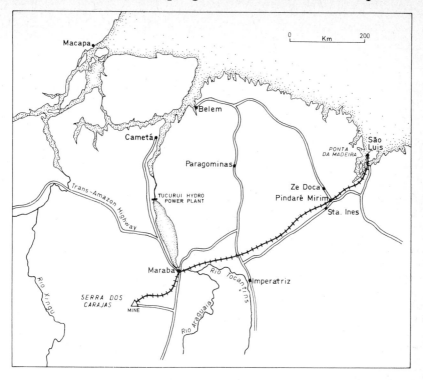

Fig. 2 Map showing the Tucuruí hydroproject and the Carajás iron ore project

Environmental aspects

A rapid but intensive reconnaissance to identify the main environmental aspects of this project was commissioned by Electronorte in 1977.[3] Since then various environmental activities have been contracted out largely to Brazil's National Institute for Amazonian Research (INPA) based in Manaus. Fonseca (1980) outlines the main features of the agreement which includes water quality, fish, aquatic weeds, study of the biota to be lost, decomposition of vegetation, diseases, soils and meteorology. Reports of all this work may be made public in the future. The major environmental aspects are outlined below.

Reservoir clearance

Nearly all the 2160 km² area to be impounded is covered by dense tropical wet forest with a mainly closed canopy about 35 m high. Even when the reservoir is full (72 m above sea level) with a mean depth of 20 m most of the canopy will be exposed. The shallowness of the reservoir and the large volume of the flow means

Table 1   Tucuruí hydroproject statistics

1   Dam

Location: latitude		3° 45′ S
	longitude	49° 41′ W
Distance from Belém (straight line)		300 km
Nominal fall		60.8 m
Firm power (first stage)		2115 MW
Earthfall dam, right bank, length		3420 m
Rockfill Dam, left bank, length		460 m
Left lateral dike		774 m
Right lateral dike		5850 m

2   Reservoir

Area (at 72 m asl)		2160 km^2
Length		200 km
Total volume (at 72 m)		34000 km^3
Live storage		23000 km^3
Normal maximum level		72 m asl
Normal minimum level		58 m asl
Drawdown, maximum		14 m
Average depths (area/volume) at 72 m		20 m
	at 58 m	16 m

3   River

Flow mean (1949–74) at Tucuruí	9208 m^3/s
Flow minimum recorded (8 Oct 1955)	1511 m^3/s
Flow maximum recorded (9 Apr 1957)	51521 m^3/s
Flow mean at mouth	12700 m^3/s
Length (source to mouth)	2900 km
Watershed above dam	767000 km^2

4   Power transmission
Tucuruí to Vila do Conde (3 circuits)

Tension	500 kV
Length	280 km
Width of right of way	100 m

Vila do Conde to Belém (2 circuits)

Tension	230 kV
Length	70 km
Width	100 m

Tucuruí via Marabá to Imperatriz

Tension	500 kV
Length	383 km
Width	100 m

Tucuruí: Marabá to Carajás

Tension	230 kV
Length	180 km
Width	100 m

After Eletronate 1976; Goodland 1977; Mermel 1982.

the retention time of water will be short. A flow of 9000 m^3/s into 43 000 × 10^6 m^3 volume discharging 6900 m^3/s gives a 2-month average retention time. To the extent the water becomes well oxygenated, decomposition of the softer parts of the vegetation is expected to be rapid, except where the water is stagnant.

In 1977, one of the main opportunities perceived was to salvage at least the more valuable timber before it was lost by inundation. The estimated 2.8 million trees and woody stems were calculated at 157 000 m³/ha to occupy 20 million cubic metres of mainly merchantable-quality timber (a figure equivalent to the volume of earth and cement used in the civil works of the dam) belonging to at least 170 named species. Since clearing contracts were let to CAPEMI (Caixa de Peculio dos Militares) only in March 1981, the concern has shifted to water quality related to multiple use of the reservoir and downstream. Rather than turning the forest into a profit (through timber, charcoal, etc.), the concern now focuses on removing enough biomass to ensure that the reservoir does not become eutrophic, dead or dangerous to use. All possibilities are being considered, including use of wood extracted from the reservoir after filling, burning the forest before filling, and even treating the forest with chemical herbicides. This latter controversial possibility was subsequently ruled out. CAPEMI's loan of US$100 million from Lazard Frères who were to have marketed the timber, was terminated in July 1982 'with mutual recriminations' (according to *Journal of Commerce* 12 August 1982), and CAPEMI filed bankruptcy. Estimates on how much biomass to remove range from 100 km² to 1850 km², with little consensus.

Adequate removal of biomass before filling the reservoir is possibly the main environmental issue at present. There is little precedent to guide planners since practically all large reservoirs have been in temperate regions or in grassland, savanna, or areas cleared for agriculture. Although very different, the most similar case is Surinam's 150 000 ha uncleared Brokopondo reservoir which closed in 1964 and was so slow in filling that the spillway was not used for the first 12 years. Alarmed at the rapid spread of waterweed and the production of hydrogen sulphide, the reservoir was aerially sprayed with herbicide, which may have magnified the problem.

Human resettlement

The Tucuruí hydroproject entails the resettlement of 5000 non-Indian families (20–30 000 people) and six small towns. The reservoir will also flood tracts belonging to the Parakanã Reserve; and the Pucuruí Indian Reservation, principally of the Parakatege or Gaviões, has been bisected by the roughly parallel highway PA70, the Tucuruí transmission line from Marabá to Imperatriz, and the Carajás railroad. The last two projects included financial compensation to the Amerindians with their agreement. Eletronorte's legal department is completing thorough cadastral surveys of the other Brazilians to be resettled.

The Northwest Region programme

Description of the programme

Recent history

The Northwest Region of Brazil is officially defined as the area of influence of the 1500 km Cuiabá–Pôrto Velho highway, thus encompassing all of Rondônia and

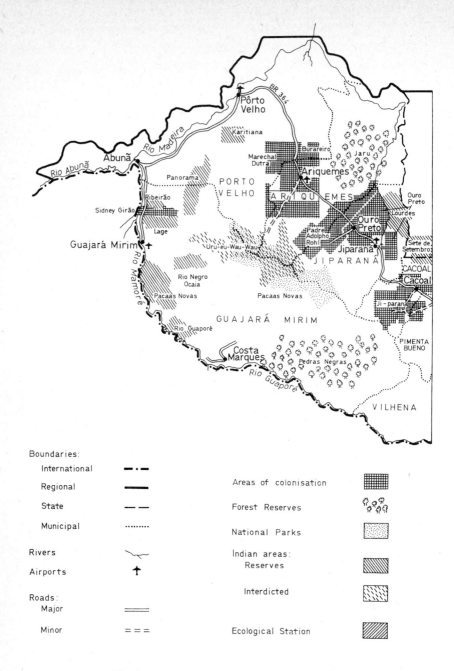

Boundaries:

International   ▬ ▬ · ▬

Regional   ▬▬▬▬

State   ▬ ▬ ▬

Municipal   ········

Rivers

Airports   ✚

Roads:
Major   ═══

Minor   ═ ═ ═

Areas of colonisation

Forest Reserves

National Parks

Indian areas:
Reserves

Interdicted

Ecological Station

Fig. 3 Map of Northwest Region Programme

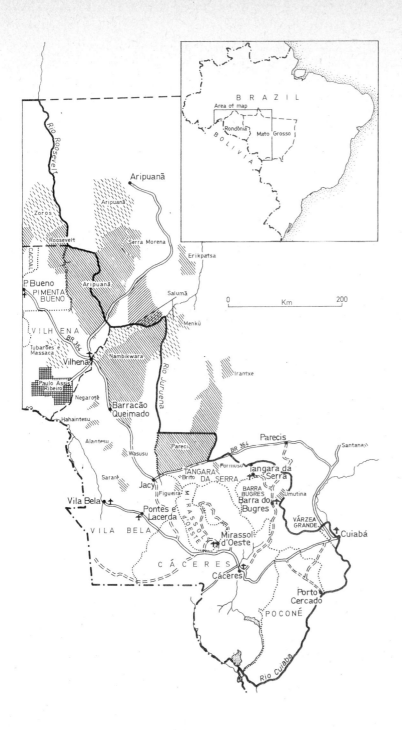

the central and western parts of Mato Grosso (Figure 3). This 410 000 km² area, about three-quarters the size of France, is sparsely populated with 1.2 million people (1981 estimate); less than three inhabitants per square kilometre.

In the early 1900s, Marshal Cândido Rondon joined Cuiabá with Pôrto Velho during construction of the telegraph, and an earth road was built in the 1960s. The road deteriorated and remained closed for weeks during each long rainy season and, even when passable, entailed very high transport costs. Distance, difficulty of access, and an environment less attractive to settlers than more accessible areas kept the region relatively intact until 1970.

Since 1970 the situation has changed dramatically. Powerful forces of frosts killing coffee in São Paulo and Paraná; droughts in the northeast; increase in mechanised export agriculture, particularly soybean production; and large-scale cattle ranching all combined to decrease rural employment and greatly swell the number of migrants. This coincided with the improvement of the BR364 road in 1969, the rapid spread of compelling and largely erroneous rumours of fertile soils in Rondônia, and the plans of INCRA to allot enormous (minimum 100 ha) holdings per family. Annual population growth soared to nearly 16% in Rondônia (a doubling time of less than five years) and almost 8% in Mato Grosso between 1970 and 1980. This was exacerbated by the abandonment in 1974 of official attempts to settle large numbers of people along the Transamazonian Highway (only four years after construction started) in favour of agro-industrial cattle ranching.

By the late 1970s, the Northwest Region was one of the most dynamic in Brazil. With 5000 people arriving per month with few financial resources, little employment, and nowhere to go, the region became volatile and unhealthy, if not dangerous. In 1979, the government invited the World Bank to survey the region, to assess the development potential, and to identify issues concerning possible financing. Following the 1979–80 survey, the Bank decided to help finance part of the Polonoroeste programme, established in May 1981.[4]

Polonoroeste

The Polonoroeste programme is a group of projects budgeted at US$ 1.55 thousand million for the 1981–85 period, of which most (57%) is for BR364, the Cuiabá–Pôrto Velho road. Settlement of new areas (23%), rural development (13%), land tenure services (3%), health (2%), and environmental protection including Amerindian affairs (3%) complete the programme. The highway component is straightforward and is well under way, several sections having been built by the army.

Land settlement, assisted by INCRA, and rural development fostered by the state governments of Rondônia and Mato Grosso establish agricultural colonies and improve existing settlements, aim to reduce crop losses through improved storage and transport, reinforce extension and research, promote use of fertilisers and biocides, regularise and facilitate land tenure and credit, improve education by teacher training and schools, and improve health by water supply, clinics and particularly malaria control. At least one member of every family in Rondônia contracted malaria in 1980 (Mahar 1982b).

Environmental aspects

Zoning

Since the soils of the region are highly variable and largely unsurveyed, appropriate land use can be designated only when soil fertility and land suitability have been ascertained. Therefore a 1:250 000 scale soil and land suitability survey is being carried out by EMBRAPA for all of Rondônia to be completed by 1984. More detailed surveys (1:50 000) will be carried out on the more promising sites revealed by the broader survey. This will enable land use to be more reliably tailored to the carrying capacity of the land, will enable colonies to be more appropriately sited, and should lead to a prudent dimensioning of each land holding.

National forests

Creation of a system of sustained-yield commercial forests in Amazonia, while planned, has yet to be achieved and will, in any event, be a complicated and drawn-out process. A forestry development team has been created within IBDF for research and field studies. Some sites have been identified for forestry development (e.g. the 30 000 ha Fionas forest, east of the Guaporé Biological Reserve). Under the programme, these were to be demarcated, protected, and inventoried, infrastructure to be planned and a pilot operation started. Four new IBDF forest control posts were to be created, staffed, and equipped and the three existing posts be strengthened and operational by the end of 1982. Other project components monitor deforestation from IBDF's Remote Sensing Laboratory, and seek to increase the efficiency of extraction and use of timber, including its possible use as fuel.

Natural reserves

In order to manage in perpetuity some samples of forest and wildlife, a conservation system of eight units (one national park, three biological reserves and four ecological stations, Table 2) totalling two million hectares will be financed by the programme. The main items are demarcation and surveillance of the boundaries of these conservation units, establishment of staffed and equipped control posts, construction of administrative and residential buildings, landing strips, aerial surveys, provision of a four-seater monitoring aircraft and vehicles, in addition to personnel and operating costs for the first five years. In the case of the ecological stations, laboratory and research facilities are included. The 5-year budget for the conservation units and national forests totals US$ 8.9 million.

Ecological research

In view of the complexity of the Amazonian ecosystems and the lack of scientific information about them, it is difficult to design management strategies for these resources. Baseline ecological studies, biotic inventories, hydrometeorological and

Table 2   Northwest Region conservation units

	Name	Type	Area (ha)	Status	Agency
1	Pacaas Novos	National park	764 800	Created, undemarcated	IBDF
2	Guaporé	Biological reserve	500 000	Awaits decree	IBDF
3	Jaru	Biological reserve	268 150	Created, undemarcated	IBDF
4	Cara-Cara	Biological reserve	70 000	Created	IBDF
5	Taiama	Ecological station	12 000	Established	SEMA
6	Serra das Araras	Ecological station	24 000	Acquired, undeveloped	SEMA
7	Ique	Ecological station	200 000	Established	SEMA
8	Cunia	Ecological station	(100 000)	To be negotiated and created	SEMA

1 This park has been found to contain the Uru-eu-wau-wau tribal group which is in process of being contacted for the first time. The whole area has been interdicted from further activity until the contacting process has been achieved and a permanent reserve can be established.
2 The precise boundaries of this reserve have yet to be surveyed and agreed with FUNAI regarding the adjacent Rio Branco Indian Reserve. The northern portion appears to contain highly endemic biota which have yet to be surveyed, owing to difficulty of access.
3 This reserve was reduced by encroachment of cocoa plantations in 1979. Encroachment from the Aripuanã side is possible until the control posts can be established.
4 Cara-Cara is expected to be incorporated into a larger (250 000) Pantanal National Park when IBDF formulates a proposal.
5 Since this is the only field facility for the entire Pantanal, overcrowding will be avoided by the extension provided.
6 This represents the ecozone between *cerrado* (savanna) and forest.
7 Although just outside the programme region, it has been included because it contains the only sample of the transitional (dry) forest available.
8 Flooded '*várzea*' forest, as well as upland forest is represented.

Sources: SEMA and IBDF publications and Bank files.

biogeochemical studies will therefore be included in the research programme. This US$ 7.0 million component will be coordinated by CNDCT (CNPq).

Amerindians

Information on the Amerindians in the Northwest Region is scarce and often contradictory. About 4600 Amerindians live in the 35 officially designated areas listed in Table 3. The total indigenous population of the region is probably 8000, since some tribal groups live outside the official reserve system, have not yet had their territory elevated to official status, or (as in at least two cases, the Uru-eu-wau-wau and the Tubarões-Massacá) the Amerindians have yet to be permanently contacted by the dominant society. There are more than 28 different tribal groups, some of which are closely interrelated. There are 58 Amerindian villages in the region; 26 in Rondônia and 32 in Mato Grosso. These groups differ greatly both in size (e.g. 10 Jabotí people; 1750 Cinta Largas) and in degree of acculturation. Some groups own and operate tractors and may even hire non-tribal labourers, while others are uncontacted or in only intermittent contact with other Brazilians.

Possibly the single most effective action to protect tribal people is to safeguard their lands, which are guaranteed by the constitution of Brazil for their exclusive use in perpetuity. To this end the programme strengthens land protection,[5] Amerindian

Table 3   Northwest Region: official tribal areas

		Population Size	('000 ha)	Status
8th Delegation of FUNAI	Rondônia	2424	2972.1	
	1 Roosevelt [a]	109	233.1	Demarcated
	2 Ribeirão	96	47.9	Demarcated
	3 Lage	162	107.3	Demarcated
	4 Lourdes	379	185.5	Demarcated
	5 Rio Guaporé	170	69.8	Demarcated
	6 Rio Negro Ocaia	193	104.1	Demarcated
	7 Pacaas Novos	621	279.9	Demarcated
	8 Sete de Setembro	109	247.9	Demarcated
	9 Karitiana	77	89.7	Demarcated
	10 Rio Branco	186	240.0	Identified
	11 Karipuna	20	202.0	Identified
	12 Tubarões-Massacá	103	63.0	Identified
	13 Kaxarari	109 (?)	83.0	Identified
	14 Uru-eu-wau-wau	n.a.	878.0	Identified
	15 Serra Morena [b]	89	141.0	Demarcated
	16 Zoros [b]	?	?	Interdicted
	TOTAL	1822	2527.3	
5th Delegation of FUNAI	Mato Grosso			
	17 Negarote [c]	31	12.2	Demarcated
	18 Santana	128	6.3	Demarcated
	19 Bakairi	237	50.0	Demarcated
	20 Umutina	137	24.6	Demarcated
	21 Sararé [c]	23	69.3	Identified
	22 Nambikwara [c]	184	912.0	Delimited
	23 Wasusu [c]	43	13.5	Demarcated
	24 Alantesu [c]	31	10.8	Demarcated
	25 Hahaintesu [c]	56	28.3	Demarcated
	26 Mamaindé [c]	59	63.4	Identified
	27 Saluma	126	640.0	Identified
	28 Irantxe	149	62.0	Delimited
	29 Pareci	416	556.0	Delimited
	30 Brito	19	2.0	Identified
	31 Figueira	12	10.0	Identified
	32 Formoso	58	19.7	Identified
	33 Waikisu [c]	23	?	Being restudied
	34 Menku	100 (?)	47.1	—
	35 Tirecatinga	?	?	—
	TOTAL	4246	5499.4	

[a] Partly in Mato Grosso.
[b] In Mato Grosso.
[c] Nambikwara tribes.

Source: FUNAI, Projeto de Apoio às Communidades Indígenas da Área de Influência da Rodovia Cuiabá/Pôrto Velho, 1980–5 (Brasília, September 1980); FUNAI (28 July 1981 updating).

lands are first marked on maps (delimitation); then they are physically demarcated on the ground (usually by a 6 m wide cleared swath), and accorded official reserve status. The programme accelerates the delimitation and demarcation process, resolves border disputes, evicts illegal settlers from within reserves, and provides surveillance to prevent renewed trespass. The programme provided $ 3.2 million for 3941 km of demarcation by the end of 1982, with additional support for personnel, buildings, boats, vehicles, aircraft and radio equipment. Health will be improved by immunisation campaigns, control of malaria and tuberculosis, augmented clinics and health workers, mobile health teams and epidemic contingency plans. Bilingual schools, teachers, and educational materials will be provided as soon as they are available under a $ 750 000 education component. A $ 5.1 million economic development component is being designed to assist the tribal people, mainly with their own agricultural activities.

Environment opportunities

Since Polonoroeste has scarcely started, it is far too early to assess its success. The forestry, Amerindian, health and conservation components represent major achievements in project design. This section outlines options for further environmental improvements regarding forestry and land use, and describes some of the predictable pitfalls to be avoided.

Forest potential

The major and by far the most valuable renewable resource of the Northwest Region is the forest. Currently, this resource is being expended as capital, rather than the interest on this rich capital being exploited on a sustainable basis. The resource can be used in three main ways:

(a) Cut and burn to create agricultural space.
(b) Cut, use the wood, create agricultural space.
(c) Manage the forest on a sustained-yield basis.

At present, most of the forest is being converted as quickly as possible to production of coffee and cacao and to a few years of rice or other annual crops. After three harvests or so, practically all non-tree forest-replacement crops on all but the most fertile sites will fail without continual use of chemical inputs (fertiliser, biocides), an option too expensive at the moment for most people in this distant region. In fact, one government-sponsored colonisation scheme in Rondônia has not achieved project goals as it was established on infertile soils. After crops fail, the whole area becomes ruinate cattle pasture or is abandoned. Institutional arrangements encourage the depletion of the forest resource. Land titles are sometimes granted after a tract of forest has been cleared, removal of forest being a sign of occupancy. The lots are so big, 100 ha and larger, that their very size encourages rapid depletion of the forest resource. Production of agricultural surpluses for export out of the region can 'mine' the soil, spending capital rather than the renewable interest on the capital resource – forest. These facts could contribute to the problems of the region if not recognised. For example, the view is widely voiced that since most of the banana or rice crop perishes for lack of access to markets, easing of access would solve the problem. From the environmental standpoint, this is questionable because it encourages the production of perishable crops at the expense of a potentially renewable resource. The situation is worse for those families on the more distant plots. It is in the interest of such families to 'mine' the forest resource as quickly as possible. The longer-term interest would be to promote optimal or at least more sustainable land use.

In some cases, the forest is used during the process of being converted to agricultural crops. Encouragement of this process creates significant environmental (and economic) advantages. Extraction of the more valuable timbers, and culling the abundant overmature stands, creates an immediate payoff which can capitalise further activities while preserving future options. Log processing, in this case by sawmills, being brought to the resource improve the results. In practice, the converse is the prevailing pattern: the wood is hauled at great expense in both roads and fuel to a central sawmill. Since sawmills can be mobile and small in size, promotion of sawmills will improve the efficiency and sustainability of resource use. Environmentally, this is such a major opportunity that there is a compelling case for small sawmills to be the basis of all forest settlements in the study area. Such sawmills are cheap to manufacture entirely in Brazil and are easy to maintain: spare parts are rarely required and if they are, they can be made by the local mechanic or blacksmith. The sawmill is easily disassembled and can be carried in manageable parts for assembly on site. There is no reliance on imported fuel which is so expensive in Brazil in general, and even more so in this region. Small-scale steam sawmills generate more and longer-term employment than cutting and burning the forest. The result is a mix of products so valuable they can profitably be exported out of the region, together with products readily saleable locally for housing, furniture, etc. This promotes secondary, forest-based industries, thus decreasing the dependence on sales of perishable agricultural surpluses. One secondary advantage of steam-powered sawmills is the production of nutrient-rich ash which can be used as fertiliser where it is produced, rather than relying totally on distant chemical imports.

Electricity is another bonus of small sawmills. Even the smallest sawmill can provide enough electricity for illumination. All but the smallest can generate electric power for processing timber into building materials on site. Such sawmills are easily run from floating barges. Settlement based on fluvial access will avoid the onerous expense of road construction and maintenance, while promoting more fuel-efficient transport modes.

Provision for using the resource in sustained-yield forest management have been noted in the section on national forests (p. 13). Promotion of forest management and forest-based industries as provided for in the Polonoroeste programme are likely to prove sustainable activities and will improve long-term development prospects significantly. In summary, from the longer-term environmental point of view, the most sustainable development model for this region is forest-based, with a significant component of perennial crops for export, together with subsistence cultivation of annual crops. This is likely to be more sustainable than the emphasis on soil-depleting, perishable annual crops.

Land use

Since physiography, moisture and fertility throughout the region are highly heterogeneous, 'geometrical grid planning' is environmentally wasteful of land and expensive in the use of resources. Optimal land use can be achieved by relying on the land suitability classification which is being provided for (p. 12) under the Polonoroeste programme.

Since land is a fundamental resource of the area, it should be managed on a renewable basis, rather than risk degradation and exhaustion. Renewable land use can be achieved by estimating the carrying capacity of the land and adjusting production to sustainable levels. Assuming production should be held constant, the variable to be adjusted is plot size. Plots too small will be depleted, while plots too large will be wastefully underutilised, supporting fewer people than could be sustained, thereby exerting more pressure on agriculturally marginal and intact forest areas. A uniform plot size wastes the resource and impedes sustainable resource management. Plot sizes approximating land suitability estimates or carrying capacity would improve resource management. Plot size is difficult to adjust after the fact. Adjustment by failure of the farm is hard on the family and damaging to the resource base; but it is avoidable.

The Carajás iron ore project

Description of the project

Most of the Carajás iron ore lies in two balding rocky outcrops about 550 km SSW of Belém (see Figure 2). These two ridges, Serra Norte and Serra Sul, are 35 km apart and rise 300–400 m above the jungle-covered lowland. They total 17 thousand million metric tons of unusually high grade ore (66% iron) which is very low in the common impurities phosphorous, silica, and aluminium oxides. Open-pit mining will start in July 1985 with the 'N4E' deposit of 1280 millions tons. This ore body is 4.2 km long with an average width of 300 m and a maximum depth of 285 m below the surface. Due to its high natural iron content, the ore requires no concentration, other than size reduction of the run-of-mine ore to sinter feed and natural pellets.

Design capacity of 35 million tons per year (tpy) planned for 1988 will be transported from the mine on a new 890 km railroad to a new port near São Luis in Maranhão. This will be the longest rail built in recent times. It is mainly flat and straight with no tunnels and only 63 bridges; the only major bridge is over the 2.34 km wide Tocantins river just upstream of the town of Marabá. The railroad will be single-track, 1.6 m gauge on a 7.6 m bed with 1850 heat- and pressure-creosoted wooden tiles per kilometre; many of these ties will be made from the forest being removed for the Tucuruí reservoir (p. 000). The standard train will have 160 ore wagons of 98 t capacity (15 680 t of ore), hauled by three 3000 horsepower diesel-electric locomotives at maximum speeds of 65 km/h loaded and 80 km/h empty. There will be eight ore trains per day in each direction, about $1\frac{1}{2}$ km long, taking 21 hours loaded and 12 hours empty. Most of the earthmoving and bed-preparation of the line had been completed in July 1982. Erosion-prone tracts have been asphalted and slopes vegetated.

The new port is 10 km southeast of the city of São Luis and 1.5 km north of the existing port of Itaqui. The minimum depth of 23 m is constantly scoured by ocean currents so that ore ships of 280 000 dead weight tonnage (about 21 m draught) can be accommodated. Two rail wagon dumpers of 8000 tons per hour will stockpile up to 3.3 million metric tons of ore, whence it will be fed to conveyors to a 16 000 tons per hour ship loader.

The 508 ha Carajás town site is on a 640 m high plateau, 12 km upwind from the mine and 170 km from Marabá (70 000 population, 1982 estimate). There are expected to be 2044 workers on site by 1988 when the 35 million tpy production is reached. These will be housed in 2720 buildings under construction. Tucuruí will supply power to Carajás via a 180 km, 230 kV line from the Marabá substation, when the first 330 MW unit comes on line in 1984.

The Carajás iron ore project is expected to cost US$ 4.5 thousand million of which 19.5% ($ 680 million) is for the mine, 53% ($ 1872 million) for the railroad, and 7% ($ 250 million) for the port. The remaining 20% includes the town sites, management, contingencies, and insurance. CVRD, a mixed-capital company with 80% owned by the government and 20% by private Brazilian shareholders, together with the government and other Brazilian sources are financing most of these costs. Foreign financing (32.9%) includes EEC, IBRD, four Japanese sources, and KfW of West Germany. Contracts to buy much of the ore have been received. The sinter feed and natural pellets produced will be exported largely to Europe and Japan, generating a cumulative foreign exchange benefit of US$ 20 thousand million over 30 years (to 2015 AD) – or $ 27 thousand million assuming expansion to 50 million tpy in 1993. The project will create direct employment for about 6000 employees and some 2000 service workers through to 1988.[6]

Environmental aspects

Since CVRD is the world's largest producer and exporter of iron ore, it has had much experience in similar projects since 1942 in solving environmental problems.[20] In 1972, CVRD assigned responsibility for environmental planning and management of the Carajás project to a division now called Environmental Coordination. More than twelve environment-related studies were commissioned between 1973 and 1981, forming the basis for environmental planning.

In January 1981, CVRD created an independent environmental group, GEAMAM, to advise on all environmental aspects of the company and, in particular, to oversee activities at Carajás (Figure 4). The group, which is composed of nine senior scientists and Amazon experts, will be kept up to strength at all times and will inspect the site systematically for the duration of the project.[7] The group

Figure 4: *CVRD–Carajas Environmental Management Organisation*

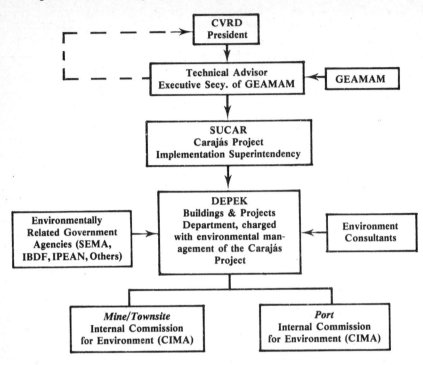

and the Environmental Coordinator prepared an environmental management manual, containing guidelines covering all aspects of contractors' activities (e.g. wildlife, tree removal, fires, erosion, stream crossings). All contractors are required to follow these guidelines as part of their contractual services to CVRD.

CVRD established permanent on-site Internal Environmental Commissions – CIMAs – for the mine site and for the railway in June 1981 and for the port site in June 1982. Two full-time environmental officers have been appointed; in November 1981 for the mine, and in July 1982 for the port. Between them they are responsible for the part of the rail system nearer to them. They are responsible for ensuring that all contractors following the environmental guidelines, and for assisting the CIMAs. These two environmental officers also alert the Environmental Coordinator to any potential environmental problems, and ensure that the various environmental studies and programmes are carried out and that their recommendations are implemented.

CVRD works closely with governmental environment-related agencies. SEMA, the Special Environmental Secretariat, is designing a series of ecological stations for the Carajás project. IBDF, the Federal Forestry Institute responsible for national parks and wildlife, has held several training courses for forest guards and has established permanent control posts at strategic locations. National park needs for the region are being addressed.

Environmental zoning

The Ministry of Mines and Energy (DNPM) undertook a resource survey resulting in a detailed map (1:250 000 scale) of the Carajás region. Based on this survey and other data, CVRD is preparing a 1:100 000-scale base map showing mineralised deposits, IBDF and SEMA tracts, INCRA areas, and FUNAI reserves and other Amerindian-occupied areas. This zoning will facilitate planning for appropriate land use, reduce the incidence of incompatible activities, and allow for systematic conservation of special tracts.

Conservation tracts and biotic inventories

Based on the results of the environmental zoning, CVRD plans to review the forest and unique iron-stone scrub areas in the concession and along the railway track in order to set aside conservation tracts where appropriate. CVRD has already acquired 20 000 ha for this purpose. Biotic inventories are being carried out by the National Research Council and the Goeldi Museum of Belém in areas where forest clearing is presently envisaged, in order to allow preservation where appropriate. Similar inventory and salvage programmes have been designed for archaeological and historic artifacts.

Green belt buffer zone

GEAMAM has strongly recommended the creation of a buffer zone to minimise the negative impact of the project on the surrounding areas. As iron ore mineralisation extends to the concession's perimeter, CVRD has requested expansion of the concession area to allow the establishment of a buffer zone around the mining area. A similar buffer zone is planned along the railway and at the port.

Pollution control

In controlling pollution, CVRD is making direct use of its environmental experience from the construction of Tubarão port, Itabira mines, and 550 km of connecting railroad in their southern operation in planning pollution control for the Carajás project. In general, pollution problems are expected to be less severe in the north than in the south for several reasons: (a) Carajás ore is sinter feed, and less dusty than the fines, ultra-fines and bluedust in the south; (b) Carajás sinter feed will be more humid (shipped wetter) than Itabira products; and (c) the prevailing winds at São Luis are from port to sea, unlike Tubarão where winds blow from the ore port towards the city. To control marine pollution, especially with regard to any flushing of oil holds by cargo ships, CVRD is undertaking a three-year port study, including a baseline marine study, to determine the optimum pollution prevention system. Due to the importance of this and other pollution studies, CVRD is preparing and will carry out a comprehensive pollution control programme.

Much of the mine site will be kept damp in the dry season by three 40 m^3 water spraying units to suppress dust. Mining process water will be discharged into settling lagoons (under construction), filtered through specially permeable barrages, and recycled back to the plant.

Amerindians

CVRD and FUNAI, the National Indian Foundation, interpret the 'zone of influence' of the project to be up to a 100 km radius from the outer limits of the mine–rail–port system. The estimated 4535 Amerindians in the large zone of influence comprise nine different tribal groups, most of which occupy the 14 reserves listed in Table 4.

An Amerindian sub-project has been integrated into the Carajás iron ore project in order to prevent immediate impact, to mitigate longer-term effects, and to buy time to allow the Amerindians to acculturate at their own pace and in the style they desire. This is consistent with Brazil's own far-sighted legislation and with the World Bank's new (May 1982) policy regarding tribal people and development projects.

The sub-project provides for the completion of demarcation of all reserves and Amerindian areas not yet reserved, the eviction of squatters from within Amerindian areas, surveillance and prevention of trespass, and the resolution of contested borders. Preventive health programmes (especially for the least acculturated Guaja people) supporting health delivery (clinics and mobile health services), water supply, and bilingual schools are included. FUNAI staff will be strengthened to enable it to carry out this sub-project which has been allocated US$ 13.6 million over 1982–6, above Funai's basic allocation for the area. CVRD have arranged with the Brazilian Anthropology Association (ABA) to contract the three most experienced anthropologists specialising in the region to study, advise, and monitor progress (see Ferraz 1982; Vidal 1982; Gomes 1982), including health (Viera Fihol 1982).

The Grande Carajás Programme

This section seeks to avoid confusion between the Carajás iron ore project (ie mine–rail–port) described in this paper, and the Greater Carajás Programme (Programa Grande Carajás or 'Carajazão'). The Grande Carajás Programme, created on 24 November 1980 (Decree Law 1.813 and Decree 85.387), has so far been outlined only in regional and general terms. The Grande Carajás Programme covers that region of Goiás, Pará and Maranhão north of 8° south, and between the Amazon, Xingu and Parnaíba rivers, an area roughly 1000 km by 800 km. The Grande Carajás Programme is coordinated by an interministerial council of eight ministers led by Planning, which appointed Dr Nestor Jost, ex-President of the Bank of Brazil, as Executive Secretary in February 1982. A Science and Technology Advisory Commission formed in June 1982 is coordinated by the National Research Council (CNDCT) and includes SEMA, IBDF, EMBRAPA, IPEA, Industry and Mining. Most publications describing the Grande Carajás Programme sum the major projects either under construction or planned for the

Table 4   Amerindian reserves in the area of influence of the Carajás iron ore project

Reserve	State	Amerindian group	Population	Area size (ha)	Area status[a]	Municipality	Number of villages
1 Cateté	Pará	Xikrin/Kayapó	263	439 150	Pending/Edital	Marabá	1
2 Mãe Maria	Pará	Gavião	170	62 000	Decree	Marabá	2
3 Parakanã	Pará	Parakanã	123	270 000	Decree+Portária	Tucuruí	2
4 Sororo	Pará	Suruí	89	26 257	Decree+Portária	Marabá	1
5 Alto Turiaço	Maranhão	Urubu-Kaapor	312	530 524	Decree+Portária	Monção	3
6 Angico Torto	Maranhão	Guajajara (Tenetehara)	1084	413 589	Decree+Portária	Amarante	8
7 Arariboia	Maranhão	Guajajara	569	?[b]	–[c]	Amarante	4
8 Canudal	Maranhão	Guajajara	434	?[b]	–[c]	Amarante	2
9 Caru	Maranhão	Guajajara and Guaja	162	170 000	Decree+Edital	Bom Jardim	5
10 Guaja	Maranhão	Guaja	29				
11 Governador	Maranhão	Gavião	208	41 643	Decree+Portária	Carutapera & Monção	1
12 Krikati	Maranhão	Krikati	297	136 000	Decree+Portária	Montes Altos	1
Guajajara	369	13 425	Decree+	Monção &	2 Edital	Bom Jardim	
14 Apinajé	Goiás	Apinajé	447	101 000	Decree+Portária	Tocantinópolis	2
Total			4535	2 203 588			37

Source: FUNAI and Freitas & Smyrski-Shluger 1982.
a All areas lack register with the 'Serviço do Patrimonio da União'.
b Unknown.
c Possibly included in Angico Torto Decree; data being verified.

region (eg. Carajás iron ore; Tucuruí, Carolina, Santa Isabel and Santo Antônio hydroprojects; Salobo copper mine; Barcarena and Paragominas aluminium smelters) with agricultural and transport plans, and arrives at a total of US$ 60 thousand million (see Sá 1982; Carajazão 1981; IBGE 1981). The Grande Carajás planning secretariat is quoted as saying: 'After CVRD and Tucuruí, our idea is to have minimum state intervention to try to teach the people to believe in the market. We grant the incentives, but the risk is the entrepreneurs'.' (*Wall Street Journal*, 28 Oct. 1982, p. 56). Further information on the Greater Carajás Programme may be found in Senado Federal (1981), Asselin (1982), Pinto (1982), Klein *et al.* (1983) and IBASE (1983).

Discussion

Environmental contrast and options

Since environmental problems have longer latency periods than most other problems, it is premature to assess the environmental precautions instituted in all three projects. All three project agencies have achieved a commendable start towards environmental improvements in the very different developments. Such improvements represent marked progress over 5 or 10 years ago. In an ideal world doubtless the environmental precautions would have been better, and in future projects they are likely to be better. This section attempts to outline options for the future and to contrast environmental aspects of the three projects.

Developers are frequently exasperated by the uncertainty of environmental projections. For example, most knowledgeable people agree that atmospheric cabon dioxide is increasing and that the consequences are likely to be more harmful than beneficial.[8] There is less agreement whether, and if so when, where, and by how much, the earth will cool down, heat up or become drier or wetter as a result. The other unattractiveness of environmental advice is that it is almost always pessimistic − it is difficult to be optimistic about acid rain, for example. In spite of these difficulties, one contentious issue is environmentally fundamental − that of ownership of natural resources.

Long-term land use

The ethic of private property became enshrined in common law when the carrying capacity of the environment greatly exceeded the population and its use of resources. People's use or abuse of land had little or no effect on their neighbours or their society, let alone on the world in general. Although that time has ended for much of the world, the ethic of ownership of natural resources, or land in particular has yet to be modified to stewardship. The present generation should manage natural resources as trustees for the benefit of ourselves during our lifetime, but maintained at constant or enhanced value for future generations. From this point of view, the sustainable and commercial benefits of power from the 2160 km² Tucuruí reservoir greatly exceed the low and short-term benefits that would accrue if the land area was settled by 2160 families on 100 ha plots. At a different scale, even if some settlers wanted to manage their 100 ha as forest, land use – deforestation – on neighbouring plots would damage the intact forest plot.

Ownership of one hundred hectares is so attractive that migratory flows into Amazonia are likely to be accelerated whenever such offers are made. Since one hundred hectares vastly exceeds the area one family can manage sustainably, this large size can be used by (a) extensive, low-management types of land use (e.g. ranching); (b) labour-, capital-, energy-intensive and mechanised methods (e.g. Jari); (c) underutilisation of the resource; or (d) conversion of the resource to the largest (but ephemeral) profit (e.g. deforestation). These trends could be reversed in favour of the two factors of production so abundant – land and labour – to the extent that the aim is the more efficient use of the resource base, for the longest term, and for the largest number of people.

Involuntary human impact is greatest in the Northwest Region, potentially affecting many and vulnerable Amerindians. At Tucuruí 30 000 people will be resettled, but this can improve rather than worsen their lot. The impact of a mineral rail is clearly much less than that of a highway or land settlement. Three Amerindian reserves will be affected (one more significantly) by Tucuruí, compared with up to 35 in the Northwest Region. Carajás impacts one reserve directly, and few people will be resettled (mainly near the port).

Irreversible losses

All three projects inevitably cause the irreversible loss of sizeable areas of intact ecosystems and probably lead to the extinction of some species, whether known to science or not. In the case of the Northwest Region, 100 000 km² of intact ecosystem may eventually be lost. This compares with more than 2000 km² at Tucuruí, and less than 100 km² at Carajás. From this point of view, the exploitation of a concentrated resource, very small in area, as at Carajás, is preferable to large-scale conversion as in the Northwest Region. Both Polonoroeste and Carajás commendably provide for conserved tracts (such as national parks) to help mitigate the loss. Conservationists probably feel that losses are scarcely compensated for, while developers may question the need for such extensive tracts of seemingly 'unused' land. Such management of wildlands maintains for posterity the aesthetic and economic potential of currently unknown or poorly known biota, together with the major benefit of regional climatic stability.[9]

The efficiency and appropriateness of resource use is similarly wide open. The *cerrado* can be developed at lower cost and less risk than the Northwest Region forest. Within the Northwest Region, 5 to 10 ha plots would be managed more efficiently than 100 ha family plots. Similarly, low-head hydroprojects could be developed at less environmental cost than the single high-head at Tucuruí. (Recent axial turbines are as large as 50 MW).

Energy considerations

Hydro v. other energy systems

Environmental problems of hydroprojects, though potentially large, are now reasonably predictable and largely avoidable if identified in time as they were in the case of Tucuruí. Brazil uses much less electricity *per capita* than industrial countries and still needs to expand supply. Environmentally, hydropower is benign since it is solar-powered (via the hydrological cycle) and sustainable in perpetuity. From this point of view, hydropower is preferable to increasing reliance on a diminishing foreign resource (oil), and min-hydroprojects (no-head, axial tube turbines) create less environmental impacts than large reservoirs.[10] Similarly, development of hydropower postpones the need for the economically and environmentally more risky and uncertain nuclear fission being developed, but now on hold, in southern Brazil (Krugman 1981). The whole world has to shift from oil as it is depleted and becomes more expensive: hydropower can be made an environmentally acceptable replacement for many uses. Special efforts should be made to design and locate hydroprojects to prevent or keep to an absolute minimum the extinction of narrowly circumscribed species, especially of aquatic life.

Wood energy potential

Much of Amazonia and the Northwest Region in particular is well endowed with solar energy and water, so could, in principle, be entirely self-sefficient in energy. However, Amazonia is at present vulnerably dependent on costly imports of petroleum. This paradox stems from the choice of highways and internal combustion as the transport and generation modes: an energy-expensive choice.

The need for expensive fuel contributes to the pressure to realise a quick profit from the forest. This need not be the case. The forest can be used as a renewable source of energy in perpetuity, or it can be used as an energy source for the mid-term, during conversion or refining to tree crops or agriculture. Forest can be converted into energy as:

    (a) firewood for heat and steam;

    (b) sawdust for steam;

    (c) charcoal (including water gas and producer gas);

    (d) methyl alcohol (methanol); and

    (e) biogas (mainly methane).

At the moment, these opportunities are not taken. Most Amazonian colonisation projects are based on diesel-fuelled electricity. In spite of preference for imported fuel, there are encouraging signs of more sustainable energy systems already being implemented privately. Ancient steam-powered sawmills are increasingly used. These consume sawdust which is otherwise wasted, and which pollutes air and water if improperly disposed of. Most of the steam engines are over 50 years old, resurrected from the south of Brazil, now that the forests, such as Paraná pine, have been removed. The life of a diesel sawmill, in contrast, is only one year or so due to the abrasive atmosphere of the surroundings. The largest wood-fuelled steam engine in Amazonia is the 700 horsepower turbine, generating 1700 kV from 120 m³/day of wood for 24 hours at the Taboca cassiterite project at Massangana in Rondônia. This was augmented to 1500 horsepower in early 1980 and now powers several dredges and beneficiation machines. The most appropriate size for much of Amazonia is approximately 10–100 horsepower, which is easily managed by one or two families and is small enough to be carried on draught animals along forest tracks without the need for highways.

Another appropriate energy system for Amazonia is charcoal. This can be made easily with readily acquired skills, from raw material (wood) available at low cost. The technology is simple, cheap and widely practised in Minas Gerais, mainly for the steel industries there. The product is light in weight so that it can be delivered to settlements and towns by draught animals, bicycles, carts or small boats. All domestic cooking and much processing can be carried out more appropriately with charcoal than with petroleum-based fuels. Eventually, fuel-wood plantations will have to be established around towns, but that need is still some way off. At a slightly higher level of technology, charcoal can be used to power trucks and buses. The skills required for this process are marginally greater than those for running steam engines, but much less than those required for diesel engine use.

Finally, biogas can be made from any and all organic wastes such as manure, water weeds, sawdust, domestic residues and sewage. These can be mixed or used separately depending on the supply. The product, biogas (largely methane), can be used on a family scale directly as a source of heat, or for agricultural drying, or it can be pressurised and used as the motive fuel for tractors and trucks. The technology and capital costs of biogas are lower than for diesel. Biogas systems are widely and successfully used throughout countries unable to afford petroleum imports such as India and China. In those countries, they range in size from small family-run units, to large facilities run from city sewage works. The smaller sizes are appropriate for Amazonia, and the State of Mato Grosso (Secretary of Industry) has advanced plans for their development.

All the above energy systems can convert regional agricultural development projects into energy self-sufficiency. In view of the small scale and low capital requirements, the development of such systems is appropriate for rural development projects. In view of Brazil's 84% reliance for petroleum on increasingly expensive imports and in view of the government's expressed desire to reduce this vulnerability, such self-reliant energy systems are valuable opportunities for Amazonia.

Highways and energy

The environmental implications of highways are mentioned for several compelling reasons.[11] One of the main justifications for highways is to facilitate access of agricultural surpluses to distant markets. Although this may appear reasonable, it has environmental costs. Facilitating access to distant markets promotes natural-resource management oriented towards these markets. This policy encourages Amazonia, including the Northwest Region, to supply food to the south of Brazil. Food production is not sustainable in much of Amazonia without fertilisers which most settlers have not yet been able to afford. Export food production in Amazonia represents a conversion of the natural resource base — forest and some soil fertility — into a short-lived surplus exported to southern Brazil. Since highways facilitate access to intact forest, unplanned settlement may damage the forest for many kilometres on either side.

Highways in Brazil are used almost exclusively by petroleum-powered vehicles, and more than 90% of all goods are transported by highway. The results of these choices are worrying the government: high and increasing transport costs, increasing dependence on imported fuels, increasing indebtedness. These can be reduced by:

(a) Promotion of a degree of self-sufficiency, rather than increasing the need for cargo transport.

(b) Promotion of more energy-efficient modes of transport. River and rail transport consumes less fuel per kilometre-ton than do highways. Rail freight is up to four times more fuel-efficient than big trucks. Airships are likely to be appropriate for parts of Amazonia, particularly in forestry industries.

(c) Promotion of highway modes that consume less petroleum than the prevailing course. Producer- and water-gas-driven trucks, vegetable-oil diesels, steam engines, biogas vehicles, together with draught animals would reduce the dependency on imported fuels.

(d) Production of storable products such as wood products, rather than perishable products such as rice and bananas.

Less conventional energy

A private corporation in northern Mato Grosso, Sinop, has 2500 ha of manioc which produces 150 000 litres of ethanol per day. Expansion to 16 000 ha is envisaged. Another land corporation, Indeco, generates electricity from a wood-fuelled steam engine consuming 70 m^{3}per 12 hours of operation. There are hundreds of sites suitable for mini-hydroprojects already inventoried by Eletronorte. These sites, distributed throughout Amazonia, with drops from 1.5 m to 20 m, possess potentials between 100 kW and 60 000 kW.

Perennials, annuals and cattle

Apart from fish, the most sustainable land management for most of Amazonia is tree-based, whether natural forest management, tree plantations or perennial plantation crops.[12] Since a shortage of mineral nutrients is the main constraint to increased production on the infertile soils of Amazonia, the mineral content of the harvest will govern the sustainability of the land use. Oligotrophic products, those with few nutrients (e.g. wood, which is essentially carbon, hydrogen and oxygen, which are abundant) can be produced more sustainably than a eutrophic harvest such as cattle, which contain large shares of mineral nutrient (e.g. phosphorus and calcium). Annual crops and cattle ranches are likely to be the least sustainable forms of land management. We now outline the options.[13]

Choice of crop

The choice of crops is environmentally important. Most Amazonian soils are so infertile that annual crops fail as soon as the ash from the burnt forest is exported out of the ecosystem in the marketed commodity, such as phosphate in cattle bones. Since import of fertilisers into much of Amazonia is too expensive for most settlers at the moment, the sooner that annual crops are discouraged and the sooner perennial crops are encouraged, the more sustainable development in the region will become.[14]

The most sustainable activity will be tree-based, as mentioned earlier, including plantations, forestry and tree crops. Although annual export crops are the least sustainable, there are four situations in which annuals are appropriate in areas of largely poor soils, high rainfall, and high year-round temperatures. These are: (a) seasonally flooded areas such as *várzeas*, (b) irrigated areas, (c) as intercrops with trees (agroforestry or *taungya*), and (d) subsistence plots. There are extensive *várzeas* near major transport lanes in Amazonia, e.g. Solimões. Because capital for intensive irrigation is more available near consuming markets in southern Brazil, irrigation is unlikely to be widespread in Amazonia in the near term. Therefore, annuals are more appropriate as subsistence crops. The whole system can be made more resilient to the extent that most families, except urbanites, cultivate subsistence crops on their own one- or two-hectare plots. Such 'home gardens', recently promoted by UNICEF (1981), and researched for decades by Soemarwoto (1976), successfully support high populations in Java (Pekarangan), the Philippines, and Central America (Chinampa and Mayan gardens). If most families can support themselves and on occasion produce a small marketable surplus from 2 ha of very similar soils and climate in Sumatra and Kalimantan, then awarding 100 ha plots in Amazonia provides resources for one-fiftieth of the population density.

Perennial crops

Most of Amazonia is suited to a wide array of tree crops. Tree crops (and forest industry) are strongly preferred on an environmental basis over annuals, to the extent that tree crops protect the fragile soils, reduce soil deterioration and nutrient depletion and produce on a sustainable basis. While all tree crops and perennials are strongly preferred over annuals, those tree crops grown with the most protective cover will conserve the soils better than those with more open canopies. Similarly, those tree crops harvested without killing the tree (e.g. oil palm and rubber) are more protective of the soils than those harvests that kill the tree (e.g. heart of palm, except the lateral shoots).

Rubber is one of the most appropriate tree crops, to the extent that the useful short dry season (e.g. in much of Rondônia) provides some protection from the leaf blight disease that is so damaging elsewhere in Brazil. Since land area is not a major constraint, yields lowered by the presence of the dry season are less an impediment. Even individual plots can be improved by inclusion of rubber trees grown in mixed stands. Elsewhere, such as in Indonesia, reforestation is promoted by the use of rubber trees. These are tapped only when the price is attractive and alternative allocation of labour and resources is less attractive. Should the price of rubber fall or the price of some other commodity rise, the rubber can be safely left alone with little or no maintenance for a few years until the situation improves. The best use will be a mixture of estate and outlying rubber, together with the 'sleeping' rubber on family plots mentioned above.

Oil palm appears to be an attractive candidate. Although soils and climate in central and southern Rondônia may not be suitable for modern industrial oil palm production without chemical fertilisers, the example of household or village-scale production so widely and successfully practised elsewhere is encouraging. The valley of the upper Madeira between Abuna and the Jiparaná confluence lies entirely within the best climatic parameters for oil palm as delimited by SUDAM. If this is so, then this 300 km long strip, almost 100 km wide provides ample space for an export industry for Rondônia.

Cocoa, being a perennial, is greatly preferred over most other crops. Cocoa production can be improved ecologically by strengthening the leguminous shade tree, hedge, and living fence components. Intercropping will further improve the sustainability of the system. Cocoa is said to thrive under Brazil nut in the Indeco project at Alta Floresta.

Coffee protects the soils somewhat more than annuals. Since it seems to be reasonably successful and the product valuable on a per weight basis, it is preferred over annuals.

Brazil nut thrives naturally throughout large parts of Amazonia and provides lucrative returns in places. To the extent this tree becomes a significant component of mixed tree crop family plots as well as in plantations with other species, it could generate useful export earnings.[15]

Babaçu grows abundantly in Amazonia and its exploitation merits examination. However, since it grows in almost pure stands in large areas of pre-Amazonian Maranhão, it should not be excessively relied upon.

Coconuts are a useful component of the mixed tree crop plots, and could be the basis for small- and medium-scale industries in the future.

Remedial tree crops

Extensive and increasing tracts of cut and burned forest will be abandoned as the yields from annual crops decline. Throughout Amazonia, a rapidly increasing opportunity, therefore, will be for remedial measures on abandoned tracts. The most appropriate land use is for tree crops, starting with fast-growing leguminous ground covers. The final mix of trees will depend on the land-suitability classification and on the degree of environmental degradation of the site to be rehabilitated. In general, early emphasis on leguminous, fast-growing species such as *Leucaena*, *Gliricidia*, *Erythrina*, and *Albizia* will improve the nutrient, especially nitrogen, status of the depleted soils. Also recent evidence suggests that *Gmelina* may improve the calcium balance (Russell *et al.* 1982; St. John and Alvim 1982). Useful product species such as Brazil nut, coconut, oil palm, and fruit trees (especially citrus), with major emphasis on native products (pupunha, cupuaçu, etc.) can be usefully grown in mixed stands since their harvesting is compatible. The greater the mix of species and products, the more robust ecologically the farm will become.[16]

Reforestation

Despite fiscal incentives, reforestation is minimal in Amazonia.[17] Cia. Rondoniense de Reflorestamento, Municipio Jaci Paraná, is planting about 2000 ha mainly with cerejeira (*Amburana cearense*, Leguminosae), higher in value than mahogany and faster growing (60–70 cm diameter in 20 years). Caribbean pine, Brazil nut, cedar, and mahogany are also planted. Exploração Florestal in Pôrto Velho municipality, on the Madeira river, has planted 400 ha of cedar, mahogany, pine and cerejeira. There is opportunity for planting valuable species on a much larger scale, particularly in areas near cheap access routes that have already been deforested.

The role of cattle

Deforestation of Amazonia for agro-industrial cattle ranching is now recognised by Brazil as so inappropriate that the massive fiscal incentives by SUDAM for this activity have recently ceased.[18] Some cattle may be appropriate for the large natural savannas around Humaitá and Lábrea, and on the *pantanal* and *cerrado* portions of Amazonia. Even so, cattle there will not create many jobs and there are equally or more appropriate sites in the central *cerrados*, nearer the markets of southern Brazil.

There is, however, a minor role for cattle in Amazonia. Cattle can provide draught power, decreasing reliance on imported petroleum. Cattle can be fed grass grown in appropriate agroforestry sites and between trees in immature plantations. Fodder brought to the tethered and stabled animal is less damaging than the more usual converse. The stabled animal can be used to recycle agricultural residues and provide manure for the home garden, subsistence plot and for biogas and fertilising sludge. Water buffalo in *várzeas* or associated with farm ponds and water bodies would also increase the resilience of land management.

Conclusion

Approach to sustainability

The world faces the transition in energy use between cheap but exhaustible resources (oil and other fossil fuels) and currently expensive but renewable resources (solar-based, including biomass and hydroelectric). In view of population pressures and the rising cost of petroleum-dependent fertilisers and biocides, the need is increasing to adjust land-use systems to improve efficiency of land use and to prevent degradation. From this point of view the Carajás iron ore and the Tucuruí hydroprojects are environmentally less costly than the Northwest Region programme.

Amazonian resources can be managed in perpetuity for the benefit of successive generations, or can be rapidly capitalised for the present generation, leaving a depleted resource base behind. In the Northwest Region programme, the forest can be converted to three years or so of annuals, followed by five to ten years of low and declining productivity cattle pastures. Forestry could be sustainable, but appears unlikely to be widely attempted under the prevailing economic arrangements. Tree crops, between these two in sustainability, appear to suffer from weak markets in the medium term (e.g. coffee, cacao). Tucuruí can be indefinitely sustainable, thus decreasing expensive imports of depleting petroleum. The mine clearly depletes the resource although this may take 50 years or more. The steel produced from the ore is recyclable – hence scarcely used up.

In the Amazon the options are open: planning and mitigating the human impacts of the transition or letting depletion dictate the transition. Traditional development has been tried: highways, colonisation, cattle ranches. Less conventional approaches may now be appropriate. A society based on renewable energy and ecologically sustainable land use is possible in Amazonia if the proper choices are made now.[19]

Notes on text and guide to the literature

1 *The New York Times* of 13 May, 1982 reporting from Nairobi the Second United Nations Conference on the Environment: 'At the first Stockholm Conference ten years ago, Brazil resisted calls for action to protect the environment as a plot by rich countries to keep the poor countries from developing. The attitude then was, "you've had your chance to pollute and develop and we must have ours". Now, according to Paulo Nogueira Neto, Brazil's environmental protection chief, "we have changed 180 degrees." ' See also references: Minter 1982; E.G. 1982.

2 Brazilian Amazonia and the World Bank. Until recently the World Bank had no investments in Amazonia. A $ 6.7 million land-settlement project – Alto Turi – approved in 1972, is in pre-Amazonian Maranhão. Since it was directed by SUDENE it was more part of the Northeast development strategy. In 1982, a follow-up project – Maranhão Land Settlement – was approved adjacent to Alto Turi. The International Finance Corporation (IFC), an affiliate of the World Bank, holds minority shares in the Trombetas bauxite project (1979), and in the Denpasa palm oil project (1977) near Belém. In mid-1982, the Bank appraised the Amazonas Agricultural Development project which focuses on agriculture in the seasonally flooded (*várzea*) zone mainly south and east of Manaus. The Bank's major Amazonian investments are in the Northwest Region programme (signed December 1981) and the Carajás iron ore project (signed August 1982). The Bank is not involved with the Tucuruí hydroproject. The World Bank's environmental requirements for development projects it may finance are outlined by Goodland (1982), and amplified in World Bank (1982b).

3 The environmental reconnaissance of Tucuruí was carried out in 1976 and submitted to Electronorte the next year (Goodland 1977). Environmental aspects of hydroprojects in tropical forest regions including Brokopondo are mentioned in Goodland (1979). Further information is available in Anon. (1980), Budweg (1982), Eletronorte (1976), E.N.R. (1980), Franco (1981), O.J.M. Fonesca (1980), and SEMA (1980).

4 The results of the World Bank's regional survey are published in World Bank (1981). Martine (1980, 1982), Mueller (1980), Muller and Gligo (1982), Schmink (1982), Schmink and Wood (1983), and Mahar (1982) comment on Rondônia's migratory flux and the policy changes regarding land settlement along the Transamazon Highway.

5 The World Bank promulgated a policy regarding tribal people and economic development projects in February 1982, and amplified in a policy document (World Bank 1982a) available from the World Bank's Publications Office for US$ 5.

6 Technical data on the Carajás iron ore project presented by Anon. (1975), AMB (1980), Diniz *et al.* (1982), Isto é (1982), Martino (1980), Paiva (1979), Sá (1982), Santos (1981), Skillings (1981), and IBDF (1977). Schubart (1981) notes potential environmental effects.

7 GEAMAM members as of 1982 are: Angelo Camargo (climatology), Azis Ab'Saber (geomorphology), Italo Falesi (soils), Frazão Medeiros de Lima (development), Paulo Alvim (agronomy), Murca Pires (biology), José Cândido de Carvalho (conservation), and Warwick Kerr (biology).

8 The role of the Amazon forest in the maintenance of regional (and possibly global) climatic patterns is discussed by CEQ (1981), Gentry and López-Parodi (1980), Lugo and Brown (1980), Marques *et al.* (1980 a,b), Salati *et al.* (1978, 1979) and global carbon dioxide by IEA (1983).

9 The global problem of species extinctions is discussed by Ehrlich and Ehrlich (1981), Eckholm (1978), USDS (1980), Valverde and Freitas (1980). Loss of Amazonian wet forest and tropical wet forest in general, which is the species-richest biome on earth, is documented by DePaiva (1980a, b), IBDF (1980), Fearnside (1982), Lamb (1980), Nations and Nigh (1978), Myers (1980), Parsons (1976), Plumwood and Routley (1982), and Sutlive *et al.* (1981a, b). Conservation of Amazonian biota is outlined in Ayres and Best (1979), Barrett (1980), Carneiro (1980), Carvalho (1979), Lovejoy (1982), Poore (1978), Prance (1982), Raven (1980), and Wetterberg *et al.* (1981).

10 Krahe (1977, 1978) discusses energy possibilities in Amazonia and the axial tube turbine mini-hydroproject at Aripuanã, formerly the Humboldt University. Harwood (1980) outlines Amazonian biogas research.

11 The environmental implications of Amazonian highways and concomitant unplanned settlement is discussed in Smith (1981a,b, 1982), Goodland and Irwin (1975), Goodland (1980), Bunker (1980, 1981), Fearnside (1980a,b,c), Moran (1981b), and Sioli (1980a,b).

12 Fish, mainly from the world's greatest river system, but also from other water bodies can be a valuable and sustainable source of protein for Amazonia, but is not dealt with here. Smith (1979, 1981c) and Goulding (1980) discuss this topic.

13 In general, the many and repeated attempts at large-scale continuous cash crop (annuals) and export cattle production in Amazonia (with certain exceptions) have failed (cf. Jordan 1982a, Sioli 1980a,b). One recent colloquium prioritising constraints to Amazonian development dwelt almost exclusively on difficulties of credit and land tenure, poor administration, deficient infrastructure, weak governmental support, inadequate market demand and so on. General refusal to acknowledge over-riding environmental constraints (infertile soils, pest and weed pressure, ecological interdependence) is striking and does not augur well for this huge region (cf. Jordan, 1982a). High-input agriculture (petroleum, chemical fertiliser, biocides) is becoming

questioned even in temperate zones with relatively fertile soils and less pest pressure, so may be less appropriate for Amazonia. Although the infertile nature of most (80% according to Sánchez 1976) Amazonian soils has long been realised by soil scientists, how the luxuriant jungle manages to thrive is only now being elucidated. Jordan and colleagues in particular are analysing the above-ground closed nutrient cycle of the Amazon forest which is so leakproof that incoming nutrient rates from rain and dust closely balance outgoing nutrient rates from leaching and streams (see papers by Jordan, Escalante, Herrera, Golley, Stark, Uhl and co-workers published in 1975, 1978, 1979, 1980, 1981 and 1982). Even forest canopy leaves scavenge nutrients from rain, and roots grow out of the soil up tree trunks intercepting nutrients flowing down the bark. The implication of this system of adaptations of the ecosystem to infertile soils is that the forest cannot be clear-cut over large areas, burned, and then be expected to produce crops for more than a few years. This applies even to tree plantations. Only four rotations are possible harvesting *Pinus caribaea* and sandy soils at Jari before all the calcium is completely mined (Russell *et al.* 1982). Even if fertilisers became affordable, there is reason to expect they will be less effective due to high rainfall (leaching, erosion), high temperature, and low nutrient-retaining ability of the soils, compared with southern Brazil and the vast *cerrado* region of central Brazil.

14 Although Amazonia is highly heterogeneous on most measures, nearly all (more than 80%) of the soil is among the least fertile in the world (Irion 1978; Sánchez 1976; van Wambeke 1978) with very small, although locally significant exceptions. Sánchez *et al.* (1982) discovered that forest can be replaced by annual cropping systems using imported chemical fertiliser for eight years in Amazonian Peru. The vast cost of building nearly 2000 km of highway across the Andes, and its onerous maintenance costs, the fact that fertilisers are heavily subsidised at present by the Peruvian government, and the need for costly biocides are scarcely mentioned. Most farmers who let the test be run on small parts of their property have not adopted high-input results. The inappropriateness of reliance on high-input agriculture (chemicals, petroleum, tractors, etc.) may now have been perceived since the programme recently started low-input research.

15 Difficulties (i.e. poor fruit set in plantations) encountered trying to cultivate Brazil nut trees illustrate the interdependence of the forest ecosystem which must be understood in order to design appropriate management systems. The pollinators of Brazil nut tree flowers are not fully known, yet the tree is an obligate outcrosser (i.e. does not self-pollinate). The flowers are visited by several species of Euglossine bees, of which *Eulaema* is a pollinator, as is the carpenter bee (*Xylocopa* spp.). Male Euglossines attract females before mating only after gathering organic compounds (e.g. pheromones) from certain species of epiphytic orchids (which are thereby pollinated), but depend on other species for food (nectar). Female bees also depend on other species of plants to collect pollen used to provision nests. Brazil nut trees flower mainly synchronously, hence leaving much of the year in which their pollinators depend on food from other species of plants. The fruit, an armoured pyxidium, can be opened possible only by agoutis (*Dasyprocta* spp.). Furthermore, flowering appears to be nutrient-dependent. To the extent this proves to be correct, successful regeneration of Brazil nut trees may need certain species of bees, bee nest habitat, other bee food plants, certain orchids and the trees on which they grow, the orchid pollinators (and all their necessities in turn), habitat for adequate populations of agoutis, and adequate nutrient levels. Smoke from forest

burning has been suspected of decreasing Brazil nut yields by interfering with the pollinators. Dr Scott Mori, of the New York Botanic Garden kindly assisted with this note.

16 Tree-based agriculture, agroforestry and ecologically based agriculture appropriate for Amazonia are discussed by Alvim (1981), Bishop (1978, 1982), Budowski (1981), Clarke (1976), Fearnside (1979a), Gliessman and Amador (1980), Goodland and Irwin (1977a,b), Goodland, Irwin and Tillman (1978), Hartshorn (1982), Hecht (1982a,b), Janzen (1973), Mongi and Huxley (1979), NAS (1982), Noda *et al.* (1978), Norgaard (1981), Peck (1979, 1982). Toenniessen (1981), Uhl, Jordan and Montagnini (1982), and Weaver (1979). Half-hectare Mexican home gardens may contain 60 species of food, medicinal or other useful plants.

17 Forestry and forest potential in Amazonia and the environmental impacts of tree removal are discussed by Ewel (1981), Ewel and Conde (1976, 1978), Hallsworth (1982), Jordan (1979), Palmer (1977), Pandolfo (1978), and Sedjo (1980).

18 The long-predicted inappropriateness of deforestation for cattle ranching on infertile soils in high temperature, high rainfall areas of low technology and management has now been carefully documented by Hecht (1980b, 1981, 1982a,b, 1983b,c). The failure of Amazon cattle ranching that contributed to reversing governmental financial incentives for cattle are noted by Denevan (1980), Fearnside (1979b, 1980d,e), and Feder (1980). Even the pasture proponents are muted or rely on fertiliser subsidies and management levels yet to be commonly achieved throughout Amazonia: Falesi (1976), Sánchez and Tergas (1979), Toledo and Serrão (1982).

19 The President of the World Bank recently presented a major environmental policy speech on the sustainability of development (Clausen 1981). The approach to and need for sustainability is discussed by Brown (1981a, b), Coomer (1981), Daly (1977, 1980), and Pirages (1977). Skillings and Tcheyan (1979) comprehensively assess the economic potential of the Brazilian Amazon. Cooperation for the development of Amazonia is promoted by the Amazon Pact (Landau 1980; Medina 1980).

20 CVRD acquired a 20 000 ha forest tract near Linhares, Espíritu Santo, starting in 1955 to supply wood for railroad ties and other uses in their southern operation. Since then, practically all the surrounding forest has been lost, so that CVRD's tract has become the largest remaining representative of the Atlantic forest ecosystem in Brazil. CVRD therefore now manages it for conservation and research only. In 1981 it was declared a permanent federal reserve. A further 10 000 ha of mainly intact forest was purchased, perhaps for conservation purposes, in November 1982 near Marabá, Pará.

2　Economic development of the Brazilian Amazon: opportunities and constraints

ROBERT F. SKILLINGS

Introduction

This paper is based mainly on information obtained while I was on sabbatical leave from the World Bank in 1978–9, as well as frequent travels and investigations in Brazil during the ten years I was responsible for the Bank's Brazil operations programme, up to 1981, and readings that I shall cite. Needless to say, the opinions voiced are my own and not necessarily those of the World Bank. However, I am indebted to my former associates at the World Bank, the Johns Hopkins School of Advanced International Studies, the Brazilian administrations both federal and state, Brazilian private citizens lofty and humble, and many others, who have informed and inspired me.

The great problem of the Brazilian Amazon is how to guide its development to further the economic growth and well-being of Brazil and its people without destroying the Amazon's contribution to the well-being of the earth. On the one hand, the Amazon's potentially rich forest and mineral resources, and in certain districts its productive soils, can contribute much to the regeneration of growth and prosperity of the potentially dynamic (though temporarily slowed) Brazilian economy. On the other hand that very growth could alter the unique ecosystem of the world's largest remaining tropical forest, eliminate plant and animal species, modify the region's (and perhaps the world's) climate, and bring disappointment and material loss to venturesome investors and the common folk whose livelihood depends on them. I do not pretend to have all the answers to these dilemmas and contradictions. What I propose to do here is to recall some of the promises and the constraints, the processes – planned and unplanned – that govern economic development of the Brazilian Amazon. I will also describe interventions by the government, some of them supported by the World Bank, that seek to compose these conflicting potentials and to achieve economic gains compatible with prudent conservation of the Amazon's transnational advantages and the orderly evolution of its indigenous population.

The constraints to development

Brazil's 'legal' Amazon comprises 57% of its land area, but holds only 4% of its population, and provides only 2% of the country's domestic product. This means that the people in the region earn on the average only half as much as the average Brazilian citizen. This is about the same as the *per capita* income in Brazil's Northeast – the area known as one of the poorest in South America.

Why is this insignificant economic performance associated with a region that appears to be so rich? Because the development of the apparent riches of the Amazon is the subject of a myriad of a natural, human and economic constraints. There are at least seven important such constraints:

(a) The *weak data base*: knowledge of both natural phenomena and economic data is fragmentary and unreliable. An engineer designing a dam does not really know how much rainfall and runoff have occurred in the past and are likely in the future. The dam may or may not produce the energy he expects. The settlement planner does not really know whether his soil samples represent the whole settlement area, or only a minor fragment – so that the farmers he wants to settle may or may not be able to produce the crops that are expected to justify the investment and sacrifice. There are innumerable other examples.

(b) The *high cost* of most economic activities, caused principally by high costs of transport over long distances with inefficient transport modes. Paradoxically, water transport on Amazonia's far-flung river network is not the cheap way of moving things that the common wisdom supposes – in fact it is too slow to accommodate the demands of most modern production and distribution systems.

(c) The *scarcity of entrepreneurial, managerial, and technical talent* (a scarcity which itself contributes to high costs): there are only three or four higher educational institutions in northern Brazil, and few middle-level technical and vocational schools. Managers, engineers, and accountants must be attracted from the south. Although many of them are willing to spend the early years of their careers in the Amazon, far from the amenities of Brazil's burgeoning southern cities, by mid-career most move back to the south where their children find better educational facilities, and they themselves find remunerative opportunities in Brazil's rapidly growing economy.

(d) The *narrow regional market*: any industrial enterprise in the Amazon has a severe handicap if its process requires mass production and its products are expensive to transport. The assembly industries in the Manaus free-trade zone have survived these handicaps by means of unusual tax advantages that cast doubt on the zone's economic justification and its industry's ability to survive if the zone is terminated, as scheduled, in 1997 (Mahar, 1979).

(e) The *scarcity of public services and infrastructure* – in part because of their high costs, as noted – and in part because of the financial weakness of Amazon states and cities, with a very thin tax base. The Jari project of Daniel Ludwig suffered because the enterprise was obliged to bear the cost of education, health, transport, security, and even amenity services that in a more established, prosperous community would be provided by public agencies or private investors. The proposed aluminium plant at Barcarena, near Belém, has been burdened by the need to build a new port, new access roads and bridges, and an entirely new town.

(f) The *uncertain land tenure* situation: state land records are confused, prior claims to land titles abundant, and land fraud flourishing. A settler or investor has to think twice before putting money into land that may be taken away by prior claimants, perhaps even by force.

(g) *Poor world market price prospects for cocoa and coffee*, the two tree crops which agriculturally and ecologically are attractive for part of the Amazon.

The environmental objectives

The physical and economic constraints to the development of the Amazon are powerfully reinforced by the widely recognised grounds for designing development so that it will be as compatible as possible with the conservation of the natural environment of the region. Those grounds have been publicised by foreign ecologists and they are being voiced increasingly in Brazil where the director of the federal environmental protection agency, Paulo Nogueira Neto, and the director of Brazil's national parks, Maria Tereza Jorge Padua, recently received awards from the World Wildlife Fund for their contributions to wildlife conservation. There is a growing body of opinion in Brazil in favour of environmental conservation measures, extending perhaps to environmental zoning. Such measures would limit economic development in each subregion to activities that do not irreversibly damage the environment. Legislation defining Amazon development policy has been drafted, after studies by a high level inter-agency commission, and has been the subject of much pro-and-con discussion in Brazil between environmentalists and those who fear that zoning would unduly inhibit economic growth, especially agricultural. The proposed legislation is still under consideration in the Presidency of the Republic. If it is finally enacted, it could make a major contribution towards harmonising economic and environmental objectives in the Amazon.

Specifically, what are the damages that are inflicted by uncontrolled economic development? Most of them stem from the consequences of widespread deforestation. These dangers include:

(a) Irreversible decline in the genetic stock of the region through the extinction of species, some of which are unidentified and many of which still have not had their economic potential identified (Lovejoy 1982).

(b) Depletion of potentially valuable natural resources. Tropical timber is lost through burning by farmers, ranchers and road builders, as well as through flooding from construction of dams and highways. Stocks of nutritionally valuable fish may be lost by destroying riverine forest, as well as by overfishing.

(c) Pollution of rivers through erosion and leaching of inadequately protected agricultural land. The eroded farms in the north of the state of Paraná, in southern Brazil, bear witness to this danger.

(d) Modification to the region's, and even the world's climate. Research by Eneas Salati and others has demonstrated that a large share of Amazonia's rainfall originates from moisture given off by the forest (Salati *et al*, 1978). And the work of George Woodwell (1978), among others, has raised a serious possibility that carbon dioxide given off by forest burning may contribute to a rising proportion of carbon dioxide in the earth's atmosphere and that, in turn, to a long-term increase in the earth's temperature. The results of such a process are still a matter of conjecture – some regions would no doubt be benefited while others were harmed – but the uncertainty of the effects of such a process surely indicate that deforestation is justified only when the economic benefits to be obtained therefrom are large and unambiguous. Philip Fearnside (1982) has recently made some arithmetic projections that suggest that if deforestation were to continue along an exponential growth path, there would be little forest left in the Amazon by the year 2000. Even if one does not accept that such an exponential expansion of forest clearing is realistically likely to happen (and I do not, given the constraints), the calculation throws into sharp relief what would happen if the Brazilian government and economic entities do not exercise restraint and caution. The enactment and enforcement of economic zoning could help significantly to slow down forest destruction.

The benefits of development

But if the limitations on economic development are so severe, why does Brazil continue to place importance on investments in the region as part of the national development effort? The reasons are psychological, economic, and social.

Psychologically, large empty spaces on a map have often become a challenge to national leaders, and one reason Brazilians want to develop the Amazon is, understandably, 'because it's there'. Moreover, Brazilian leaders and writers have always been fearful that if Brazil did not fully 'occupy' the Amazon, someone else would (Reis 1960). There is a long history of incidents that lend credence to the Brazilian belief that international greed threatens Brazil's control over its portion of the Amazon.

Economically, it is part of the common wisdom in Brazil that the Amazon region contains untold riches. This is an exaggeration, but there are indeed many valuable natural resources. The principal developments likely to occur are as follows.

(a) Exports of 35 million tons a year of iron ore from the rich and extensive Serra dos Carajás deposits will begin about 1986.

(b) Exports and domestic use of the important bauxite deposits on the Trombetas river and in other parts of the State of Pará.

(c) Growth in tin production, especially in Rondônia.

(d) Some increase in gold production, though probably not as much as was eagerly expected during the gold rush to the Serra Pelada a couple of years ago.

(e) Gradual expansion in exports of tropical timber: such an expansion depends on finding economic extraction methods. Experiments now going on at the Amazon Research Institute (INPA) in Manaus and long advocated by the Superintendency for Amazonian Development (SUDAM) are seeking to develop methods of timber extraction that assure natural regeneration, or even enrichment, of commercially valuable species (Pandolfo 1978).

(f) Expansion in the production of tree crops – cocoa and rubber in Rondônia, coffee in Mato Grosso (replacing production that is expected to decline in the frost-prone areas of southern Brazil), palm oil and kernels in the Belém area, in Amapá and at Tefé on the upper Solimões. Although world cocoa and coffee prices are predicted to be depressed in the next decade, production costs on the better soils should be low enough to induce increases in production. There may also be some increase in the production of indigenous perennials like *guaraná* (Alvim 1981), but the quantities involved, while useful, will still be very small in the medium term.

(g) Among industrial products, the best prospects for increases are in alumina and aluminium from plants being built near Belém and São Luiz. Possibly by the end of the decade there may be output and exports of refined mineral products from installations in the Carajás region – the first of these 'Grande Carajás' projects may be a ferromanganese plant. Hopes for expansion of wood pulp and paper production at Jari have been dampened by the finding that growth of *gmelina* and Caribbean pine planted in areas cleared of tropical forest is slower than hoped. Planting of pine on the savanna land of Amapá, by the company whose manganese mine will be depleted by the end of the decade, may result in additional pulpwood production.

(h) In the early 1970s great hopes were placed on production of cattle and meat on ranches cleared from forest and *cerrado* in Mato Grosso and southern Pará, with the help of tax incentives granted by SUDAM. Such ranches have serious ecological disadvantages and may not be as profitable as their sponsors hope because of soil fertility problems (Fearnside 1980e).

Together with some associates, I made a calculation a couple of years ago that if all the various mineral, agricultural, and industrial projects that seemed then to be practical possibilities were to materialise, they would improve Brazil's balance of trade by some US$ 3.8 thousand million between 1980 and 1990, both through increased exports and savings on imports (Skillings and Tcheyan 1979; Doren 1981). Exports from the Amazon could amount to 5–7% of Brazil's total projected exports in 1990, compared to 2% of total exports at present. Although these developments will make a welcome contribution to Brazil's economic growth, they are evidently not going to transform Brazil's economy fundamentally.

Socially, there is also strong motivation for development of the Amazon. In part, this concerns the local population, some living in poverty and isolation along the thousands and thousands of miles of rivers and creeks, and others in the crowded *favelas* of Belém and Manaus. In part, the Amazon has seemed an attractive settlement area for low-income people from other parts of Brazil. The vast empty spaces, with some identified patches of relatively good soils, have attracted the hopes of Brazilian leaders that overpopulated districts elsewhere, especially in the northeast, might be relieved through migration programmes. The disappointing experiments in organised settlement along the Transamazon Highway are well known. On the other hand, in Rondônia a multitude of spontaneous migrants from the south have found what promises to be productive farm life. But the areas of productive soils are not large enough to accommodate more than a small fraction of Brazil's low-income population.

Harmonising development and environmental objectives

How can the economic development possibilities be pursued while affording reasonable protection to the natural environment and the indigenous population? A few practical examples drawn from the experience of the World Bank family in the Brazilian Amazon provide some indications.

Some of the examples are to be found in the POLONOROESTE programme (World Bank 1981), the ambitious regional development programme in Rondônia and northwest Mato Grosso which is estimated to cost US\$ 1.5 thousand million equivalent over the 5 years 1982–6. The World Bank has made four loans, totalling US\$ 346.4 million, to support this programme. The principal economic activities are as follows. First, the reconstruction and paving of the 1400 km Cuiabá–Pôrto Velho highway, providing more satisfactory access for the hundreds of thousands of migrants who moved spontaneously into the area in the past ten years, and an economical evacuation route for their products. Second, the programme provides agricultural services and feeder roads to enable the newly settled population to increase its production and incomes. Third, the programme will support health services, including research into ways of controlling malaria, an extremely serious problem in Rondônia. Fourth, the programme includes the creation and equipment of two ecological research stations, organisation of a national park, and the creation of adequate staff and equipment for the Brazilian Institute for Forest Development (IBDF), to enable it for the first time to monitor and enforce compliance with restrictions on deforestation. Fifth, the programme includes basic research projects to be carried out by INPA and other agencies, designed to improve knowledge of the natural environment, of the hydrology of the region, and of the effects of agricultural and other developments on water runoff and river water quality. Finally

– though not financed by the World Bank – the POLONOROESTE programme includes actions by FUNAI, the national Indian foundation, to protect the many Amerindian groups whose health and living conditions might be threatened by the spread of agricultural settlements and the construction of highways. At the start of the programme, special measures were taken to enlarge and demarcate the lands of the Nambiquara Indians in the Guaporé Valley of Mato Grosso. POLONOROESTE has been strongly criticised by humanitarian groups as detrimental to the Indians. No development activity would fail to have some effect on those groups, but before making its finance available, the World Bank satisfied itself that the Brazilian government was taking all reasonable steps to protect the Indians potentially affected.

Another example of development designed to be compatible with environmental constraints is an agricultural project in the State of Amazonas. Most of the project consists of economic and social support services to small farmers, designed to increase production on *várzea* (floodplain) lands south and east of Manaus and smallholder oil palm production near Tefé. The project includes research to identify the natural resource potential of the area, including the preparation of topographical maps and hydrological maps of *várzea* areas. There would be five hydroclimatological observation stations and studies to identify areas suitable for biological and forest reserves. Finally, the project would provide funds to monitor the possible introduction into the area of schistosomiasis and chagas disease by future migrants.

A third example of Brazilian efforts to harmonise economic growth projects with environmental concerns is the large Carajás iron ore, railway, and port project. The project is estimated to cost almost US$ 5 thousand million, financed by a group of Brazilian and foreign institutions, including a World Bank loan of US$ 304.5 million signed in August 1982. The Companhia Vale do Rio Doce (CVRD), the mining company that is carrying out the project, began in 1972 to commission studies of the project's environmental impact. In 1981 CVRD created a special environmental studies and advisory committee, composed of nine senior scientists and Amazon experts, to review and monitor all environmental aspects of the project. This committee will issue periodic reports that will be reviewed by the World Bank. The latter will also make field inspections. Parallel with efforts to minimise the effects of the project on the natural environment, the government's Indian agency, FUNAI, is undertaking a special US$ 13.6 million programme to protect the estimated 4500 Amerindians living in 37 villages within 100 km of the project. World Bank staff, accompanied at all times by FUNAI personnel, will have access to the Indian areas to observe the progress of the Amerindian project.

Conclusion

There is no doubt that Brazil's efforts to settle the Amazon for the benefit of its economy and its people will continue. There is also no doubt that these development activities will alter the environment, by reducing the area of natural tropical rainforest and by affecting climate, water resources, soils, and wildlife to some degree. They may also accelerate the pace at which the indigenous Amerindian population is acculturated, though there can be little doubt that whatever happens these groups would be engulfed by Brazilian society within the next century.

What is encouraging is that the Brazilian authorities recognise the adverse effects that economic growth can have on the natural Amazon forest and its original inhabitants and have shown themselves determined to reduce and, wherever possible, prevent such effects from occurring. The record of protective measures incorporated into specific development projects has recently been quite good. It will be substantially improved if the region-wide environmental zoning programme, now under consideration, is adopted.

3   Major projects and human life in Amazonia

ARMANDO DIAS MENDES

Major projects

The major enterprises now in progress in Amazonia, especially in the eastern part, can be described from many different points of view.

Brazilian Amazonia, considering only the area covered by *hyleia* forests, is about 3.5 million km², but 'Amazônia Legal', as defined in regional planning, covers 5.0 million km² – 60% of Brazil. Independently, it would be one of the largest countries in the world, the largest in South America and in all Latin America.

Its population is as yet relatively small: 6 million inhabitants, according to the 1980 census, which was restricted to 'natural' Amazonia. In 'Amazônia Legal' there are 12–13 million people. However, many countries in Spanish-speaking America, even among Brazil's neighbours, have a smaller population.

Eastern Amazonia is about 2 million km² in area. Within it, the land devoted to just one major programme, the Carajás project, is approximately 0.8 to 1 million km². I refrain from giving other facts about its jungles, hydrographic network or the extent of its borders, since they are sufficiently well known and of minor interest to this study.

This region, especially the State of Pará, contains the greatest mineral deposits in Brazil, and possibly in the world. The variety and volume of underground mineral resources already known or estimated are fantastic: iron, aluminium, copper, tin, manganese, nickel, gold, kaolin, limestone, are all found in impressive numbers. To give just one example, the haematite of Serra dos Carajás consists of solid deposits of the order of 18 thousand million tons, and the indications are that the total will reach 50 thousand million tons or more.

The projects in progress are principally the mining or iron, aluminium, manganese, gold, kaolin and limestone. Other projects beginning are the mining of copper, nickel and other minerals. It is intended in the near future to mine, process and export quantities such as 15 million (and shortly 35 million) tons per year of iron ore; 3.5 to 8.0 million tons of bauxite (subsequently to be refined into alumina – a third stage will produce aluminium); 60 million tons of manganese (including that which has already been mined for over twenty years in the Federal Territory of Amapá); 6 million tons of copper.

The Tucuruí hydroelectric plant is being constructed on the Tocantins river. It will be the fourth largest in the world and the largest in Brazil (if one omits the binationally developed Itaipú plant which is the largest in the world). In its first stage beginning in 1984, Tucuruí will generate about 4000 megawatts, the major part of which has been consigned to the plants which will process and refine bauxite. When it reaches full capacity, it will generate about 8000 MW per year. Another six hydroelectric plants are being planned upstream of Tucuruí on the Tocantins river, and they will provide some 13 000 MW. It has been estimated that the hydroelectric potential of the Amazon basin and its tributaries is of the order of 100 000 MW.

In order to transport the iron ore from Carajás to the port of Itaqui, a railroad of some 900 km is being built. At Tucuruí a lock system is being built to permit regular navigation on the Tocantins, making possible river transportation of some of the resources to be mined at the Carajás complex. Entire cities, to house tens of thousands of people, will be or are being constructed close to the sites of the major enterprises.

It is hoped that these enterprises will solve some of Brazil's greatest problems. The principal economic difficulties are, besides inflation: chronic instability of balance of payments and the consequent accumulation of foreign debt. Thus, rapid decisions have been made and international obligations assumed which are of impressive size. It has been roughly estimated that the Greater Carajás programme (of which iron mining and metallurgy is only one component) has already required between US$ 60 and 90 thousand million. But, most important of all, the whole infrastructure has to be finished in approximately five years, demanding investments of some US$ 22.5 thousand million or more. Added to these are the investments made in Tucuruí (US$ 5.6 thousand million) in Trombetas and in Villa do Conde (bauxite, alumina, aluminium – US$ 2.7 thousand million plus US$ 400 million, not including ALCOA in São Luiz), in Tapajós (gold), Rondônia (manganese, ranching, forestry), in Jari (cellulose, forestry, ranching, kaolin), in Balbina and Samuel (hydroelectric plants), in the Carajás–Itaqui railway (US$ 1.7 thousand million).

Brazil's national resources are clearly inadequate for such a great effort. This is especially so when we consider the other major investments in progress outside Amazonia, such as Itaipú, the Nuclear Programme, the railway system, the subways of Rio and São Paulo, and so forth. To these should be added the nationalisation of the Jari project. In this way, it is becoming imperative to negotiate the participation of major transnational economic groups. They would be associated with Cia. Vale do Rio Doce (CVRD), the nationalised company that is managing the process, and is a major world mineral exporter with 24% of the market. Loans are being arranged, on a guarantee of mineral ores being produced by 1985, by means of commodity futures at agreed prices which can be readjusted. The iron ore of Carajás has a basic price of US$ 20 a ton, although it is the highest grade known (about 66% pure on average).

Once the export of these ores begins, it is supposed to signify relief for Brazil's trade balance and balance of payments. However, the first few years, from 1985, will not provide sufficient relief to meet international debts. In fact, to refer again to the most conspicuous example, the Carajás iron ore: if 15 million tons a year are exported and the price is the present base price, the total revenue will be only US$ 300 million. When the goal of 35 million tons per year is reached, the total amount received will rise to US$ 700 million. But it must be taken into account that, besides the debt accumulated up to now (and everything indicates that this will not stop growing during that period) new amortisations, interest and royalties will have to be arranged to service the loans taken out to make Carajás viable. As an illustration: the Carajás iron mining and metallurgy project must absorb some US$ 3.3 thousand million. If this amount is borrowed from abroad and the interest and repayment of the loan is 20% annually, the totaly will be US$ 600 million a year.

Naturally, one must take into account the total exports generated by the different projects in progress, and also the imports that will no longer be necessary (aluminium, manganese, etc). In the time remaining until the year 2000, the final balance does not seem to indicate a definitive solution for the instability of the Brazilian external debt.

It is, however, certain that these investments will generate new jobs, directly and indirectly, on a comparable scale. In Tucuruí alone, there are about 35 000 technicians and labourers. At Carajás there will be a town of approximately 11 000 inhabitants. Ponta de Madeira, part of the port of Itaqui, should add 250 000 persons to the existing population of São Luiz. In the last ten years, great migrations have explosively increased the populations of some towns in the south of the State of Pará, the north of the State of Mato Grosso, and in the Federal Territory (now a State) of Rondônia. The city of Marabá has increased from 25 000 to 73 000 inhabitants, Conceição do Araguaia has grown from 28 000 to 130 000, becoming the third largest city in Pará; Tucuruí has grown from 10 000 to more than 67 000; Rondônia jumped from 113 000 to more than 500 000 in a decade; Manaus now has almost 700 000 inhabitants; and Belém has reached the million mark.

In part, the rapid increase in population is directly tied to the major projects in process. Just the new town constructed by Electronorte in Tucuruí to house its directors, technicians and workers will have about 40 000 people. Other major projects, such as ranching, have little capacity to increase employment. But the headquarters of the Jari complex, Monte Dourado, is a new town of more than 35 000 inhabitants.

There are now some 350 agro-business projects using fiscal incentives (as do the industrial projects), with a total investment, at current values, of the order of Cr$ 27 billion. But these investments are concentrated: *nine* of these projects absorb *one-third* of the total investments. In 1967 SUDAM estimated that more than 680 000 jobs would be needed to carry out the projects. But, at present, only about one-seventh of this number have been created.

Major effects

Major enterprises have major effects, but it is necessary to examine whether they are wholly 'good', or maybe partially (and, perhaps, predominantly) 'bad' and 'perverse' in various respects. Naturally, the standard used to decided the relative degree of goodness in any economic act is highly subjective. If we use the economic concept of efficiency or success of a venture, we can obtain a result. If we consider the effects from the viewpoint of economic growth, expressed in the indicator of national accounting, the result is different – whether or not it coincides with the first. And if we ask who is the beneficiary and how the benefits were attained from these ventures, we can have a third result totally different from the previous ones.

I am most interested in this last analysis: starting from the basic principle that it is man that evolves or not. His development is physical in the most inclusive sense (hygiene, health, well-being, life-expectancy, etc), but is also spiritual, equally in its most complete sense (involving cultural, 'social', intellectual, mental, and moral considerations). Economics – scientific and political – assumes a merely instrumental and mediating role: it is the means, method or mechanism to achieve goals which are not economic, but human. With this in mind, I can present some thoughts on the effects of the major projects already introduced into the landscape of Amazonia.

The first fact to mention is that for over a decade the projects have been one cause of significant migration into Amazonia. Some indications on this subject have already been given. Now they must be developed.

It should be noted that between 1970 and 1980 the population of Brazil grew at a yearly mean geometrical rate of 2.7%. The population of Amazonia as a whole grew by 5.0%. But within Amazonia, if we consider the basic political-administrative units, we can see that there were cases, such as Rondônia, in which this rate reached 15.8%. The State of Pará, which witnessed most construction of great enterprises, grew by 4.67% to a population of 3.5 million in September 1980. But, within it, particularly in the Araguaia–Tocantins region, there were towns in which the rate of demographic growth was higher than that of Rondônia: 19% to 20% per year, cumulatively. Whole towns, such as Redenção, non-existent ten years ago, sprang up with more than ten thousand inhabitants. Such examples can be repeated many times.

The migration movements come mainly from the south and southeast of the country. *Capixabas* (natives of the State of Espírito Santo), *Mineiros* (from the State of Minas Gerais), *Baianos* (from the State of Bahia) and people from the northeast in general have also been attracted to certain areas. There are official projects, now relatively inactive, and private projects, by major economic groups, for the colonisation of extensive areas. But a substantial number of these people migrate spontaneously and set themselves up on their own initiative, and at their own expense. Inevitably, conflicts over the possession of and title to land are becoming quite frequent. A certain rigidity in the actual supply of land in Amazonia occurs, on the one hand, because of the immense reserves created by law in favour of INCRA, and on the other hand, because of land speculation by large property developers and the presence of squatters ('*grileiros*') who came before the opening of roads or the benefits directly caused by them. There is also the presence of the major agro-business projects encouraged by SUDAM. There are numerous cases in which different land titles obtained in different ways lead to disputes about the ownership of property. In Conceição do Araguaia, for example, the total area of land titles is greater than the land available.

The role of major agricultural properties must be emphasised. This is particularly true of cattle firms which incorporate large expanses of land in a vast scheme of semi-intensive ranching. The total of jobs generated is extremely small. For example, 27 farms registered by INCRA contain 1.7 million hectares but employ only 500 families. Access by small farmers to the land necessary for their subsistence is precarious, if not impossible. In the area covered by these 27 farms it would be possible to established 17 000 small farmers and their families on plots of 100 hectares each. The agricultural enterprises are given fiscal incentives to form their capital, using resources derived from corporation tax paid by existing companies and others associated with them, as well as fringe benefits. They thus absorb substantial resources which would otherwise be at the disposal of the Treasury or of some political or social agency capable of guiding these funds to investments better justified on human or collective grounds. It has been estimated that in the past 15 years SUDAM has given incentives to projects, the majority of them agro-businesses, to a total historical value of 50 thousand million cruzeiros. In 'real' currency in December 1981, this would be approximately US$ 10 to 12 thousand million.

The predatory activities of large enterprises are well known. They involve the indiscriminate destruction of native vegetation in order to obtain a reduced amount of commercially saleable timber. They also involve cutting down the forest to make room for grazing land for cattle as part of major agro-business projects, and the destruction that small farmers cause along roads and rivers by penetrations which necessarily involve the opening of clearings for small plantations or the extraction of timber. These involve primitive farming methods, which lead to the abandonment of the original areas of settlement three or four years later. And so on, successively, using low-productivity agriculture.

The statistics, in this respect, cannot be trusted. There are specialists who estimate that in 30 years, if the rhythm of destruction of recent years is maintained, all of Amazonia will be a vast desert. Others, basing their information on satellite imagery, are of the opinion that the *hyleia* has barely been touched by deforestation. SUDAM is just starting to worry aboutestablishing more rigorous regulations and controls to stop or punish abuses resulting from indiscriminate destruction. The IBDF has the task of preventing deforestation from exceeding the limits prescribed by law, which are related to established productive activity; but it has very few forest rangers, considering the dimensions of the area to be patrolled and the physical difficulties of access to many places.

Into this picture, there are now to be added the major mining enterprises. Even if they are by nature located in relatively small areas, their geographic situations must be taken into consideration. In the case of Carajás, located about 1000 km from the coast, the railroad under construction is destroying the forest with its embankments, bridges and other works, calculated at more than 11 km width and requiring considerable earth movement. Centres of population will be installed alongside the railway, and each will be a base for greater penetration of the surrounding forest. On the other hand, the Carajás programme is a complex which involves the creation of agricultural and agro-industrial developments. This means that, depending on what they will grow, areas must be cleared to make room for these new plantations. Also, these tend to be oversized, out of scale with the region where the programme is taking place. This does not take into account the fact that there are already populated areas there, spontaneously settled and with their own agricultural activities.

It is important to add certain statistics. We are talking about the use of 15.5 million hectares, of which 10.2 million will be given over to various forms of agriculture (especially cereal grains), 3.0 million to ranches of 10 000 hectares each, and 2.3 million for reforestation (supposedly by eucalyptus trees, with which the CVRD has experience in Minas Gerais and Espírito Santo, whose soil, climate and ecology are totally different to those of Amazonia). Such use should yield results such as 10 million tons per year of cereal grains, almost one million tons of rubber, as much again of 'pellets' of manioc, 5.4 thousand million litres of alcohol, 25 million cubic metres of timber and 390 000 tons of meat. These estimates are greater than the corresponding total from projects approved and assisted by SUDAM over a period of 15 years from 1967.

It is important to recall that (as mentioned above for communities in the Araguaia region) in certain places the area of property title deeds exceeds the total extent of the local Armando Dias Mendesities in which they are located. Therefore there are only unoccupied public lands available for these projects and these are scattered and inadequate. There is also the fact publicly stated and reconised by the programme's directors, that extensive parts of this territory are not fit for the agricultural uses implicitly desired by the planners. Systematic soil studies by EMBRAPA/Pará have shown that these parts should have been used for agricultural purposes other than those required by the programme. On the other hand, there are native babaçu palms growing on about 8.6 million hectares. The CVRD has not decided what to do with these despite the importance of babaçu oil in activities such as iron and steel manufacturing.

At the same time, population expansion in Amazonia is being felt in the cities. Until very recently, the whole region had only two cities of any size: Belém and Manaus. Besides these there were a certain number of small towns and a larger number of small population centres which did not have the minimum urban equipment to be designated as true cities. They had the political and administrative status of municipalities solely because of their land area. One could not describe this as an urban network. Now Belém has a population of more than one million inhabitants and Manaus has almost 700 000. There is a significant number of towns with between 100 and 200 thousand inhabitants. If we consider Amazônia Legal which includes such urban centres as São Luiz and Cuiabá, besides rapidly expanding cities in the hinterland (such as Imperatriz in the State of Maranhão which has increased from 81 000 to 228 000 between 1970 and 1980), this category becomes even more significant.

We are here involved with the social problems of people who live on the fringes of society: slum areas and related factors which afflict major urban centres. Ease of access, demonstrated by an expanded network of highways, air travel and telecommunications, all help to uproot people, customs and ideas. Some of the migrants who originally moved to the interior are now arriving in the cities and are entangled in difficulties about possession of and title to the land.

This is the major challenge of present-day Amazonia: the region is seen by many as a great internal economic frontier which Brazil can use to resolve its problems of land distribution and food production. These problems stem not only from an excess of population in the more developed states, but also from the tendency to replace small and medium-sized farms run by one family by large, highly mechanised plantations producing on a commercial scale for the external market. This is how in the southern states there appeared the '*boia fria*', a salaried field hand, without land, who follows the seasonal needs of the large agricultural enterprises. It is no wonder that, apart from its capital, the State of Paraná lost population in almost all its towns between the censuses of 1970 and 1980. The population of Paraná has not reached a growth rate of one per cent a year. The same situation is found to a lesser extent in the State of Rio Grande do Sul and in other southern and southeastern states.

In these places, land has become too valuable for subsistence agriculture or even cattle ranching. The incentive to grow products such as soybeans for export to the great international markets, has caused large parcels of agricultural land to be used for this new function. To some extent, *pro-alcool* has played the same role in some regions. All these factors have combined to create a suplus of rural population which has generated the migration of those who saw in Amazonia their Eldorado. To these migrations were added many family members who, because of their own family's growth, could no longer be sustained on their original property which was usually destined to go to the eldest son. These migrations go to Rondônia, the State of Acre and the north of the State of Mato Grosso along the Brasília–Cuiabá–Pôrto Velho highway (with connections originating in the south or southeast to Brasília, Campo Grande and other important junctions). Or they go to eastern Amazonia, which includes the north of the State of Goiás, the south of Pará and the southeast of Maranhão, by the Belém–Brasília highway with transversal penetration by the Transamazon Highway.

An ambitious programme of colonisation was started alongside the Transamazon Highway about a decade ago when it was at the peak of its construction. Its goals involved the movement of 100 000 families from the northeast of Brazil, but these were far from being achieved. The agro-towns that were built have prospered and declined. In any case, the road made possible penetration by other migrants coming from the most distant parts of the country.

A number of workers joined or left these migrations, which were directed to major enterprises of mining or exploration of natural resources other than those of the forest or soil. It was thus possible to gather those people together into great anthills while they are building Tucuruí, Carajás, Itaqui, Vila de Conde, etc. At the same time parasitic agglomerations grew up around these centres, to provide such socially questionable 'services' as prohibited diversions, prostitution, etc. Such is the field of action of the federal, state and municipal governments, directly or through intermediary offices of every kind created to face the rising problems. At times, especially in eastern Amazonia with the Greater Carajás programme, their jurisdictions were superimposed. The available resources were often insufficient or badly administered. Almost always and notably in Rondônia, solutions have been found to be outdated in relation to the extent and diversity of the problems to be faced – so great is the number of persons who are *daily* added to the existing population. Until quite recently in Gi-Paraná, an average of *30 migrant families* arrived daily.

The attempt to develop a solution to this situation has inevitably been gigantic. In 1981, more than 100 000 deeds were distributed by INCRA. They embraced an area equivalent to a country the size of Spain. In 1982 INCRA sought to distribute about 240–300 000 new deeds – which far exceeds the total accumulated up to now. A the same time, pressure for land and present and potential sources of conflict are being tackled by the new law of Special Usufruct (*Usucapião Especial*). Not only does this reduce the time limit for occupation to five years, but lands which were previously exemp are now included: public lands in general including the frontier zones.

But, understandably, some 'solutions' in fact attract more people and aggravate the problems. Each road that is opened, each area that is urbanised, each occupation that is made official, means a new hope for the masses who still aspire to such benefits – these masses may already be installed in the region, or live in other regions, but have lost any hope of enjoying these benefits without leaving their original homes. These solutions still seem insufficient and disproportionate to the size and rhythm of the challenges. It would be necessary to put the Land Statute into practice quickly and forcefully, for immediate utilisation of the vast landed patrimony held by the federal institutions. Only thus could the frontier be 'opened' again and absorb the surplus population of other Brazilian geo-economic areas. This does not involve the more ambitious project of altering the present economic model and guiding it for the immediate and direct satisfaction of the most urgent needs of the people.

Major errors

Unwillingness (or lack of will) is the root of the major errors that result from 'development' based on giant enterprises. Obviously, the deepest roots of this complex situation did not originate in Brazil. In this as in many other respects, Brazil is suffering from the effects of a group of ideas or 'ideocracy' that has also devastated most of the countries improperly called 'western'. Thus, the observations that follow cannot be understood or discussed outside a wider context, which is that of the international economy and its national ramifications. This economy is usually described as capitalist, and it is from this concept that analyses are made and conclusions drawn. What I want to examine is the zone of contact between the capitalist and socialist worlds and some of the practical approximations generated by it – to the point where it is permissible to speak plausibly, but only in this sense, of 'the end of ideologies'.

One attitude disregards as less important, or at least not susceptible to 'scientific' manipulation, any aspects of reality that cannot be quantified. On an economic level, the most immediate form of this attitude is a tendency to see in increasing growth the highest goal of human activity. This gives rise to the phenomenon which can aptly be called *growth mania*. There must be growth at any cost. No attention should be paid to the destruction of nature and other (not quantifiable) values: of traditions, of ways of seeing things, of life-styles that are crushed by the projects of growth.

These projects are generally quite large. They are a phenomenon which correlates with the cult of gigantism, something that we might call *Goliathphilia* (some people propose calling it *macrophilia*); Goliath is better than David for the simple fact that he is bigger. This phenomenon is linked to the rise of manpower-efficiency techniques in central economies designed for large internal or foreign markets.

Naturally, some system of measurement is needed to express the things that must be quantified and made to grow until paroxysm is reached. This system must be dynamic, in order to reflect rapid transformations. It has produced *index worship*. All of us are seized with paranoia in the development of the Gross National Product and related indices. We feel frustrated when they do not repeat excellent performances of past years or when, sadly, they are zero or even negative. On the other hand, when they rise above historical averages we feel that the nation has taken a further step towards a collective happiness – even if this growth resulted from anti-social or predatory activities.

Such are the bases of the major errors. But the greatest of all and the cause of all the rest is industrial error. Of course I do not advocate a return to a 'pastoral' style of life, with the renunciation of those technical achievements which make man's life easier and increase his capacity for work and production. But it is important to review the industrial phase in the history of humanity over the past 300 years. Borrowing from others' recent work, I believe it valid to draw attention to such thoughts in the case of Amazonia.

In both the capitalist and socialist worlds, the dominance of industry shapes and leaves its mark on society and on each of its members. *Specialisation* and its consequent professionalisation is one of these, as well as *standardisation* of goods and services with which it is closely associated. With it comes the standardisation of habits, ways of thinking and living, attitudes and suffering. Standardisation, in turn, demands synchronisation and 'timing' of operations, so that the specialised productive process is subdivided, which brings about the *robotisation* of mankind.

What needs to be done is to demythicise this vision. Nonquantifiable, extra-economic values must be give due weight. Such values must guide economic calculations instead of resulting from them – which inevitably happens when purely material, statistically manoeuvrable objectives are given prime importance as ends in themselves. This is the atmosphere in which the industrial system prospers.

It is evident and worth repeating that this critical vision will not 'absolve' the ills of capitalism. It seems valid to assess the dominant presence of major multinational capital from the example of such an obscure corner as Amazonia. Even when its action is formally developed through a state-owned company such as CVRD, the sheer size of such enterprises and their economic, technical and political power make the participation of these major protagonists inevitable. Their manipulations are well known and are increasingly coming under close examination at home and abroad.

But there must be limits to such an assessment. The first is not to attempt to understand a region such as Amazonia by using interpretive models based on a more complex and evolved socio-economic context than exists there. Along with recent capitalist formations, precapitalist or even acapitalist formations persist. The important new factor which dominates everything in Amazonia is the introduction of an industrial dimension – and its capitalist form, of course.

The other limitation is not to criticise real capitalist industrialism simply by means of so-called socialist theory. Some considered practical (as opposed to 'ideal' of hypothetical) socialist experience would introduce a wholesome element of humility in proposing solutions — which cannot be found on the supermarket shelves of the social sciences. This error occurs very frequently from a failure to identify the presence of the quantitive fetish in systems which try to be socialist. Before suggesting supposedly more effective and equitable alternatives to the model now in force, it would be realistic to attempt an evaluation of the experiences attempted.

Major challenges

Major projects and their errors inevitably lead to major challenges of vision for the future. These result from the national and worldwide context in which projects are developed. The first major challenge is precisely what attitude to assume about the current situation. A comfortable, but essentially sterile, attitude is simply to condemn all deviations from what is considered desirable, hence to imagine an alternative future which would be a return to the Lost Paradise. It is a comfortable attitude, because it frees people from offering concrete solutions to concrete situations. Everything is put off to an imaginary future.

Let us adopt the more realistic view that some factors cannot be substantially changed. We must therefore think of other challenges. One is a possible 'compromise' between large and smaller businesses. To compromise does not mean to subordinate small businesses or to imagine some form of peaceful coexistence free from tensions. It means to attempt systems that ensure that small family, individual, group, or small community enterprises can survive with relative autonomy. At the same time they fulfil an unmistakable and essential social role. It should be possible for a small farmer or cattle rancher to organise his family business without being under the crushing pressure to which they are increasingly subjected by the major enterprises. There must be full support for their possession of and title to the land, with conditions which permit them to live off it and also to produce a surplus for market. And, what is fundamental, they must be able to reach decisions on the basis of the best possible knowledge of the general economic and social conditions in which they live.

A small productive property generally attends to its own needs and those of local markets. A larger productive unit is inevitably tuned to the major national or world market. The former cannot entirely escape this crushing reality, but can coexist with it. In many respects the productivity of these small units exceeds that of the major units. Those are also responsible for a disproportionate share of the consumer market.

The second challenge must distinguish between decisions which can and must be made at regional level within Amazonia, and those which are necessarily assumed by the federal government or even by transnational firms. In countries like Brazil, in the last few decades, there has been a tendency towards growing centralisation of decision-making on economic policy. It is easy to understand why: the scale of production and marketing of products increasingly transcends the limits of local or regional markets. Technical and scientific development has established a model of production based on the major enterprises. This model requires a corresponding political model and tends to centralisation and concentration.

Nevertheless, recent studies show that micro- and mini-productive organisations can flourish spontaneously and fulfil roles not met by the major enterprises. The challenge we are talking about requires that decision-makers have a very clear perception of this fact and take a favourable attitude towards the small producers. It also requires a less centralised political model, with safeguards for autonomy and proper options for different social, ethnic (and this embraces the problems of indigenous communities), cultural, and other groups.

We thus come to the most difficult of the 'compromises': the reconciliation of private aspirations and collective needs. This compromise questions the extent to which initiatives and actions are left to individuals and lesser social groups, or whether they must be subject to wider decisions and imposed on all. This is not a new question, for it is the essence of the unending battle between hopes for freedom and the constraints of necessity. Total freedom would be chaotic and unthinkable in modern economic life. But it is not impossible in some specific situations. On the other hand, total planning would be drastic and equally unthinkable. This is not the moment to make a final proposal about this. It must flow naturally from the play of negotiations, pressures and counterpressures, debate, alliances, and disputes, compromises and partial transactions which are capable of leading slowly but surely in the desired direction.

Equally this is not the time to present a list of policies to apply this scheme to the concrete situation of Amazonia. I can however, suggest some methods perfectly compatible with the constitutional and legal instruments now in force and which can be adopted. Such are: the reformulation of the Single Tax (*Imposto Unico*) on minerals, the creation of 'royalties' or similar means in favour of a region producing non-renewable natural resources, the establishment of favourable tariffs (facilitating physical and economic access to prosperous markets, including access to further knowledge), the creation of special incentives for work that is directly productive and autonomous (including the possession of and title to land), a subsidy for absolute poverty, and so forth.

The ultimate ends of a 'list' of this nature would be the type of development which it makes possible. This development will not be brought about solely by a major enterprise. On the contrary, the intrinsic logic of major projects suggests that favourable treatment of real human beings tends to be neglected. Inevitably, those who work directly in these major enterprises form an isolated and privileged class. There are numerous examples of this among the mining firms.

By way of illustration, it can be shown that even with a basic selling price for ore of US$ 20 per ton, it is estimated that the gross profit of CVRD will be about US$ 9 per ton. If an export rate of 15 million tons a year is reached, it will yield revenue of US$ 135 million. If export reaches the predicted goal of 35 million tons, this will rise to US$ 315 million. If a 'royalty' of 10% were established (as was done recently by the government of Peru which established a percentage in favour of the 'jungle zone' of revenue from petroleum taken from it), we would have, respectively, US$ 13.5 million and US$ 31.5 million (or in Brazilian currency of late 1981, approximately Cr$ 1.8 thousand million and Cr$ 4.1 thousand million). The first figure corresponds to a tenth of the total current budget of Pará – including both its own revenues and transfers from the federal government. The second figure would correspond to almost 23% of this income.

The establishment of 'royalties' of up to 20% to be divided between the State and municipalities affected by the programme would not be unthinkable. Doubling the above percentages would mean a great deal to a state with as little revenue as Pará which will remain short of revenue even when the mining enclaves are producing at full capacity according to present estimates. This withdrawl of funds would mean very little to CVRD, if we appreciate that we are talking about 10% and 20% respectively of gross profits, not about costs. The estimated profit is in the order of US$ 9 on an export price of US$ 20 per ton, representing a margin of 45%. Thus the proposed 'royalties' would represent 4.5% and 9% respectively of the export value. This would still be less than the 10% charged by Peru.

Conclusion

Our thoughts can be summarised as follows:
  (a) Prevailing activity in Amazonia is concentrative – spatial, economic, social and demographic.
  (b) It therefore creates conditions that attract strong contingents of migrants.
  (c) These dispute the available land, with consequent legal, administrative and political confusion.
  (d) Large companies take profits out of the region through their national and transnational divisions.
  (e) Relatively few suitable jobs are created.
  (f) Those who secure these jobs enjoy benefits which do not spread to the rest of the population.
  (g) At the same time, the implantation of major projects imposes new responsibilities on local government (both state and municipal) that are not matched by new revenues, at least not in corresponding proportion.
  (h) The contrast between the privileged ghetto of the major enterprise and the

'outside world' tends to be aggravated – augmenting social inequalities and tensions.

(i)   Many factors combine to make it unthinkable that Brazil or Amazonia, in the context of the real world, could be free from major enterprises.

(j)   But it is imperative to develop incentives to guarantee small and medium-sized producers and consumers the freedom of option needed for dignified human life.

(k)   This need involves numerous compromises: participation schemes and firm political decisions, beginning with the definition of certain basic values extrapolated from a pure economic state.

(l)   The issue therefore is not one of economic efficiency but of social equality.

(m) For this reason, the most important factor must be extra-economic; in the final analysis, it must be a question of ethics.

4 The effects of deforestation in Amazonia

HARALD SIOLI

Ecological peculiarities

An exposé on the effects of deforestation in Amazonia has to start with an introduction into the most important peculiarities or principles of the ecology of the region. I shall restrict myself to the high-forest-covered *terra firme* of the Amazonia lowlands.

The first scientist to recognise and outline the most striking basic ecological characteristics of that area was the Swiss Hans Bluntschli who stated that '. . . *wind* and *plain*, *forest* and *water* act intrinsically together. We perceive that everything in Amazonia must come under their influence, from the smallest living being to the activity and behaviour of mankind . . ." (Bluntschli 1921, p 51; translated by H.S.). As a comparative anatomist, Bluntschli observed with eyes schooled in structural interrelations that the forest and water 'act intrinsically together ', depend on each other and are mutual expressions of one another.

Chemical poverty including lack of nutrients

Bluntschli, however, did not make any chemical analysis of water and evidently did not know that Katzer had already discovered the surprising chemical pureness and weakness of most Amazonian waters (Katzer 1903). Otherwise, that keen observer would have discovered deeper and more revealing interrelationships.

Systematic research on Amazonian water chemistry started only after 1945 and still continues. It confirmed Katzer's early discovery and extended it to by far the largest areas of the whole forest-covered Amazonian region: the 'hylaea' of Alexander von Humboldt (Sioli 1950, 1954, 1955; Schmidt 1972; Furch 1976; Junk and Furch 1980).

The only exceptions to that general rule are a few small local zones with peculiar geology and lithology (Sioli 1963). It is especially true of the strip of land of the Andean foothills with its projections along the whitewater rivers and the alluvial lands of their '*várzeas*'. Here we find chemically richer waters, signs of richer, more fertile soils, and conditions completely different from those of the *terra firme*. Most Amazonian waters, however, prove to be so pure and poor in electrolytic content that they are best compared to distilled water of low quality and almost equal to rainwater.

In a climate as humid as that of the Amazonian hylaea, and under a mature forest cover, i.e., with a biomass constant over a long period of time, all soluble substances are liberated from the soil by weather processes and are being washed out. Since they are nowhere retained or accumulated, as would happen with an increasing mass of vegetation, they must appear in the ground, spring and creek waters. But since these waters are chemically as pure and poor as I have described, we must conclude that the soils are correspondingly poor and do not contain appreciable quantities of substances, including nutrients for plant growth, that could be mobilised by weathering. By implication this means that those soils are extremely infertile.

Chemical analyses of soils (Camargo 1948; Sombroek 1966; Falesi 1972) confirmed the conclusion drawn from the water chemistry.

These results enable us to understand one fact or principle which is basic for the forest ecosystem of by far the greatest part of the Amazonian hylaea: the poorness in nutrients of its soils, or in other words their infertility.

Recycling of nutrients

Despite their infertility, an exuberant forest stands on the Amazonian soils. At first glance this seems a paradox and must be clarified. The answer is that the living part of that forest ecosystem, the forest vegetation itself, responds to that challenge by strictly closed circulation of nutrients within the living biomass (Stark 1969; Klinge and Fittkau 1972). This constant recycling of the same nutrient molecules through generations of forest organisms must be understood as one of the basic principles in the functioning of the Amazonian forest system.

This principle alone does not, however, explain how the forest manages to realise and maintain its closed nutrient cycle. Studying it in detail, we find that nature has applied all possible means to achieve that aim: to reduce to a minimum the loss of nutrients by leaks from the cycle. There is no appreciable humus layer on top of the Amazonian forest soil. Instead, the root system of the trees is shallow, usually restricted to the uppermost 20–30 cm, and on average three times as dense as that of a temperate forest (Klinge 1973a). This indicates that the nutrients are never temporarily retained or stored in dead matter on top of this soil (from which they might easily be leached by the high rainfall) but are rapidly reabsorbed from the forest litter – and from the droppings and remains of animals – which rapidly decompose in the hot humid climatic conditions. Stark (1969) was the first researcher to discover that the decomposition of dead forest litter, and hence the recycling of nutrients within the forest system, is performed by fungi. Herrera *et al.* (1978) were even able to show fungi with one end of their hypae inside a decomposing litter leaf and the other end inside a living root. And Singer (in press) recently found specific details and conditions of the mycorrhiza.

The intensity of nutrient recycling in the Amazon forest has also been shown by W. Franken (verbal communication) by comparing the chemical compositions of rainwater, of water falling from the canopies, of stem runoff, and of groundwater in a forest near Manaus. While the rainwater was chemically as poor as would be expected in an area far from industrial civilisation, the canopy water and the stem runoff were very rich in dissolved matter including nutrients, whereas the groundwater was practically as poor as the rainwater. This means that the dense mat of roots of the forest trees acts as a highly effective filter. It retains all dissolved substances from the canopy water and the stem runoff, and immediately recycles them back into the living trees without losing any into the groundwater, creeks and rivers which would finally carry them into the ocean to be lost forever from the forest ecosystem (see also Klinge and Fittkau 1972).

The chemical richness of the subcanopy water and the stem runoff is explained, not only by the leaching effect of rainwater on the leaves and epiphytic and epiphyllic plants of the forest trees, but far more importantly by the fact that probably the greatest part of Amazon forest fauna lives in or on the canopies of the trees: insects, birds and up to the coatis and monkeys. They not only feed but also defaecate there and their 'manure' is washed down by the rains. The fauna is thus perfectly integrated into the general nutrient recycling process within the life of the forest as a whole: it simply adds a lateral extension to it, as does all the fauna of the forest ecosystem.

Tightly closed and rapid recycling is all the more essential for the forest's existence, since *terra firme* soils consist of up to 80% or even more of fine quartz, the rest being kaolinite as the only clay mineral present (Irion 1976, 1978). Because of the low absorption capacity of kaolinite, the soil would never retain nutrients, even those liberated by decomposition of inorganic and organic matter. The first rains would extract such nutrients from the soil and carry them beyond the forest ecosystem into the groundwater, creeks and finally into the sea.

Protection against soil erosion

Good percolation capacity of the soil under high forest cover reduces surface runoff to practically zero, and the dense canopies of high forest inhibit surface erosion. The dense surface mat of tree roots not only recovers nutrients for the living vegetation. It also immediately soaks up a high percentage of fallen rainwater to be evapotranspired again by the evergreen latifolious trees and quickly returns it to the atmosphere where it condenses and falls once again as new rain. Salati *et al.* (1978, 1979) found that about 50% of rains in Amazonia consist of water recycled within the region. The pluvial climate of Amazonia favours uninterrupted growth of vegetation, through its annual average rainfall of some 2500 mm and its absence of an arid season (Koppen types Af and Am). But it depends on that portion of the rainwater which is recycled thanks to the existence of latifolious forest with its high evapotranspiration capacity. That is the final implication of Bluntschli's early observation.

We thus see why recycling processes are essential for the existence and survival of the forest ecosystem in Amazonia.

Diversity of the forest ecosystem

Once these recycling processes have overcome the basic difficulty for perpetuating the Amazon forest ecosystem – that is the lack of a steady supply of fresh nutrients – nature has developed here the most diverse ecosystem we know on earth (see Fittkau 1973; Klinge 1973b). The greatest number of plant and animal species we are aware of (estimated at between 1.5 and 2 million species) divides the big, general nutrient cycle into an immense number of subcycles. Indigenous man in his native cultures is perfectly adapted to and integrated in that system. The diversity of species may be taken as yet another 'principle' of the Amazon forest ecosystem.

The enormous number of plant and animal species means not only that there is an equally vast number of ecological niches occupied and utilised by those species or nutrient subcycles intercalated into the major closed cycle. It also means that these plant and animal species, together with the abiotic environmental conditions, by their mutual interaction and feedback form a single complex that includes an even greater number of homeostatic cycles, from very tiny to large ones, all of which interact and influence one another. At the same time, they all depend on the fact that the greatest homeostatic cycle of that system – that of the tightly closed cycle which results from the cooperation of the smaller ones – functions with a minimum of loss. The whole system may be loosely compared to the circulation of an organism in which there are blood vessels of the most diverse sizes, from capillaries to the main arteries.

This extremely complex, diverse and rich Amazon biota has developed over millions of years, uninterrupted by glacial periods or general aridification. It represents the greatest genetic pool and reserve we know on earth, and is at the same time the basis and the starting material for future biotic evolution.

Effects of deforestation

With these basic ecological peculiarities or principles of Amazon *terra firme* and its ecosystem in mind, we may attempt a survey of some consequences to be predicted when current 'development' projects are undertaken. All of them interfere with the Amazon forest and involve large-scale deforestation, almost all for export purposes.

Circulation and reserves of nutrients

Deforestation interrupts the tightly closed recycling of nutrients within the ecosystem. The inorganic components of the biomass, particularly the nutrients, are liberated by burning the felled forest and are contained in the ashes since they are not fixed in the soils, as already shown. Most are then washed out by the first rains and removed from the environment by surface runoff from the denuded areas or through the groundwater. The rest are absorbed by crops or through the grasses by cattle, and are exported with the harvest or the beef.

The word 'colonialism' is used nowadays as a synonym for the exploitation or pauperisation of one region for the benefit or enrichment of another. Deforestation and export of the resulting products can only be termed neo or endo colonialism. I must also mention that cattle ranches, which have already destroyed tens of thousands of square kilometres of forest and transformed them into artificial steppe, need relatively few personnel and are thus of no advantage to the local population.

The result of such activity is impoverished soils, deprived of the stock of nutrients contained in the former living biomass. Carrying capacity of artificial pastures in a former hylaean section of the Belém–Brasília highways decreased from 0.9–1 head of cattle on young pastures to only 0.3 head after some six years (H. O'R. Sternberg, verbal communication). Nutrients are one basis of constant biological productivity. Their irreplaceable loss reduces and limits not only harvests but also biological production.

Surface erosion and compaction of the soil

The soils, sediments and thick weathering layers of the Amazon *terra firme* are easily eroded. With deforestation, these soils and layers are deprived of the protection of the dense forest canopy and exposed to the direct impact of heavy rains and tropical thunderstorms. The substitution of forest by short-cycle crops or by planted grasses removes the former protection. In the case of planted pasture, we must also consider that there is no tropical grass perfectly resistant to trampling by cattle. Besides, during the dry seasons, pasture grasses dry up, the sod is exposed still more, and the bare soil is strongly heated, destroying its microflora. There is a danger that the region may develop into a new 'dust-bowl' – dust, formerly unknown in Amazonia, is already common on the new roads during the dry season.

Also, formerly porous forest soil is compacted by deforestation (Schubart 1977). Through general and especially slope clearing, deforestation increases surface runoff. With the onset of the first heavy rains of the next rainy season, the unprotected dust-dry soil will be eroded with unprecedented violence and washed away into the creeks and rivers.

Sandification

Sandification on the bare surface layer of the soil is another effect. The direct impact of heavy raindrops causes what can be called 'selective erosion', washing away the finer clay particles while the coarser and heavier sand is left behind. This effect can also be observed on small areas left without protective vegetation for a longer time. The most striking example of that type of selective erosion is the famous 'sandy campos' behind Santarém which the famous British naturalist Henry Walter Bates (1892) described in the last century. With time, 'sandification' proceeds deeper into the soil, thereby reducing its water-retention capacity. This new edaphic condition is especially hostile to young seedlings of forest trees and finally prevents the regrowth of a forest.

Climatic change

This will be one of the most serious effects of large-scale deforestation in Amazonia. Small and temporary clearings ('*roças*' of the native people, Indians as well as *caboclos*) are mere pinpricks in a coherent forest, which soon heal and cicatrise after abandonment and do not noticeably affect the general recycling of nutrients nor reduce the generally high evapotranspiration of the whole forest. But the effect on it of great clearings will be worse, the more extensive the deforestation. With the reduction of rainwater re-evaporating from the original forest, the rate of its recycling will also diminish. Evapotranspiration of steppe is estimated to be only a third that of latifolious evergreen forest, and the availability of water for evapotranspiring steppe plants is reduced in the same proportion. The consequence will be that the total annual rainfall will decrease considerably when a certain percentage of Amazon forest has been destroyed, and the seasonality of rainfall will become more pronounced. This will probably have a disastrous effect on the survival of spared forest areas which are intended as 'nature reserves' or the like.

With longer and more severe dry seasons, the supply of rainwater to the generally surface root systems of the forest trees will be interrupted for longer periods. Since the groundwater level of Amazon *terra firme* is usually very deep and not reached by the roots of most trees, these depend on having only short periods without rain, just the relatively dry seasons called 'summer' in Amazonia. Through climatic change, it is inevitable that the planned limited forest reserves will automatically also die.

Rivers

More intensive surface runoff and soil erosion, and seasonal changes in the pluvial climate on the regime, will have obvious effects on the sediment load and sedimentation processes of the rivers. We must certainly expect more sudden and higher floods, lower water levels during the dry season, greater turbidity and increased bottom freight, and partial silting of the river beds in unpredictable places.

Global consequences

Large-scale deforestation of Amazonia must also be taken into consideration. Determination of the biomass of the Amazon high forest (undertaken in a subregion near Manaus that is poor in nutrients and with a noticeably weak developed forest) has revealed that the dry vegetable matter amounts to about 500 tons per hectare, which corresponds to about 250 metric tons of carbon fixed in a steady-state equilibrium (Klinge 1976). Extrapolated for the whole Amazonian hylaea of nearly 5×10^6 km^2, this means that about 115×10^9 tons of carbon are retained in the forest matter. That is of the order of nearly 20% of the carbon of the entire atmosphere's CO_2.

Removal of that forest biomass and replacing it with artificial steppe (pasture) or short-cycle crops means that at most 20% of the C-content of the former forest biomass will be fixed in the new vegetation. The rest will be oxidised, by burning or by rotting etc., and will enter the atmosphere as carbon dioxide. Experience during recent decades indicates that about half that additional input of CO_2 into the atmosphere will disappear into the sink of the oceans. There would thus be a net increase of about 8% in the CO_2 content of the global atmosphere if the entire Amazon forest were replaced by a much less voluminous, manmade vegetation. Together with the increase of about 16% of CO_2 in the atmosphere already observed since the last century, that new addition would contribute to the greenhouse effect of the CO_2 in the atmosphere. (For more details see Sternberg, in press.)

Trying to relate the existence or disappearance of the Amazon forest to the O_2 content of the atmosphere, or to hold that forest responsible for up to 50% (!) of the oxygen production on earth, is naturally nonsense and invented only for propaganda reasons.

The annihilation of the enormous number and diversity of species of organisms which make up the unique Amazonian forest ecosystem will probably have a most incisive effect on all life on earth and its future. Not only will its present diversity, richness and beauty be impoverished, but a very high percentage of the global genetic stock and reserves will be irretrievably exterminated by large-scale deforestation and with it the basis for their future evolutionary potential will be cut off.

'Life' on earth does not consist only of the metabolic processes occuring in the organisms or in the flux rates of matter and energy through the ecosystems. Perhaps the most striking essentials of life are its diversity and polychromy. That peculiarity ranges from the number of possible combinations of amino acids in protein molecules (compared to which the mass of the whole universe expressed in the lightest hydrogen atoms is infinitely small) (Eigen 1979) to the insight that 'the purpose of the world is not the best possible general welfare but richness in potential' (Kleinschmidt 1930, translated by H.S.).

With this statement we leave the realm of pure classic natural sciences and enter another spiritual dimension of such qualities as beauty and, more essentially, ethics. In this context let me quote the American anthropologist Ruy Rappaport who said 'knowledge will never replace respect in the attitude of men vis-a-vis ecological systems, since the latter are so complex that sufficient understanding of their content and structure may never be at hand to permit predictions about results of their actions' (Rappaport 1969, cit. from Sternberg 1980).

These words are clearcut, but they are not observed by modern 'development' schemes. These envisage and take for granted only hoped-for quantitative production, mostly of export goods. They fail to consider the losses which will occur when the Amazon forest ecosystem, evolved over millions of years and maintained by its native peoples in their adapted cultures, is destroyed within a few decades.

The question thus arises: what is behind the risky projects whose proponents show no 'respect' for that ecosystem, but aim only to exploit Amazonia?

Life, in an ecological sense, can be defined as the mutural interaction between an organism and its environment, from which a new function unit results (see Sioli 1973a). 'Development' is the interaction by the organism, man, on the environment, the Amazon forest ecosystem. Since we have hitherto considered only the response of the environment, we must now look at man who performs that interaction in order to understand the whole process in truly ecological terms. Only then can we comprehend what is happening in that part of the tropics.

It is only too obvious that the 'development' ideas come from non-Amazonian people, be they in Europe, North America, Japan, or in the modern centres of southern Brazil. They come from a mentality evolved in temperate climates and under different geographical, historical and social conditions, culminating in the present 'highly developed' industrial–commercial civilisation (see Sioli 1972). The plans are conceived and elaborated solely to serve that civilisation all over the world. They are not for the local population of Amazonia (whether Indians, *caboclos* or other Amazonised inhabitants), and are not intended to safeguard the basis of these people's future. This is nothing but a new wave of conquests now sweeping over the last vast tract of land spared by the original and subsequent European conquests.

What is needed is to care about the local population, which is also multiplying, and about its needs and its future. Current projects of giant enterprises for export, and of mega-colonisation by foreign settlers, are obnoxious to the people of Amazonia and to future generations.

Instead, a really rational and lasting utilisation of Amazonia must benefit her true inhabitants and must be based on strict observance of the well-known ecological peculiarities of that country. That means the reverse of the present ideas. The diverse Amazonian forest must be maintained as a continuum, in space and time. Inside it, population centres of limited size and number should be built as 'islands' of human civilisation separated from each other by the forest. As much as possible should be recycled, with just enough produced for export to enable the people to purchase undeniably necessary goods (for more details see Sioli 1980a). As a basic concept for such true development, in a humane sense for a growing number of people, without destroying the extremely fragile landscape, its diversity and sustainable bio-productivity, the ideas of Schumacher's '*Small is Beautiful*' (1973) may be taken as a guideline. Some groping experiments in that direction have already started. May they be successful and triumph over the destructive objectives of instant profits for foreign regions and peoples!

5 Development in a water-dominated ecosystem, or Amazonian ecology in a time of change

THOMAS E. LOVEJOY

Heralded by the Transamazon Highway development of the 1970s, the late twentieth century is a turning point in Amazonian history. A major new emphasis has been placed on occupying and developing Amazonia, particularly by Brazil, which of course occupies the largest part, as well as by Peru and Ecuador. This inevitably spells a major impact on the ecology of the world's largest river system and largest tropical rainforest. The challenge, as noted by Skillings (this volume) and others, is to determine scientifically and socially how to guide this development to protect the ecology of Amazonia. This is requisite if Amazonia is to maintain its ability to contribute to human welfare, both for those living within the region as well as over the remainder of the planet.

Water is a dominant element in Amazonia. Its river system is estimated to contain twenty per cent of all the world's river waters and to discharge 175 000 m^3/second into the Atlantic (Smith 1981). It is not surprising with so much water that hydroelectric schemes are currently under way, but it is regrettable that they have been planned with so little understanding of their impact, and executed so haphazardly as far as ecological problems are concerned.

The Amazon fishery, recently estimated at a standing stock of roughly 10^6 metric tons is a critical (and delicious) source of animal protein for Amazon residents. Migratory patterns of major food fishes are close to unknown, and virtually no provision has been made to learn about them let alone to plan hydroelectric projects to minimise their disruption. Projects such as Tucuruí are likely to forever impoverish the waters of the Rio Tocantins and its fisheries, hardly a sensible course in a world increasingly concerned about feeding an ever larger, even more hungry population. This is not to say the potential of the Amazon fisheries is enormous for it is not (Goulding in Moran in press), but neither is it negligible.

Hydroelectric projects in tropical areas are subject to a number of problems (Goodland), some of them because there is no turnover, or seasonal mixing, of waters in tropical water bodies (although in very shallow lakes wind-generated mixing can occur). These conditions produce oxygen-deficient (anaerobic) conditions with vegetation decomposition producing hydrogen sulphide, which in turn creates dilute acid solutions corrosive to turbines and susceptible to combustion. The record in effective vegetation clearing in advance of flooding has been very poor to date, in part because of a lack of ready market for the timber. Even less attention has been given to biological salvage schemes. These vary greatly in their potential: wildlife capture and release schemes are generally unproven in their worth and could well often be mostly self-satisfying but unproductive; there is unlikely to be ecological 'room' for animals released into forests already occupied by wildlife.

Perhaps most serious of all, is the poor attention accorded the need for watershed management. Occupation is being ignored or permitted in the Balbina watershed near Manaus. There is no systematic plan to protect the watershed at Tucuruí, and the firm contracted for vegetation clearing there would seem to have been rewarded for its poor performance by a 2000 ha concession for cattle ranching within the watershed. Given the attentiveness of Panama to the siltation problem estimated to be on the order of 13.5×10^6 m^3/year (Smythe) were the Panama Canal watershed to be deforested, the lack of attention to this problem in Amazonia is curious and disturbing. There seems so little point in expenditure of huge sums of money for hydroelectric projects which will destroy vast areas and impoverish a fishery, when so little effort is made to keep the lifespan of the project at its maximum potential.

The fisheries of the Amazon are in a state of virtual non-management, the relevant agency being thinly spread and preoccupied with marine fisheries problems. In the past decade the overfishing problem has become more than apparent in the vicinity of population centres such as Manaus (Goulding in Moran). The Manaus fleet must venture hundreds if not thousands of kilometres distant to achieve the necessary catch.

Tied to this problem is the remarkable relationship, long known but only recently detailed to any extent, of the floodpain (*várzea*) forests and many of the commercial fish species (Goulding, 1980). The productivity of the fisheries of the Amazon and its tributaries is in many instances considerably higher because of a nutrient-transfer process from the terrestrial ecosystems to the aquatic. This is achieved by fishes swimming into the floodplain forests at the high-water times of year and feeding on fruits, seeds and other living matter dropping from the trees. Human welfare, in terms of fish protein, is dependent on this curious relationship. Yet it is threatened by plans to develop *várzea* lands even further than deforestation has already affected them. They are naturally attractive for agriculture because of annual deposits of silt. What is clearly needed is a zoning plan for *várzea* lands which can focus agricultural development on already deforested lands, explore alternative land uses, e.g. for fish culture, and protect sufficient floodplain forests to maintain the integrity of the fishery.

Water is as dominant an aspect of terrestrial ecosystems and aerial ecology in Amazonia as in the river system itself. The vegetation formation is of a sort characteristic of the wet tropics and very dependent on rainfall. That rainfall, however, is in turn very dependent on the vegetation. Salati and his Brazilian colleagues have demonstrated for the first time in history that forest generates rainfall. Using a number of lines of evidence including isotopic analysis of rainwater they have demonstrated that water is recycled as air moves across the Amazon Basin from the Atlantic towards the Andes, and that roughly half of the rainfall in the basin is generated by the forest itself and is not of oceanic origin. There is clearly a limit to how much conversion of the Amazon landscape can take place without disrupting this relationship. The limit itself is not known, but the means to estimate it through research have been identified. A major basin-wide study is needed to pin this down, and to avoid the risk of initiating an irreversible drying trend in Amazonia. The implications of such a climatic change are not limited to the Amazon, nor do they extend only to central Brazil. The possible effect on global heat budgets, in which cloud formation plays an important role, is a matter of concern.

On land, assuming the forest–rainfall relationship remains intact, there are still problems of sustainable forms of development (Skillings this volume; Lovejoy and Schubart 1980). They also need to be compatible with protecting the important segment (at least 10%) of the planet's biological diversity occurring there. Protecting biological diversity, while usually the responsibility of individual nations, is none the less a topic of overwhelming international importance as recently reviewed by the United States Department of State (Strategy Conference on Biological Diversity).

The majority of the Amazonian flora and fauna can only be protected in a system of national parks and reserves. Relatively few species will be able to survive in agricultural areas or monocultures such as forest plantations. Many might be able to survive in managed forests but little is known either about the Amazon forest management or which species would find such forests adequate for survival.

A great difficulty in choosing areas for protection is the very fragmentary knowledge of the Amazon flora and fauna. The majority of species have not been described by science and only a few groups such as birds and butterflies are known in any detail. The only basis for proceeding at this point is the recognition in these better-known groups of clusters of species of restricted distribution (endemics) thought by many to represent areas where the Amazon forest was able to persist during the cold dry periods of the Pleistocene (see Prance 1982). Current conservation efforts in the basin are proceeding on the basis of these so-called 'Pleistocene refugia' as defined by birds, two subfamilies of butterflies, reptiles, and four plant families. The not-very-secure assumption is that conservation areas taking care of these particular animals and plants should take care of all the rest.

Clearly more and better data on plant and animal distributions are needed before anyone can feel confident that conservation units in Amazonia are able to measure up to the task of protecting the significant fraction of biological diversity within the basin. The Flora Project of INPA (Instituto Nacional de Pesquisas da Amazônia) and the New York Botanical Garden, is making an important contribution to this.

Within a short time it should be amenable to computer analysis. Attempts are afoot in Brazil to mount a complementary Fauna Project, but are encountering funding difficulties.

A difficulty with such efforts is to decide when the accumulation of data is enough for conservation purposes. Here the purposes of conservation can be seemingly at odds with more traditional academic undertakings. Instead of highly detailed distribution maps worked up from expeditions stretching over years if not decades, preliminary atlases would do for conservation purposes. Some fieldwork might in fact be indicated to fill in important blanks, but ultimately patterns should be clear enough to indicate priority areas for conservation units. These should of course be investigated in the field to verify that the species do in fact still occur at proposed locations. The problem of size of protected areas is important too, but has been discussed in detail elsewhere.

In the meantime, despite shortcomings of refugia for conservation (Lovejoy 1982) and the inadequacy of the data, it is important to press ahead. In recent years, Brazil has been notable in doing so (Wetterberg *et al.* 1981), with 8 million km^2 set aside as parks or ecological stations since 1980. There has been little activity during this time in other Amazon nations. The Brazilian approach, understandably, has been to establish conservation units now and worry about their protection later. Notable omissions in the Brazilian programme so far have been in the southeastern quadrant (which includes the important Belém refugium) where creation of parks and reserves is admittedly politically more difficult. An important precedent was set in Rondônia where two ecological stations and a national park were established with help from the World Bank as part of a major development project. A similar approach should be taken with the major Carajás development in Pará and Maranhão.

Brazil's major advances have recently been recognised by the award of the distinguished J. Paul Getty Wildlife Conservation Prize to Special Secretary of the Environment (SEMA) Dr Paulo Nogueira Neto and Director of National Parks Dr Maria Tereza Jorge Padua. The most important is yet to come: the Amazon forest policy legislation, with economic and ecological zoning, which has long been promised by President Figueiredo. Not only would such legislation make a critical stride towards a national development plan and a proper balance of economic and ecological objectives, it could have considerable influence, via the Amazon Pact which Brazil, after all, initiated, on all Amazon nations. Like a half-formed dewdrop not quite ready to fall, the future of this water-dominated ecosystem hangs in the balance.

6   Environmental change and deforestation in the Brazilian Amazon

PHILIP M. FEARNSIDE

Abstract

Brazil's Amazon rainforest is being rapidly felled, continuation of recent trends leading to complete clearing in most of the region's states within a few decades. The deforestation process is too complex to allow simple projections of recent trends, but evidence suggests that much of the forest area will soon be converted to other uses. Environmental changes linked with deforestation, most of which are undesirable, should be of concern to decision makers responsible for policies affecting both forest conversion rates and development choices for converted areas. Informed debate on environmental concerns is essential, as exaggerated or unfounded claims are often used by proponents of unwise development schemes as a means of discrediting valid criticisms.

Soil degradation processes following clearing include leaching of cations, fixation of phosphorus, and decomposition of organic matter. Soil compaction, as well as granulometric changes, affect physical structure, and erosion exposes less fertile lower layers. 'Laterisation', or the formation of plinthites, has been exagerated as a general phenomenon, but unfounded claims should not obscure the phenomenon's importance in locations where impeded drainage and other required conditions exist.

Macro-ecological concerns which have been raised include:
(a) Depletion of global oxygen supplies (not a real problem).
(b) Increased atmospheric carbon dioxide causing global warming due to a 'greenhouse effect' (a valid global concern, although the role of clearing rainforests is eclipsed by fossil fuel combustion).
(c) Changes in the hydrological cycle leading in the direction of dryness both within and outside of the tropical regions being cleared (a major and increasingly well-documented concern), and
(d) Loss of genetic diversity through the extinction of species and ecosystems. Deforestation also implies the disappearance of indigenous cultures and populations dependent on the presence of rainforest.

INPA's ongoing research programme in the Brazilian Amazon, including the

Estimation of Human Carrying Capacity of Amazonian Agroecosystems project, are producing information which might be hoped to help place the debate over environmental changes on firmer ground. The pace of deforestation makes such information an urgent priority.

Brazil's shrinking rainforest

Brazil's Amazon rainforests are rapidly shrinking. The form of the increase in cleared areas in the state of Rondônia indicated by Landsat images gives some indication that clearing may have been occurring in an exponential fashion between 1973 and 1978 (Fearnside 1982). Although no such simple algebraic equation is adequate to predict the path of clearing, the nature of exponential growth would lead rapidly to complete deforestation of the region, assuming a constant exponential rate, even with the large areas of forest currently remaining. Along with the false impression of infinite size, another illusion engendered by Amazonian forests is that deforestation would have little environmental effect because secondary vegetation would reconstitute losses to effectively negate deforestation effects (e.g. Lugo and Brown 1981, 1982; but see Myers 1982). Unfortunately, many of the changes are not reversible (Gómez-Pompa *et al.* 1972).

Reliable information on clearing rates over time is scant for the Amazon. Estimates for Brazil's 5×10^6 km^2 Legal Amazon from Landsat images taken in 1975 and 1978 indicated that 1.55% of the total area had been cleared by the latter date (Tardin *et al.* 1980). Despite indications that the figure is somewhat underestimated, the conclusion that cleared area was small in relation to the total area of the region is sound. If the cleared area has increased exponentially at a constant rate since, it would have reached 5.8% of the Legal Amazon by 1982. Unfortunately, information more recent than 1978 is not available. Brazil's National Institute of Space Research (INPE) no longer monitors deforestation, having transferred the task to the Institute for Forestry Development (IBDF). A reorganisation of IBDF has since resulted in all research activities being passed to the Brazilian Enterprise for Agriculture and Cattle Ranching Research (EMBRAPA). Meanwhile, no clearing estimates have been released.

The rate of deforestation is controlled by complex interactions among components in the region's ecological systems, including the area's human populations and their agricultural resources. Analytical expressions like the exponential cannot reflect the opposing forces influencing a process like deforestation, the study of such problems being more suited to computer simulation (Fearnside 1983a). Work in progress at the National Institute for Research in the Amazon (INPA) in Manaus, may eventually supply information on this and related human ecological problems in a form that provides a framework for use in development planning.

The future course of deforestation depends on a network of interrelationships, some representing forces that speed the process and others that slow it. At present, forces leading to rapid clearing appear to dominate the process, but as felled areas and rates of clearing increase in the future, forces limiting the process can be expected to play an expanded role. One of the forces presently driving deforestation is a positive feedback relationship between road building and migration of settlers: building or improving roads encourages the entry of more settlers to a region, and the presence of more settlers justifies the construction of still more roads. As Brazil's Second National Development Plan states: 'The occupation of new areas should continue ... in view of the fact that the gigantic highway system, already constructed, has placed at the disposition of the [agricultural] sector immense areas ... in Amazonia.' (Brazil, Presidência da República, 1974: 41). In addition to drawing new migrants, the arrival of access roads augments deforestation by spurring settlers already in place to dramatically increase their land clearing rates. Such increases are readily apparent in data being collected in the Ouro Preto colonisation area in Rondônia. Another process linked to road improvement is the turnover of colonists in settlement areas. Original settlers sell their land or claims to land to new arrivals, especially when improved access causes land values to rise and potential buyers to appear. Newcomers bring greater material resources and plant larger areas of crops than do the original settlers they replace (Fearnside 1980a). In their first four years after arrival, newcomers fell virgin forest at almost twice the annual rate of the original occupants (Fearnside nd–a).

One of the primary forces driving deforestation is the rapid increase in the region's human population. A part of the increase is due to reproduction (Brazil's population grew by 2.4% annually between the 1970 and 1980 censuses), but far more is due to migration from other parts of Brazil, especially for migration foci like Rondônia. Rondônia's population grew at 14% per year during the 1970–80 period (data from Brazil IBGE 1981). Deforested area grew even faster, increasing at an exponential rate of 41% per year between 1975 and 1978 (data from Tardin *et al.* 1980; see Fearnside, 1982). Clearly the relationships are more complex than simple population growth, although population is of central importance.

Rapid clearing is closely linked with land-use choices. Cattle pasture is both a cause and a result of rapid deforestation. Pasture is the cheapest and quickest way of occupying felled land, which is important in establishing land-tenure claims (Fearnside 1979a). Establishing such claims for speculative purposes is a major motive for deforestation. Pasture also requires much less human labour to maintain than other non-forested land-use choices, thus allowing settlers who specialise in ranching to clear much larger areas before limitations of available labour and economic resources inhibit further expansion (Fearnside nd–b).

Forces which can be expected to exert upward pressure on clearing rates in the future include the consequences of unsustainable land uses, such as pasture, now occupying most cleared areas. Unsustainable practices mean that land will have to be left fallow or in low-intensity uses in the future, thus freeing the settler's resources for further clearing in virgin forest.

Other probable factors fuelling deforestation in the future in this century include increased timber exploitation once dwindling rainforest areas in southeast Asia cease to supply world markets. Another is anticipated surges of economic development in parts of Amazonia favoured by mineral and hydroelectric resources, such as the development pole associated with the Grand Carajás project, occupying approximately one-sixth of Brazil's Legal Amazon (Fearnside and Rankin 1982).

Forces which should act to decrease felling rates in the future include the progressive decline in quality of remaining land. The best agricultural land in the Amazon has already been cleared: the two major occurrences of the relatively fertile soil *terra roxa* (Alfisol) at Altamira (Pará) and Ouro Preto (Rondônia) are, for all practical purposes, fully occupied. By the same token, land with the easiest access has already been cleared. Areas with river access have long been settled, and land nearest the major trunk highways is also fully claimed. Distances which must be travelled on precarious lateral feeder roads to reach available land from major thoroughfares should increase on average.

As Amazonia becomes more settled, the behaviour patterns of farmers living in the area should gain in relative importance compared to the annual count of new migrant families entering the region. Blocks of occupied lots exhibit markedly different trends in deforestation from larger geographic areas where the entry of new migrants dominates clearing statistics. In a ten-year time series for occupied lots in Ouro Preto, Rondônia, cumulative felled areas increase following a linear trend for the first six years, after which a plateau is reached (Fearnside nd–a). The linear portion of this pattern has also been observed for data from the first four years of occupancy at Altamira (Fearnside, 1982). A linear/plateau trend for individual properties, without changes in ownership, would contribute to slowing regional trends in a future, more fully settled, Amazon.

Another factor that may impede continued felling at present explosive rates is the delay necessary for settlers to move from deforestation foci in Rondônia and southern Pará to new areas, once the present areas of concentrated felling are deforested. Areas with slower clearing rates and more uncut forest, such as Amapá and Amazonas, are also father from access routes to Amazonia for new migrants from southern Brazil.

Future deforestation trends could not hold to an exponential pattern up to its logical end point of complete clearing, since factors other than the availability of forest would slow the trend. Labour and capital availability would limit the very fast felling implied by the final years of an exponential trend. Migrant source areas in southern Brazil, while supplying millions of new migrants to Brazilian cities and to Amazonia, cannot be expected to produce ever-increasing fluxes of new entrants once the present process of agricultural mechanisation and land-tenure concentration has progressed further in the source regions. As the Amazon frontier 'closes', its relative attractiveness to potential migrants in search of unclaimed land would also decrease. Infinite availability of resources needed for greatly increased felling, especially petroleum, can also not be assumed.

All of this means that one cannot foresee with confidence how many decades would be needed to clear all or almost all the Amazon rainforest. More importantly, such a prediction would be of little utility as compared to the urgency of gaining better knowledge of the environmental consequences of deforestation. It matters little whether rainforests last a few decades more or less, given that ample evidence is available that probable trends, in the absence of swift changes in governmental policies and controls, would lead to a speedy end to the forest. Better understanding of the environmental effects of deforestation could, or should, move decision makers to set more rational policies regulating development in rainforest areas.

Soil degradation concerns

Leaching and fixation of nutrients

Following clearing of rainforest, the soil loses through leaching and fixation many of the nutrients originally present or added from ash when the forest is burned. Some of the nutrients are retained in the system after uptake by crops or secondary vegetation, but a significant portion is lost irretrievably in the first years after clearing. Cations such as calcium, magnesium and potassium are leached by the heavy rains, many of the soils having low capacities to retain these ions due to the lack of appropriate sites on clay particles (Irion 1978). Studies of soil changes following clearing show declines in available cations (Nye and Greenland 1960; Brinkmann and de Nascimento 1973; North Carolina State University Soil Science Department 1974–8). Available phosphorus, a limiting nutrient for plant growth in much of Amazonia, is removed from the soil by 'fixation', or conversion to compounds that cannot be used by plants. Fixation rates are inversely related to the concentration of phosphorus, ranging from 26.8 to 51.6% in 6 hours at 100 ppm P in a variety of Amazonian soils (Fassbender 1969) to 83% in 7 days at 53 ppm P in *terra roxa* (Alfisol) of the Transamazon Highway (Dynia *et al.* 1977). Available phosphorus soon falls below plant requirements in even the best of Amazonia's principal soil types, such as *terra roxa*.

Soil organic matter declines rapidly after soil is exposed by clearing (Cunningham 1963; Nye and Greenland 1960). Unlike soil cations, organic matter is not added to the soil at the time of burning, but rather begins its decline as soil temperature increases and shifts the equilibrium between accumulation and decomposition. In soils where a forest root mat is prominent (e.g. Herrera *et al.* 1978), the decline in organic matter is steepest after the roots of forest trees have decomposed in the years following clearing.

Soil compaction and clay migration

Exposed soil in rainforest areas become compacted within a few years as spaces between soil particles collapse. The soil becomes hard (increasing, for example, resistance to a penetrometer), bulk density increases, and infiltration rate and porosity decrease. Mechanised clearing results in immediate soil compaction (Seubert *et al.* 1977; Van der Weert 1974), but fortunately this practice is rare in the region. Traditional clearing methods avoid compression of the soil column under the weight of a bulldozer, but cannot prevent the ensuing compaction of the exposed soil. Compaction occurs even without agricultural use (Cunningham 1963), and proceeds more quickly still with cropping or especially cattle pasture (Schubart *et al.* 1976; Dantas 1979). Loss of organic matter following clearing decreases pore volume and contributes to compaction. Compacted soil inhibits the growth of plant roots, thus contributing to low crop production and retarded or deflected successions. Compaction also increases the susceptibility of the soil to erosion, as rain is unable to infiltrate into the soil column, thereby increasing runoff.

Soil physical structure is also altered after clearing by migration of clay particles to deeper levels in the soil profile (Scott 1975). The clay migration leaves a sandier soil surface. Since different Amazonian soils present a complete range of granulometric compositions, virtually from pure sand to pure clay, the clay migration may either represent an improvement or a form of degradation. Heavy clays have reduced porosity, with consequent susceptibility to erosion, and offer physical resistance to plant growth, while very sandy soils have both reduced water retention and reduced capacity to bind and hold needed cations.

Erosion

Erosion is another problem that plagues agriculture in the Amazon. Many people not familiar with the region harbour the illusion that the Amazon is flat, an impression encouraged by the appearance of the forest from the air. Although some parts of the basin are indeed quite level, much of it is dissected into steep slopes. Erosion causes significant soil losses when the soil is exposed for cultivation, with soil surface often dropping one or two centimetres per year under annual crops (Fearnside 1980b; see also McGregor 1980; Scott 1975). Erosion has a detrimental effect on soil fertility, since the soil quality on the Transamazon Highway is generally worse at lower depths than at the surface (soil profiles in: Brazil Ministério da Agricultura IPEAN 1967; Falesi 1972; Brazil Ministério da Agricultura DNPEA 1973a,b; Brazil Ministério de Minas e Energia Departamento de Produção Mineral Projeto RADAM 1974 Vol. 5). This effect contrasts with the situation in some other parts of the world where erosion can improve soil quality by exposing less weathered material (Pendleton 1956 cited by Popenoe 1960; Sánchez and Buol 1975).

Erosion would be likely to constrain agricultural production most quickly in systems which leave soil exposed repreatedly. One such system is a proposed technology for obtaining continuous production of annual crops (Sánchez *et al.* 1982; Valverde and Bandy 1982; Nicolaides *et al.* 1982). Erosion is one of a number of potential problems making widespread use of the system difficult (see Fearnside nd–c). The 'flat Ultisol' of Peru's Yurimaguas experimental station (Nicolaides *et al.* 1982) differs from much of Amazonia, especially the areas undergoing intensive colonisation in the Brazilian Amazon. A land use survey of the Amazon Basin indicating that half the region has slopes of more than 8% (Cochrane and Sánchez 1982 p 151) is often cited by proponents of continuous cultivation of annuals (e.g. Sánchez *et al.* 1982). The 50% figure is deceptive, however, due to the large-scale maps used to classify topography and other constraints. For example, in a 23 600 ha area on the Transamazon Highway where a detailed slope map was made based on field measurements at 225 points, 49.3% of the tract has a slop of 10% or more (Fearnside 1978 p. 437, nd–d). The entire area was classified as greater than 8% slope by Cochrane and Sánchez (1982: 149).

Laterisation

'Laterisation', or more properly the formation of plinthites, has been an overstated danger in many popular accounts of agricultural problems in the Amazon. The idea that this hardened material, largely composed of iron oxides, covers much of the tropics had its origin in early reports by nineteenth-century temperate-zone soil scientists visiting the tropics and emphasising laterite due to its novely (Sánchez 1976 pp. 52–4). More recently, fears that vast areas of the Amazon would turn to pavements of brick upon clearing have echoed through the popular press. Mary McNeil's (1964) widely read article on the subject in the *Scientific American* encouraged this impression. One text asserts that laterisation on the Transamazon Highway will turn the Amazon into 'the world's largest parking lot' (Ehrlich *et al.* 1977 p. 627). The prospect of hardening of plinthite over large areas of rainforest with deforestation is remote (Bennema 1975). The laterite problem can be a real one in some areas, but the extent of these areas is now thought to cover less than 7% of the tropics as a whole (Sánchez and Buol 1975) and 4% of the Amazon (Cochrane and Sánchez 1982). Care must be taken in these areas; recommendations have occasionally been made that such soils be cleared in the Brazilian Amazon (e.g. Brazil Ministério da Agricultura EMBRAPA-IPEAN 1974 p. 46). It is important that the problem of laterite not be dismissed as an over-reaction to the exaggerations of the past.

Aerosol nutrient supply

Nutrient stocks in agricultural systems usually decline following forest clearing, unless replaced through fertiliser applications. The balance of losses and inputs may have a link, however, with the proximity of natural stands of vegetation. Recent studies of nutrient transport as aerosols indicate that significant quantities of sulphur, and possibly other nutrients may be transported in the air from forest edges into adjacent cleared areas (R. F. Stallard, press comm. 1982, Stallard and Edmond, 1981). Such transport occurs at best over distances of a few hundred metres, so most cleared areas are deprived of this nutrient source in the Brazilian Amazon due to the present pattern of clearing vast expanses of cattle pasture.

Production systems concerns

Upland agriculture

Agriculture in the *terra firme*, or unflooded uplands, is linked in many ways to the amount and pattern of clearing that surrounds it. Forms of agriculture which require regeneration of second growth, as in the case of shifting cultivation, are likely to be modified when surrounding forest has been cleared. The modifications often involve shortening of the fallow period to a point where vegetation and soil quality are degraded, jeopardising the system's sustainability. The process of succession on fallow land is affected by both the reduced fallow time and the long distance to rainforest seed sources. The principal danger is the successional path's switching from one leading to woody second growth to one leading to a grassland dysclimax. In southeast Asia this has occurred over millions of hectares throughout the region forming low-value expanses of *Imperata cylindrica* grassland. In Indonesia alone, 16 million hectares of *Imperata* have been formed in this way (UNESCO 1978 p. 224). Return of primary forest dominants has been observed to occur in that country only when clearings are less than 1000 m² in area (Kramer 1933 cited by Richards 1966 p. 42). Very fortunately for the Amazon, this highly aggressive grass species has not arrived, but a somewhat less implacable relative, *Imperata brasiliensis*, does occur (Scott 1978 pp. 49–50). Other grass genera, such as *Adropogon*, tend to dominate New World savannas. Many present savanna areas are believed to have resulted from human agricultural activities (Budowski 1956; Sternberg 1968). The trend to large cattle pastures can be expected to discourage woody regrowth due to soil compaction, depletion of soil seed stocks, and removal of seed sources, as has been suggested in the case of Volkswagen's Vale do Rio Cristalino Ranch (Uhl, University of Florida seminar 1982; see Uhl 1982). Elimination of mycorrhizal associates of rainforest species is another factor inhibiting the return to forest vegetation (Janos 1975). Both the rapid rate and the frequent speculative motivation of rainforest clearing in Amazonia lead to pasture as the land-use choice (Fearnside 1979a). This choice has poor chances of sustainable production (Hecht 1981; Fearnside 1979b, 1980c), as well as increasing the likelihood of an eventual non-woody dysclimax.

The present pattern of deforestation, which discourages small farmers and the production systems they employ, nevertheless allows substantial tracts to be occupied by small farms. This situation may change with the eventual elimination of significant areas of uncleared land. The closing of the frontier which can be expected to be followed by continued consolidation of small holdings into larger properties has been the repeated pattern in Brazil (see Wood and Wilson 1982 for current trends). Such large holdings frequently opt for non-sustainable land uses, especially pasture, as the primary exploitation pattern. At the same time, areas secured by small farmers are subdivided into uneconomic *minifundios*, as has occurred in the *Zona Bragantina* near Belém (Hébette and Acevedo 1979 pp. 117–21), contributing to unsustainable increases in agricultural intensity and consequent failure of these areas to 'fix the man to the land' (Penteado 1967).

Floodplain agriculture

Deforestation can be expected to have its most direct effects on agriculture in the annually flooded *várzea* by alteration of the flooding cycle. Watershed deforestation invariably results in faster runoff after a rain, as less water is retained by the vegetation and its associated porous soil.

Measurements of changes in the flooding cycle from deforestation so far have been inconclusive. One report of increased flooding in the Peruvian Amazon (Gentry and López-Parodi 1980) has been criticised for ignoring alternative explanations of increased flood stage at Iquitos, including a probable unstable discharge/stage relation due to shifts in the river bed, and the possibility of superannual cycles such as those on the order of 12 years observed on the Rio Negro at Manaus (Nordin and Meade 1982).

High variability in flooding behaviour even without deforestation makes detection of changes difficult, as in the case of changes in rainfall. Nevertheless, the higher floods from 1970–8 as compared with 1962–9 are suggestive, and the logic linking higher floods with deforestation is impeccable. The unpredictable occurrence of higher than normal floods has long been the principal drawback of farming this fertile habitat, as many riverside inhabitants discovered when they lost their jute crops in 1982's unusually high flood. The variable timing and duration of the flood peak assumes an importance on a par with the flood height, while the variable time that farmable land remains exposed during the low water period is of even greater importance (J. G. Gunn pers. comm. 1982). One hotly debated anthropological theory even hypothesised the evolution of a variety of cultural characteristics as adaptations to the 'risky' nature of *várzea* agriculture which 'set a ceiling on cultural development' (Meggers 1971 p. 149; see critique by Roosevelt 1980 pp. 13–24). *Várzea* agriculture is likely to become more risky with continued deforestation of river watersheads.

Inland fisheries

Deforestation can be expected to negatively affect fisheries of many of the most important commercial fish species in the Amazon. Fish are essential in providing a relatively inexpensive source of protein to the population of the region. Among the poorest residents of Manaus, fish supply 37% of the total protein in the diet (Amoroso 1981 p. 28). Fish species such as the tambaqui (*Colossoma macropomum*) spend part of the year in inundated *várzea* forests of whitewater rivers consuming the fruit produced by a variety of tree species. Goulding (1980) has shown how the tambaqui and 34 other fish species utilise fruits of 40 plant species in flooded forests in Rondônia. Tambaqui alone supplied approximately 20% of the total protein consumed in Amazonian cities such as Manaus in 1973–4 (Giugliano *et al.* 1978 p. 40), although overfishing since that time has caused a dramatic reduction in the size and quantity of this species caught. The removal of these forests could be expected to eliminate one of the most important links in the human food chain in the region. Flooded forests provide food directly or indirectly to an estimated 75% of the commercial catch reaching Manaus (Goulding 1980 p. 253).

Forest production

Deforestation eliminates production of forest products such as Brazil nuts (*Bertholletia excelsa*), natural rubber (*Hevea brasiliensis*), rosewood oil (*Aniba duckei*) and timber. Areas with concentrations of such potentially renewable natural resources are, in many cases, deforested preferentially for conversion to cattle pasture. Brazil nut stands in the State of Pará, for example, often have a sort of title dating from the nineteenth century, granting the land to *castanhalistas* (Brazil nut barons), which raises the value of the land for sale to speculators (Bunker 1981 p. 52, 1982). The same is true for land documented for *seringalistas* (rubber barons) in Rondônia and Acre.

Clearing rainforest closes forever the option of sustainable management of forest resources (Fearnside 1983b). Many pharmaceutical uses of these products have barely begun to be tapped. Loss of rainforests, for example, is considered a major setback in the effort to find anti-cancer drugs (Myers 1976).

Macro-ecological concerns

Oxygen: a straw man

The purported threat to the world's oxygen supply from tropical deforestation is one of the more unfortunate misconceptions related to rainforest use, especially in Brazil. Oxygen levels are actually quite stable (Van Valen 1971), and are not dependent on rainforests, which use up as much oxygen as they produce (Farnworth and Golley 1974 pp. 83–4). The idea that the Amazon rainforest is responsible for the world's oxygen supply has gained particular force among the popular press in Brazil, where the Amazon is called the 'lung of the world'. This belief came into prominence after a popular Brazilian periodical conducted a transoceanic telephone iterview with Dr Harald Sioli, and later misquoted this distinguished figure in Amazonian research (Sioli 1980a). After exposing the oxygen argument as fallacious, it is usual to imply that all arguments linking deforestation with climatic change, including the important questions of carbon dioxide and rainfall, are 'alarmist' and unworthy of serious attention.

Carbon dioxide: 'greenhouse effect'

Carbon dioxide is an object of worldwide concern due to its role in the balance controlling global temperature. Atmospheric carbon dioxide classically is considered the cause of a 'greenhouse effect', where energy in the form of visible and ultra-violet rays from the sun passes through the atmosphere freely but is unable to escape when re-radiated in the form of infra-red radiation. (Note: the analogy of carbon dioxide with a greenhouse is somewhat misleading as the latter has most of its effect as a barrier to convection rather than to long-wave radiation.) An increase in carbon dioxide would result in the earth's climate warming as more energy was trapped by the atmosphere. Atmospheric carbon dioxide increased linearly from 1850 to 1960, but has since been increasing exponentially. By 1978, CO_2 levels had only increased by 18% over the levels of 1850, but they are now expected to have doubled by early in the next century.

Predicting future CO_2 levels and their effects is complicated by other climatic factors that could act to cancel some of the global warming, as they have done since 1940. One of the several existing simulations for modelling global climate finds the net result of deforestation to be overall global cooling, mainly due to increased albedo, or reflectivity, of cleared land as compared with forest (Potter *et al.* 1975; see also Saga *et al.* 1979). The rash of contradictory predictions with respect to future climate under different scenarios should not obscure recognition of the delicate balances on which these processes depend, and the woeful lack of data on some of the most important parameters, especially in the tropics. In addition to lack of reliable data on deforestation rates, biomass, and non-living carbon pools such as charcoal, climate models have shown themselves to be particularly sensitive to such poorly quantified parameters as atmospheric CO_2 levels before the industrial revolution (Björkström 1979 pp. 446–52) and the rate of mixing of the ocean layers serving as sinks for both carbon (Björkström 1979) and heat (Dickenson 1981 p. 433).

Much of the carbon dioxide increase has historically resulted from burning fossil fuels. The biosphere has been singled out as a key factor by several studies (Bolin 1977; Woodwell 1978; Woodwell *et al.* 1978). Marked seasonal oscillations in CO_2 levels, especially in temperate zones, testify to the importance of the biosphere in maintaining this delicate balance. Since tropical rainforests are estimated to contain 41.5% of the world's plant mass of carbon, and tropical seasonal forests another 14.1% (calculated from data from Whittaker and Likens 1973 p. 358), the future development of the world carbon problem could be affected by the fate of tropical forest.

The incomplete burning of forest biomass, a substantial amount of which remains as charcoal, moderates the effect of forest burning (Crutzen *et al.* 1979). Lacking data from the tropics, Seiler and Crutzen (1980) used an estimate of unburned biomass based on observations following a wildfire in a temperate stand of ponderosa pine (*Pinus ponderosa*) to estimate the size of the world carbon sink in elemental carbon remaining in burned areas. This sink, estimated at 0.4–1.7 thousand million metric tons, together with estimates of the rate of deforestation lower than those used by other modellers, plus a substantial sink in afforestation, led Seiler and Crutzen (1980) to conclude that the land biota could be either losing or gaining 2 thousand million metric tons of carbon per year (Table 1). This figure is much lower than the loss estimates of 4–8 thousand million metric tons per year calculated by Woodwell *et al.* (1978). The root cause of such sharp discrepancies is the rudimentary nature of data available, especially on tropical deforestation, forest

Table 1   *Estimates of annual carbon release*

Authors	Tropical deforestation	All terrestrial ecosystems
Woodwell *et al.* 1978	3.5 (1–7)	4–8
Dickenson 1981	1.0	–
Loucks 1980	1.5	–
Hampicke 1979 p. 230	3.6	1.5–4.5
Hampicke 1980, cited by Henderson-Sellers 1981 p. 456		
Based on historical evidence	1.8–4.0	–
Based on socio-economic development	1.3–2.3	—
Based on remote sensing measures of forest decreases	1.5–2.5	–
Adams *et al.* 1977	–	0.4–4
Bolin 1977	1.5	0.4–1.6
Wong 1978	–	1.9
Moore *et al.* 1981	–	2.2–4.7
Seiler and Crutzen 1980	–	−2–+2

* In thousands of millions of metric tons (gigatonnes)

biomass and carbon content, growth rates of tropical second growth, and burning efficiencies. Research to fill these gaps in knowledge should be a top priority, especially in the Amazon where rainforests represent an estimated 20% of the planet's carbon reservoir in living biomass (Salati 1979; Salati and Ribeiro 1979).

The amount of warming that would result from a doubling of atmospheric carbon dioxide is not known with certainty. One simulation predicts global temperature increases of 2 to 3 ° to result from this development (Stuiver 1978). A United States National Academy of Sciences expert committee has estimated an effect of 3 °C + 1.5 °C (cited by Wade 1979). The Academy estimated that current trends would lead to a doubling of 1979 CO_2 levels by 2030, with a 'few decades' more needed for saturation of the heat-absorbing capacity of deep oceans before uncontrollable temperature rises take place (Wade 1979). Other estimates for the mean effect of doubling CO_2 vary from 4 °C (Goodland and Irwin 1975a p. 35) to 2 °C (Manabe and Wetherald 1967). Models of Manabe and Souffer (1979), which include seasonable insolation fluctuation and a less idealised modelling of geography than earlier models (Manabe and Wetherald 1975) show a mean warming of 2 °C, but with significant regional and seasonal asymmetries. Regional differences can have a much greater potential effect than the value for the mean warming itself. Woodwell (oral communication, INPA seminar, 1980), who expects a 1.2 °C mean warming from a doubling of CO_2, products virtually no temperature change at the equator compared to 5–10 °C at the poles. Greater effects at the poles result from a positive feedback relationship between temperature and albedo, which is decreased by melting snow and ice or vice versa. Some controversy surrounds the amount by which polar effects are enhanced in relation to global means. The more than doubling of sensitivity to climatic change at the poles suggested by Budyko (1969) has been re-examined by Lian and Cess (1977), who expect enhancement of sensitivity by only about 25%.[1]

Using the US National Academy of Sciences estimate of 3 °C + 1.5 °C, the possibility that a mean warming by even 1.5 °C could result in melting of polar ice caps has concerned a number of meteorologists. The disproportionately higher temperature increases at the poles are especially worrisome.

> According to most of the recent research, the Arctic sheet can just maintain itself under present climatic conditions. Therefore, significant further warming would cause a complete transformation by the creation of an open sea in place of the Arctic ice sheet; an open Arctic Ocean should result in the drastic movement of all climatic zones several hundred kilometers northward ... The effect of such a shift would be especially noticeable in the belt which presently has a sub-tropical climate with winter rains (California, Mediterranean, Near East and Punjab), which would then become arid steppe. (Flohn 1974 p. 103).

Some uncertainty exists as to the rapidity and magnitude of the rise in sea levels that would result were polar ice to begin melting. The contribution of Antarctic ice is particularly uncertain, as much of it is poorly mapped and lies below sea level (Thomas *et al.* 1979). Typical estimates of the potential rise in ocean levels range from 4–8 m (United States Council of Environmental Quality 1980 cited by Marshall 1981) to 5–6 m (G. Woodwell, oral communication, INPA seminar 1980) to 10 m (Salati 1979). Goodland and Irwin's (1975a p. 35) figure of 35 m appears high. Mean sea levels have risen by 12 cm over the past century (Gornitz *et al.* 1982), and floating sea ice has been decreasing for the past several decades (Kukla and Gavin 1981), presumably primarily as a result of CO_2 increase (Etkins and Epstein 1982).

Although more reliable and detailed data, especially from the tropics, are needed before firm conclusions can be drawn on the future of world temperatures, the simple doubt that major and irreparable meteorological changes could occur should give pause to planners intent on promoting massive deforestation.

Nitrous oxide: ozone depletion

Rainforest clearing appears to be one of the contributors to a global increase in atmospheric nitrous oxide (N_2O). This gas is known to react in the stratosphere to produce nitric oxide (NO), which in turn serves as a catalyst in the breaking of ozone (O_3) molecules. Evidence for a strong catalytic effect comes from observations in nature (Fox *et al.* 1975), although rates for these reactions are quite low (Ruderman *et al.* 1976 note 6). Stratospheric ozone acts to absorb incoming ultra-violet radiation, shielding the biosphere from intense UV radiation.

The injection of N_2O into the stratosphere by proposed supersonic transport (SST) aircraft was a subject of heated debate during the mid 1970s. Ozone depletion effects of fluorocarbons from aerosol propellants and refrigerants became a public issue during the same period. Unfortunately, the potential ill-effects claimed were occasionally exaggerated, causing many to cease worrying about ozone depletion in subsequent years. Loss of public interest in stratospheric ozone was also partly the result of a widely publicised summary of a report by the US government's Climatic

Impact Assessment Program (CIAP) which 'conceals the logical conclusions of the study' (Donahue 1975). The understatement of effects identified during the course of the original study was later bitterly pointed out by the atmospheric scientists involved (see exchange of letters in *Science 187* 1145–6, 28 March 1975), but could not undo the effect on public perceptions stemming from wide press coverage of the CIAP report's 'Executive Summary' (Grobecker *et al.* 1974). Even more unfortunately, the realities of nitrous oxide and ozone depletion are still with us and are likely to increase.

Increased UV radiation could be expected to increase substantially the incidence of skin cancer (basal cell carcinoma, squamous cell carcinoma, and melinoma) in humans; a 10–20% reduction in ozone could be expected for example to increase UV radiation by 20–40% raising skin cancer incidence by about 20% among the Caucasian population of the world (Donahue 1975), More recent estimates double the effect of ozone depletion on skin cancer, each 1% depletion leading to 2–5% rise in skin cancer incidence averaged over the US population (US National Academy of Sciences 1982 cited by Maugh 1982). Any possible behavioural changes in UV-oriented insects should be determined by actual testing before making claims to that effect. Effects on aquatic ecosystems are numerous, and deserve close scrutiny due to the key role of aquatic organisms in many food chains and biogeochemical cycles (Calkins 1982).

Possible effects in agriculture due to increased rates of mutation cannot be predicted with confidence with available knowledge, but the disastrous consequence of negative impact on any of the staple grain species is ample cause for avoiding exposure. DNA's absorption maximum is at 260 nanometres, only slightly below the 286-nanometre present lower limit of solar radiation reaching the earth's surface (Eigner 1975 p. 17).

The impact of rainforest burning on nitrous oxide flux to the atmosphere, as well as the seriousness of expected changes, are areas of current debate. The debate illustrates both the minimal level of our present understanding of many fundamental global processes, and the near total absence of relevant data, especially from the tropics. The concentration of N_2O in the troposphere has been increasing at about 0.2% per year (0.5 parts per thousand million by volume per year) over the past 20 years (Weiss 1981). All known sources of N_2O are at ground level, and many are linked to human activities. One source is the decomposition of organic materials in low oxygen environments, such as much human waste deposited in the anoxic conditions of dumping sites or sewage water (McElroy *et al.* 1976). In addition to wastes and compost, agriculture produces nitrous oxide through aerobic nitrification of fertiliser nitrogen (Bremner and Blackmer 1978). Combustion of fossil fuel is a major source, believed to account for about half of the total 1.1×10^{11} moles N_2O annual anthropogenic input (Weiss 1981; Weiss and Craig 1976). Nitrous oxide production from deforestation is believed to be significant from two sources: combustion of the felled biomass (Crutzen *et al.* 1979) and increased production in bare soil as compared to forest (Goreau 1981). Forest soils have been found to produce significant fluxes of N_2O through oxidation of ammonia by nitrifying bacteria, with rates increasing at low oxygen levels (Goreau *et al.* 1980; Goreau 1981). Cleared land, however, produces much more N_2O than does the same area under forest cover.

The contribution of fertiliser to global N_2O flux needs to be better understood as a check on the share attributed to deforestation. The importance of oxygen concentration gradients in nitrifying environments has recently been demonstrated by Goreau (1981). Much of the N_2O produced through denitrification at deeper (less well oxygenated) layers in the soil is never released to the atmosphere, but rather is consumed within the soil as an electron acceptor in respiration reactions (Goreau 1981 p. 78). Much of the work done with fertilised agricultural soils has not taken this uptake into account (T. J. Goreau, pers. comm., July 1982). The implication of this is that estimates of N_2O production in fertilised soils probably exaggerate the N_2O derived from fertilisers – and a larger share of the observed atmospheric increases must therefore be explained by other sources, such as deforestation.[2]

Nitrous oxide flux measurements from the tropics are non-existent. Several indirect indications, however, suggest the conclusion that deforestation in tropical forests results in larger N_2O fluxes than temperate equivalents. Low counts of nitrifying bacteria are characteristic of acid soils under tropical forests (Nye and Greenland 1960; Jordan *et al.* 1979), but the nitrifiers greatly increase in numbers when clearing and burning raises soil pH (Nye and Greenland 1960). When the humus, root mat, and detritus are oxidised in the exposed soil, increased nitrification would release corresponding amounts of N_2O.

The long-term contributions of rainforest felling are unclear. One reason is the large amount of rainforest converted to cattle pasture. Initial conversion to pastures would result in release of N_2O as with all clearing. The lower equilibrium organic matter content of soils under pastures as compared with tropical forests (see Fearnside 1980c) would contribute to this, as soil nitrogen is approximately 98% organic (Russell 1973). Grasslands are known for low nitrification rates (Nye and Greenland 1960; Russell 1973), which would mean that further releases of N_2O from the soil should be relatively small once the initial conversion had taken place. Nitrous oxide would continue to be released from combustion; however pasture is burned frequently while it lasts, and after being invaded by second growth can be expected to undergo cutting and burning at intervals of a few years until weeds, compaction, and soil-fertility degradation force abandonment of stock raising. Savannas are often burned as a matter of cultural tradition in Brazil, even when no immediate economic use is intended.

Hydrological cycle: desertification

The issue of 'desertification' is an emotional one, especially in Brazil with reference to the Amazon. A tendency toward decrease in rainfall in the region, even if not crossing the threshold of annual precipitation that defines a desert in climatological terms, is a possibility which cannot be dismissed as a consequence of deforestation (Fearnside 1979c). One reason is that in the Amazon, far more than in other parts of the earth, rainfall is derived from water recycles into the atmosphere through evapotranspiration, rather than being blown into the region directly as clouds from the Atlantic Ocean.

Estimates for the contribution of evapotranspiration to the precipitation in the Amazon Basin as a whole range from 54% based on an estimated annual total precipitation of 12.0×10^{12} m^3 and river discharge of 5.5×10^{12} m^3 (Villa Nova *et al.* 1976) to 56% based on water and energy balances derived from average charts of wind and humidity (Molion 1975). More detailed studies of the area between Belém and Manaus have produced estimates of the evapotranspiration component in rainfall in this part of the Basin ranging from 48%., based on calculations of precipitable water and water vapour flux (Marques *et al.* 1977), to up to 50% (depending on the month), based on isotope ratioing (Salati *et al.* 1978).

Hydrological work near Manaus has shown that a mean of 66% of evapotranspiration is transpiration rather than evaporation (calculated from Leopoldo *et al.* 1982a). Both evaporation and transpiration are positively related to leaf area. Clearly the much greater leaf area of rainforest as compared with pasture crops or second growth indicates deforestation will lead to decreased evapotranspiration and consequently decreased rainfall in the region. Western parts of Amazonia, such as Rondônia and Acre, depend on evapotranspiration for a greater portion of their rainfall than does the Belém–Manaus area where estimates were made, and therefore would be expected to suffer greater decreases when forest is felled.

Other consequences of deforestation, such as increased albedo, also affect rainfall. Some models predict decreases in rainfall in temperate regions as a result of increased albedo with tropical deforestation which leads to lowered heat absorption, reduced evapotranspiration and heat flux, weakening global air circulation patterns and reducing rainfall in the 45–85 ° north and 40–60 ° south latitude ranges (Potter *et al.* 1975).

However, the magnitude of changes in albedo resulting from deforestation is a matter of debate. Problems arise from differing definitions of albedo (the ratio of reflected to incident light), and from use of unrealistic values for forest albedos prior to clearing. Forest vegetation reflects only a small amount of visible light, as indicated by its dark appearance. However, a large amount of reflectance occurs in the near infra-red region of the spectrum, making forest albedos much higher if infra-red radiation is included in the measurement. Dickenson (1981) has criticised studies such as that of Potter *et al.* (1975) for using visible spectrum albedo values (Posey and Clapp 1964) derived from measurements made in the temperate zone between 1919 and 1947 (List 1958 pp. 442–3). Widening the spectrum included in albedo measurements, and using a suitable average of more recent values from the tropics, approximately doubles the albedo of forest from 0.07 to between 0.12 and 0.14 (Dickenson 1981 p. 421). Combined with the assumption that forest is replaced by green secondary vegetation, albedos of these areas increase by only 0.02 to 0.04, or one-half to one-fourth the increases assumed by Potter *et al.* (1975) and others. The assumption is critical that evergreen vegetation replaces primary forest, however, as open savanna or grassland resulting from decreased rainfall in dry periods (e.g. Salati *et al.* 1978) and repeated burnings by humans (Budowski 1956) could well be a more likely future for these areas.

The illusion must be dispelled that, because annual rainfall totals in the Amazon are quite high, a significant amount of drying could be tolerated. The dry season in the Amazon already poses severe limits on many agricultural activities. During the dry season of 1979, Manaus went for 73 days without a single drop of rain. Soil water levels fell to very low levels both in the open and under forest cover, where trees continued to transpire from large leaf areas. Since plants react to water levels in their root zones on a day-to-day basis, and not to the abstraction of annual rainfall statistics, effects of even small increases in the severity of the dry season could be dramatic. Natural vegetation which does not tolerate severe water stress could be expected to gradually give way to more xerophytic *cerrado* (scrubland) vegetation over time. Such a change would have the potential for becoming a positive feedback process, where the resulting further reduction in evapotranspiration would increase dryness and accelerate vegetational changes (Table 2).

Table 2   *Possible macro-climatic effects of Amazonian deforestation*

Item	Change	Effect
Oxygen	Not significant	Not significant
Carbon dioxide	Increase	Global temperature increase (note: contribution of rainforest is subject of controversy)
Nitrous oxide	Increase	Global temperatures increase (slightly) ultra-violet radiation increases at ground level
Albedo (reflectivity)	Increase	Decreased rainfall in temperate zones
Evapotranspiration	Decrease	Decreased rainfall in Amazon and neighbouring regions: temperature increase due to decrease of heat-absorbing function of evapotranspiration
Rainfall	1) Decrease in total 2) Increased length of dry season (more important)	Vegetation changes: climatic regime becomes unfavourable for rainforest. Reinforces trend toward still drier climate

Genetic diversity: extinction of species and ecosystems

The genetic diversity of the Amazon rainforest is legend. One hectare inventoried 30 km from Manaus had 235 species of woody plants over 5 cm in diameter (Prance *et al.* 1976). Many of the Amazon's species of plants and animals have never been collected or described, and each new collecting expedition reveals several new species (Prance 1975; Pires and Prance 1977). A high degree of endemism exists among Amazonian species: many species occur in limited ranges. This endemism means larger deforestations automatically ensure extinction of many species. The potential loss of genetic diversity from deforestation in the Amazon has been a major concern of biologists worldwide (Lovejoy 1973; Myers 1976, 1979, 1980; Oldfield 1981, Eckholm 1978; Ehrlich 1982; Ehrlich and Ehrlich 1981). Whether or not this fact represents a reason for restraint is a question dividing many people concerned with Amazonian development. Some reasons for conserving genetic diversity include potential for discovery of new organisms of economic value, or new uses for already known organisms; these include new crop plants, and varieties. The continuing evolution and dispersal to new areas of crop pests and diseases means that need for new germplasm will never cease. A good example is the vital input of coffee germplasm from the remnants of forest in Ethiopia as a means of obtaining resistance to leaf rust (*Hemileiz vasatrix*) in *Coffee arabica* (Oldfield 1981). Destruction of stands of disease-tolerant, if low-yielding, natural rubber trees in Acre and Rondônia is one of many such losses occurring due to Amazonian deforestation. The same applies to need for new pharmaceutical chemicals in the face of continuing evolution of human disease organisms. The rush to obtain natural quinine when malarial parasites evolved resistance to chloroquine is a case in point (Oldfield 1981). The value of rainforest as a resource for fundamental scientific research has also been argued (Budowski 1976; Poore 1976; Jacobs 1980).

Ecological diversity, as well as genetic diversity in the strict sense, is quickly destroyed by deforestation. Often complex coevolved associations go extinct long before the last individuals of the species involved disappear (Janzen 1972, 1974b, 1976).

Indigenous peoples: disappearance of human cultures and population
When the Transamazon Highway was announced as a way to bring 'people without land to a land without people' the statement was tragically in error. Virtually all of the Amazon was already occupied when the highway construction programme was launched. The large areas not settled by Portuguese-speaking 'Luso-Brazilians' were occupied by Amerindians (Davis 1977). The incompatibility of colonisation with the maintenance of indigenous populations in these areas is obvious. Locations of Amerindian tribes with relation to proposed highway routes are described in chapter 5 of Robert Goodland and Howard Irwin's (1975a) book *Amazon Jungles: Green Hell to Red Desert?*[3] The resolution of conflicts of interest between highway construction and indigenous populations has rarely been a non-destructive one for the Amerindians (Davis 1977; Bodard 1972; Ramos 1980; Hanbury-Tenison 1973; Brooks *et al.* 1973; Bourne 1978 de Oliveira *et al.* 1979).

Most are agreed that since indigenous cultures are not compatible with 'development', the solution is to separate Amerindian groups from settlement areas through provision of adequately sized, located, and protected reserves. It is a question of bitter debate as to where reserves should be placed, how large they should be and whether reserves should be respected when land is desired for highway routes, mineral deposits, ranching, agriculture and land speculation.

The tropical rainforest is regarded as a resource for pioneer farming by the Brazilian government, as well as by the thousands of individuals and groups that have set out to replace rainforest with agriculture in the Amazon. Characteristics of the rainforest ecosystem, changes that occur after it is cleared and planted, and environmental and other considerations tied to the massive scale of these alterations, all must be considered in planning colonisation programmes and other forms of development.[4]

Conclusion

Most changes resulting from deforestation in the Amazon are bad from the human point of view, especially if the wellbeing of future generations in the region is given the weight that it deserves. Although not all of the ill-effects ever attributed to deforestation are likely, effects for which reasonable scientific grounds exist are numerous and severe. Exaggerated or unfounded claims of deleterious effects are to be deplored, as is the frequent oratorical use made of such statements by persons anxious to discredit by association the many valid concerns related to rainforest destruction. Soil degradation concerns include nutrient leaching and fixation, organic matter decomposition, compaction, and erosion. Production systems in upland and floodplain agriculture, inland fisheries, and forest extraction depend on rainforest. Macro-ecological effects include logical expectations of changes in the regional hydrological cycle. Global hydrological changes are more debated, but the severity of any consequences to the planet's major agricultural production systems justifies both caution and intensive study. Contributions, by amounts not well determined, are also made by deforestation to global carbon dioxide and nitrous oxide problems, both of which, when considered along with the contributions of humanity's industrial activities, imply disastrous potential environmental effects. Climatic concerns are especially dangerous since delays inherent in the natural systems mean that many of the effects may not be detectable before irreversible processes have been set in motion. The extinction of species and ecosystems and the disappearance of human cultures and populations associated with the rainforest are not less important and irreversible. The weight of evidence indicating unfavourable environmental changes as the result of deforestation should provide ample ground for decision makers to take immediate and far-reaching steps to slow the process and prevent its occurrence in significant areas of the region. The fact that many consequences are poorly understood should, in no way, justify postponing or diminishing such action. Such uncertainty, combined with the magnitude of some of the potential changes, should motivate an even more cautious approach to developments involving deforestation.

Notes

1 Some investigators have reported findings implying a substantially lower effect on global temperatures from a given increase in atmospheric CO_2. Using meteorological observations accompanying a volcanic eruption as a natural experiment rather than computer simulations used in other studies, Newell and Dopplick (1979) estimate that temperature increases resulting from a doubling of atmospheric CO_2 would be no more than 0.25 °C in tropical latitudes. Another experimental study (Idso 1980a,b) calculates a value for global mean warming of up to 0.26 °C. A number of investigators regard these estimates as low (G. Woodwell, oral communication, INPA seminar, 1980; P. Crutzen, pers. comm., 1980; Schneider *et al.* 1980; Leovy 1980), differences in results apparently being due to assumptions regarding humidity and altitude of cloud cover. Absorption of solar radiation by water vapour, and subsequent re-emission as infra-red, create a positive feedback process increasing ocean warming and atmospheric humidity (Ramanathan 1981). Omission of this feedback loop in models (Newell and Dopplick 1979), or by using short-term observations over continental land masses (Idso 1980a,b), leads to underestimation of CO_2-induced warming (National Academy of Sciences 1982b; see Kerr 1982). Two much higher estimates, 10 °C (Möller 1963) and 5.3 °C (Bryson and Dittberner 1976), have mistakenly ignored latent heat exchange with the surface (Manabe and Weatherald 1967; Watts 1980a,b).

2 The insignificant role of denitrification means that only about 0.3% of N applied would be released as atmospheric N_2O (Goreau 1981 p. 126); this corresponds to 5% of the total global flux, whereas a 1 per cent higher yield would account for 20% of the annual flux (Keller 1982 p. 30).

3 This chapter is not included in the Portuguese language edition (Goodland and Irwin 1975b).

4 I thank the Burgess Publishing Co., Minneapolis, Minn. for permission to use those passages of the present paper appearing in *Carrying Capacity for Human Populations: the Colonization of the Brazilian Rainforest* (Fearnside nd-e).

7 Hydrological aspects of the tropical rainforest in the central Amazon

PAULO RODOLFO LEOPOLDO, WOLFRAM
FRANKEN, EIICHI MATSUI

Summary

Annual runoff, loss by interception, transpiration and evapotranspiration of two watersheds in the Amazon rainforest of the *terra firme* type in central Amazonia, were estimated.

The first watershed, Barro Branco, has an area of 1.3 km^2 and is situated at Reserva Ducke by the Manaus–Itacoatiara highway, 25 km^2 from Manaus. The results obtained indicated that of the 2075 mm rainfall in one year, about 18.7% was intercepted by forest cover and re-evaporated into the atmosphere, 62% transpired by the forest, 80.7% evapotranspired and 19.3% represented runoff.

The second watershed, the 'model basin', has an estimated area of 23.5 km^2 and is located about 80 km from Manaus, near the Manaus–Caracarai (Brazil–Venezuela) highway. In this watershed, for a precipitation of 2089 mm, also observed for one year, the average corresponding to forest interception was 25.6% while those due to transpiration, evapotranspiration and runoff were estimated at 48.5%, 74.1% and 25.9% respectively.

These results show, therefore, the significant importance of the forest to the present ecological balance of the region, which may be seriously altered if uncontrolled and unplanned deforestation continues.

Introduction

The Amazon ecosystem which represents the greatest forest reserve in the world, is still relatively little studied and is practically in the initial phase of human exploitation. However, since the objectives of exploration should be rational and adequate to the region, it is clearly important to gather as much data as possible on the Amazon forest ecosystem, aimed at establishing models for use of land and natural resources in accordance with local conditions.

Many researchers have observed that intensive destruction of the forest might cause serious and irreversible ecological disturbance by various means. Among these disturbances it is believed that the hydrological cycle of the Amazon Basin might suffer great change following intensive deforestation, with serious modification to the interaction between water and environment. In view of the great quantity of water involved, not only from rivers but also from the mass of foliage which returns a considerable volume of water vapour to the atmosphere through transpiration, the hydrological cycle is a highly important aspect of this region.

General aspects of the Amazon region

The Amazon Basin, with an area over 5.8×10^6 km^2, drains about 33% of South America and involves six of the thirteen South American countries (Figure 1). From

Fig. 1 The Amazon Basin

this total, approximately 3.8×10^6 km^2 are in Brazilian territory and account for about 45% of the country's area.

The Amazon Basin is bordered by three great ecological structures of the continent: the Guiana plateau to the north, with an altitude of 1000 metres although at some points it can reach 2500 m; the Brazilian plateau to the south at an altitude of 700 m; and the Andean Mountains to the west with heights of over 5000 m. The voluminous river Amazon lies on a quaternary plain surrounded by tertiary plateaux (Figures 2 and 3) (Soares 1977), and is the main channel for the Basin's waters.

Oltman *et al.* (1964) estimated that the volume of the water drained through the Basin by the river Amazon is of the order of 5.5×10^{12} m^3 per annum. This volume, which corresponds to an average outflow of 175 000 m^3/sec, represents 15% of the total fresh water in the world. Its discharge rises slowly, from a minimum at the end of October or beginning of November to a maximum at the end of May or beginning of June (Figure 4).

According to Magalhães Filho (1960), the main channel is that of the Amazon–Ucayali–Urubamba rivers, with a total length of 6577 km and rising at over 4000 m altitude. In its profile, three-quarters of the Amazon is on sedimentary plain. When it enters Brazilian territory at Tabatinga, over 3000 km from the Atlantic Ocean, it is at an altitude of only 60 m, so that it has an imperceptible downwards slope of 2 cm/km.

The greatest part of the Amazon Basin is occupied by the Amazon rainforest. In Brazil, this forest covers an area estimated at 3.6×10^6 km^2, which corresponds to 42% of Brazilian territory. As for Amazon flora, about 23 000 are already classified and it is believed that many others are still to be classified. With the construction of new roads followed by possible irrational deforestation, it is evident that the fate of many species, like rosewood (*Aniba rosaedora*), is extinction. The same will happen to animal species unless drastic protection measures are put into force. In general, the Amazon region is characterised by a high pluviometric index and high temperature, most of the soil being poor. The region's temperature shows a certain spatial and temporal homogeneity with a small but insignificant seasonal variation. The same is not true of rainfall, as can be seen in Figure 5 which shows the annual isoyets for the region.

Table 1 includes data on monthly average precipitation observed in different places in the Amazon Basin, as a function of the period of observation. As can be seen, short dry periods occur in some regions of the Basin, generally from June to September or even October, while in other regions rainfall distribution is relatively high throughout the year. Practically all types of climate are found in the Amazon Basin, ranging from warm and humid in the Amazon plain to cool and dry in the Andes.

Bibliographic review (Amazon hydrology)

Interest in the hydrological cycle of the Amazon Basin has increased recently because of the possibility of change in water balance as a result of intensive deforestation.

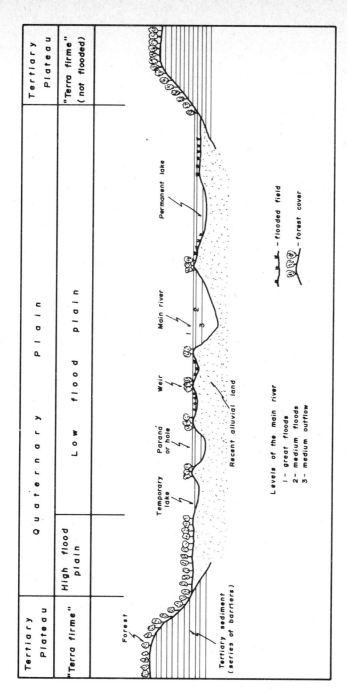

Fig. 2 Typical section of a sediment-transporting Amazon river ('whitewater' river)

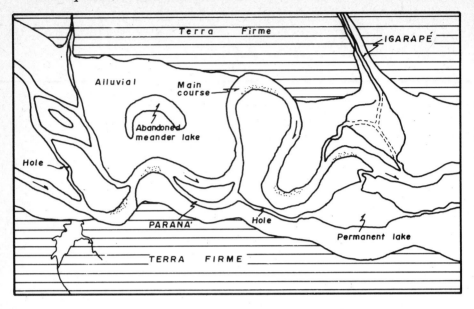

Fig. 3 Characterisation of the main draining elements of the Amazon floodplain

According to Villa Nova *et al.* (1976), the Amazon Basin, at a preliminary estimate, functions as a system receiving through precipitation 12×10^{12} m^3 of water per year, of which 5.52×10^{12} m^3/year are discharged into the Atlantic Ocean. True evapotranspiration resulting from this balance is estimated at 6.48×10^{12} m^6/year, corresponding to 54% of the rainfall. Using the Penman method adapted to forest conditions, these authors calculated the average potential evapotranspiration for the whole Amazon Basin at about 1.460 mm/year, which corresponds to 4 mm/day, and that for many regions the potential evapotranspiration is close to total.

Ribeiro and Villa Nova (1979) using the Thornthwaite and Mather method to calculate water balance and with data from the period 1965–73, obtained from the Ducke Forest Reserve an estimate of potential evapotranspiration of 1536 mm/year and true of 1508 mm/year, for an average precipitation of 2478 mm/year. They also observed that for this site the potential evapotranspiration is equal to the real for almost the whole year, except for the three months in which a soil-water deficit occurs.

Using the aerological method, Marques *et al.* (1977) observed that 52% of the rainfall in the region between Belém and Manaus comes from water vapour from the Atlantic Ocean, while the remaining 48% is water vapour from the forest through forest-cover transpiration. The true evapotranspiration estimated by this method for the Belém–Manaus section was 1000 mm/year.

The components of atmospheric water vapour flux in the Amazon region were

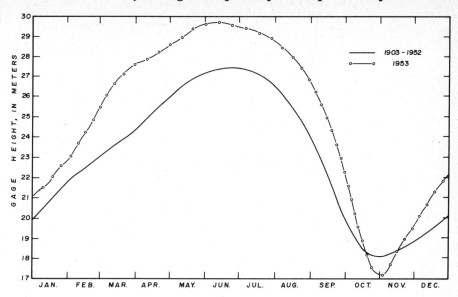

Fig. 4 Gauge height above sea level of the Amazon river, near Manaus, in the periods 1903–52 and 1953 (reprinted from Oltman *et al.* 1964)

studied by Marques *et al.* (1979a) using radio-soundings. Their results lead to the observation that the Amazon region exports part of its water vapour to the Paraguayan Chaco and central Brazil, mainly in the months of March and December. This conclusion, as noted by Salati and Ribeiro (1979) is very important, since all changes in the water regime of the Amazon Basin may have direct consequences in the rainfall of the central Brazilian plateau which feeds the heads of the main hydrographic basins.

Salati *et al.* (1979) and Dall'Olio *et al.* (1979) noted, using ^{18}O data, that there is important water recycling within the Basin, confirming the importance of re-evaporated water for the water balance throughout the Basin. A comparison of ^{18}O data for advective humidity with those from river water disproved the concept of complete condensation of all vapour entering the Basin, as noted by Salati *et al.* (1979). According to their calculations, 44% of the advective humidity leaves the Basin as water vapour, while Marques *et al.* (1979b) found that the mean recycling time of the water vapour is around 5.5 days. The length of time that surface waters remain in some hydrographic basins of the Amazon region was studied by Gonçalves (1979) using ^{18}O data. Depending on the basin, he found values varying from 1.1 to 2.3 months. Based on experimental data, Salati and Ribeiro (1979) suggested that deforestation in the region will among other things reduce the time that water remains in the Basin, and that a 10–20% reduction in

Table 1 Monthly average precipitation as a function of site and period of observation (mm)

Site	Observation period	Jan	Feb	Mar	Apr	May	Jun	Jul	Aug	Sep	Oct	Nov	Dec	Total
Altamira	1961–73	223	241	344	269	204	95	81	22	22	33	46	130	171
Alto Tapajós	1931–60	408	375	434	285	128	26	11	33	138	235	315	329	271
Barcelos	1931–60	172	145	174	256	276	234	169	118	105	118	111	125	199
Benjamin Constant	1951–60	340	280	350	280	210	140	120	140	200	220	250	280	281
Carauari	1961–77	330	173	227	336	245	152	89	157	186	230	310	269	270
Coari	1931–60	315	274	280	283	226	134	88	75	99	158	188	222	234
Fonte Boa	1931–60	298	237	278	336	314	238	175	149	150	194	186	247	280
Humaitá	1962–73	261	277	319	250	163	54	21	60	107	184	255	283	223
Yuauretê	1931–60	259	246	295	363	389	356	350	278	266	237	227	237	350
Macapá	1968–73	256	325	394	291	349	208	173	99	56	1	66	147	237
Manaus	1931–60	276	277	301	287	193	98	61	41	62	112	165	228	210
Parintins	1961–73	250	279	324	356	346	200	112	88	41	77	142	16	237
Pôrto Velho	1961–73	265	307	283	254	14	39	27	42	111	186	226	228	215
Rio Branco	1969–73	202	252	227	175	99	31	28	48	88	154	226	236	176
Santarém	1931–60	179	275	358	362	293	174	112	50	39	46	85	123	209
Tefé	1970–73	220	213	289	299	229	166	221	102	112	128	177	160	232
Uaupés	1931–60	274	250	285	267	317	250	246	195	148	173	202	305	291
Belém	1931–60	318	407	436	382	266	165	161	116	120	105	90	197	276
Imperatriz	1931–60	241	256	309	219	89	19	10	6	40	92	152	198	163

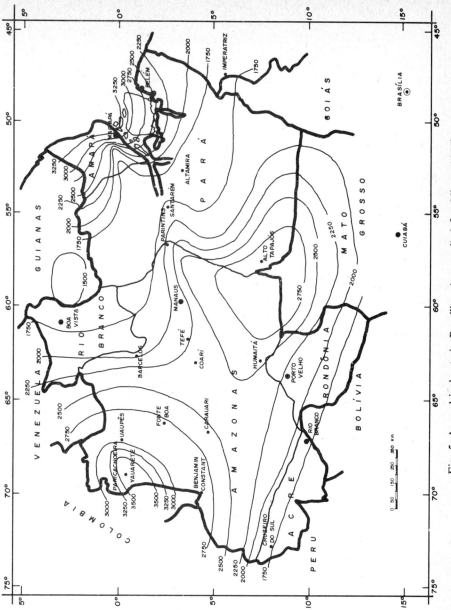

Fig. 5 Annual isohyets in Brazilian Amazonia (after Nimer 1977)

precipitation will be sufficient to cause very severe alterations in the present ecosystem.

The forest also plays an important role in the retention of part of the region's rainfall, which is intercepted by the forest cover and returns to the atmosphere by evaporation. Jordan and Heuveldop (1981) studying the tropical rainforest of the Amazon in the region of San Carlos (Venezuela) noted that of a 3664 mm/year precipitation, 87% represented throughfall, 8% stemflow, 5% interception by forest cover; and transpiration was estimated at 47%. These Leopoldo, Franken & Matsuis observed that the 8% stemflow is relatively high when compared with that observed by other researchers and that the 5% interception loss is smaller than results obtained for interception in similar forests.

A recent study by Franken *et al.* (1981) in the 'model basin', on a portion representative of the *terra firme* Amazon forest, showed that for 1706 mm/year precipitation, interception loss was estimated at 22%, precipitation that reached the forest soil (throughfall) was 77.7% and stemflow only 0.3%.

Goodland and Irwin (1975b) note that intensive destruction of the forest might cause serious ecological damage with serious modifications in the interaction between water and environment, as shown in Figure 6.

As reported by Kuhlmann (1977), the Bragantina region (where the forest was completely removed with the installation of colonies along the Belém–Bragança railway) gives an idea of what might occur in the whole region: the soils are exhausted after a few years' use, are hardly fit for poorly yielding cassava crops, and are revegetated with undergrowth of meagre shrub. Before these bushes can be of any benefit to the soil they are burned down. And after successive utilisation, the soil is turned into pure, almost barren sand.

Methodology

The following equation was used as a basis to determine the water balance in the two watersheds:

$$E = P-Q \tag{1}$$

where P = precipitation (rainfall)

Q = runoff

E = evapotranspiration

Loss due to deep percolation was considered nil in equation (1) and it was assumed that of the total water filtering into the soil, part was transpired and part drained off through the *igarapé* (stream). The variation in the quantity of water stored in the soil was ignored since the water balance was determined for a period of one year (WMO, 1967).

According to Jordan and Heuveldop (1981) and Villa Nova *et al.* (1976) the loss due to direct evaporation is negligible when compared with the rate of transpiration:

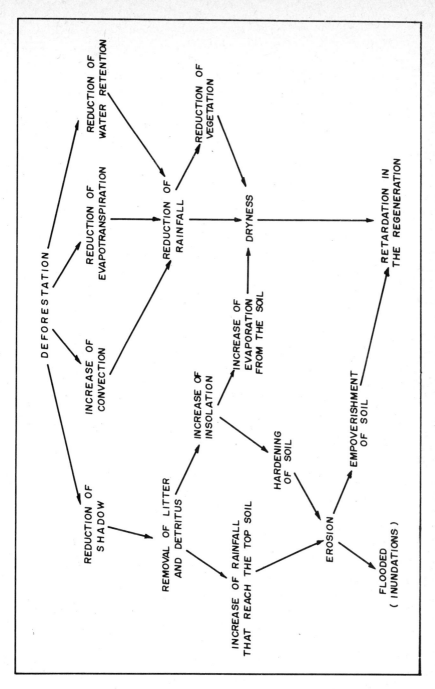

Fig. 6 Ecological disturbs that may be caused by deforestation (after Goodland and Irwin 1975b)

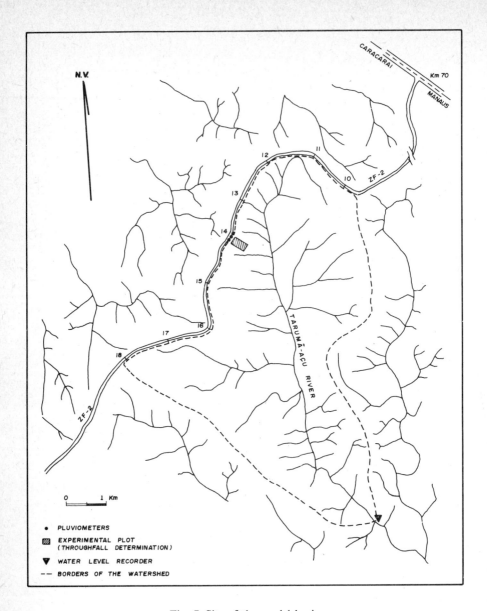

Fig. 7 Site of the model basin

$$E = I + T \qquad (2)$$

where I = loss due to interception

T = transpiration

substituting the E value given in equation (2), in equation (1), gives:

$$T = P - I - Q \qquad (3)$$

Description of the experiment carried out in the model basin

Figure 7 shows a map of the hydrographic basin called the 'model basin', located approximately 80 km from Manaus, close to the Manaus–Caracarai (Brazil–Venezuela) highway. This watershed has an area of 25.5 km^2 and is drained by the *igarapé* Tarumã-Açu. Runoff (Q) for this watershed was obtained by using a waterlevel recorder installed at its outfall, as shown in Figure 7. The period to obtain the necessary data was from 2 February 1980 to 10 February 1981, a total of 374 days.

The forest cover in this area is characterised by Amazon rainforest of the *terra*

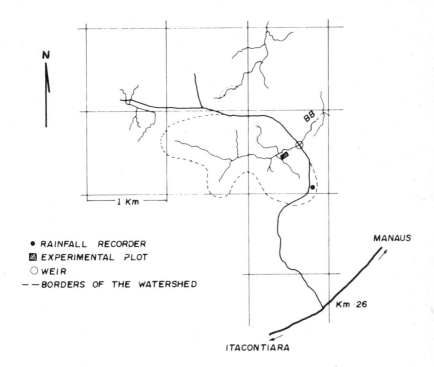

Fig. 8 Site of the Barro Branco watershed (Reserva Ducke)

firme type, and is completely undisturbed. Precipitation values were obtained using 3 pluviometers pleaced outside the forest cover, installed together at km 14 of Highway ZF–2, while throughfall values were determined by randomly installing 30 pluviometers in the interior of the forest. Thus term I (loss due to interception) in equation (3) was calculated using the following equation:

$$I = P - Pt \qquad (4)$$

where I = loss due to interception

P = total rainfall

Pt = throughfall

The stemflow was neglected, as according to Franken *et al.* (1981) its mean value is of the order of 0.3% of the total precipitation.

Description of the experiment carried out at Barro Branco watershed

Figure 8 is a map showing the location of the Barro Branco watershed, in Reserva Florestal Ducke, 26 km from Manaus, close to the Manaus–Itacoatiara highway. Its 1.3 km² area is covered by *terra firme* forest, although drainage takes place through the *igarapé* Barro Branco. The rain that fell in this watershed during the period under study (23/9/1976–25/9/1977) was determined using one pluviometer installed at an open site, while throughfall was measured using 20 pluviometers installed at random in the interior of the forest. As in the model basin, the term I was

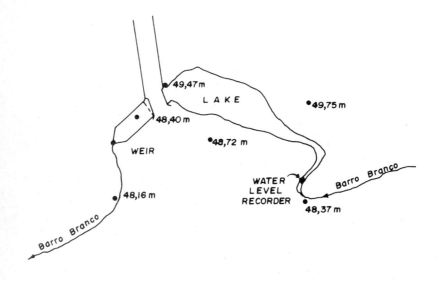

Fig. 9 Details of the runoff measuring site

Table 2 Summary of the results obtained by different researchers on the hydrological cycle of the Amazon Region

Researchers	Rainfall mm	Transpiration mm	%	mm/day	Evapotranspiration mm	%	mm/day	Runoff mm	%
Marques et al. 1980	2328 [1]	–	–	–	1260 (r)	54.2	3.5	1068	45.8
	2328 [2]	–	–	–	1000 (r)	43.0	2.7	1328	57.0
	2328 [3]	–	–	–	1330 (p)	57.1	3.6	998	42.9
Villa Nova et al. 1976	2000 [4]	–	–	–	1460 (p)	73.0	4.0	540	27.0
		–	–	–	1168 (r)	58.4	3.2	832	41.6
	2101 [5]	–	–	–	1569 (p)	73.4	4.3	532	26.6
Molion 1975	2379 [6]	–	–	–	1146 (r)	48.2	3.1	1233	51.8
Ribeiro and Villa Nova 1979	2478 [7]	–	–	–	1536 (p)	62.0	4.2	942	38.0
		–	–	–	1508 (r)	60.8	4.1	970	39.2
Ipean 1972	2179 [8]	–	–	–	1475 (r)	67.5	4.0	704	32.5
		–	–	–	1320 (r)	60.6	3.6	859	39.4
DMET 1972	2207 [9]	–	–	–	1452 (p)	65.8	4.0	755	34.2
		–	–	–	1306 (r)	59.2	3.6	901	40.8
Jordan and Heuveldop 1981	3664 [10]	1722	47.0	4.7	1905 (r)	52.0	5.2	1759	48.0
Leopoldo et al. 1982a	2089 [11]	1014	48.5	2.7	1542 (r)	74.1	4.1	541	25.9
Leopoldo et al. 1982b	2075 [12]	1287	62.0	3.5	1675 (r)	80.7	4.6	400	19.3

Observations: (r) = real, (p) = potential evapotranspiration; (1) aerological method applied to the entire Amazon Basin, from 1972 to 1975; (2) idem, for the region between Belém and Manaus; (3) by the Thornthwaite method for the region between Belém and Manaus; (4) Penman method, mean for the period 1931 to 1960; (5) idem for Manaus region; (6) climatonomic method for entire Amazon region, mean for the period 1931 to 1960; (7) water balance by Thornthwaite and Mather method for the Ducke Forest Reserve, mean for the period 1965 to 1973; (8) Thornthwaite method for entire Amazon region and estimated for a period over 10 years; (9) idem, for various periods; (10) water balance, with transpiration estimated by class A panevaporation for San Carlos region; (11) model basin water balance and (12) Barro Branco water balance (Ducke Forest Reserve). It can be seen from Figures 10 and 11 that transpiration and evapotranspiration rates depend in practice on total rainfall, involving a relatively rapid process i.e. trees with superficial root systems quickly remove the water that penetrates the soil.

estimated using equation (4). To determine the runoff (Q) through the Barro Branco *igarapé*, a 0.8 m width rectangular spillway was used at the watershed outfall and a water level recorder as shown in Figure 9. Figures 10 and 11 show values of rainfall, throughfall, transpiration and evapotranspiration for the model basin and Barro Branco watershed, respectively.

A résumé of the results obtained by different authors in hydrological-cycle studies of the region, is included for comparison in Table 2, as well as results obtained in the present work. Runoff data for studies (1) to (10) were obtained by deduction between total precipitation and evapotranspiration, while for (11) and (12) they were directly measured.

Considering that the potential evapotranspiration is very close to real, the values found for the model basin are in agreement with those found by other authors, mainly Villa Nova *et al.* (1976). It should be noted that these authors found for Manaus an evapotranspiration of 4.3 mm/day while in the present work this value

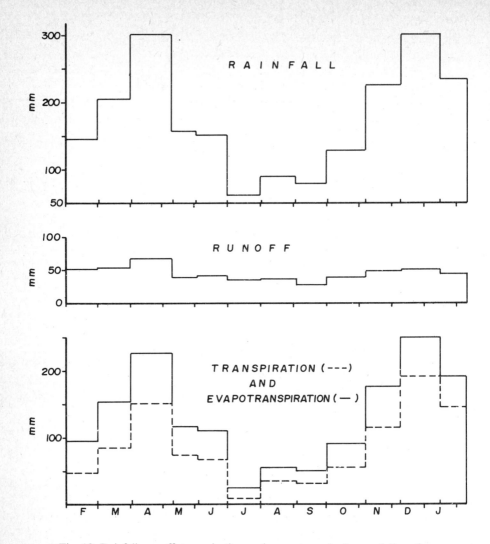

Fig. 10 Rainfall, runoff, transpiration and evapotranspiration variations for the period 2 Feb 80 to 10 Feb 81, of the 'model basin' watershed (note: $I = E - T$)

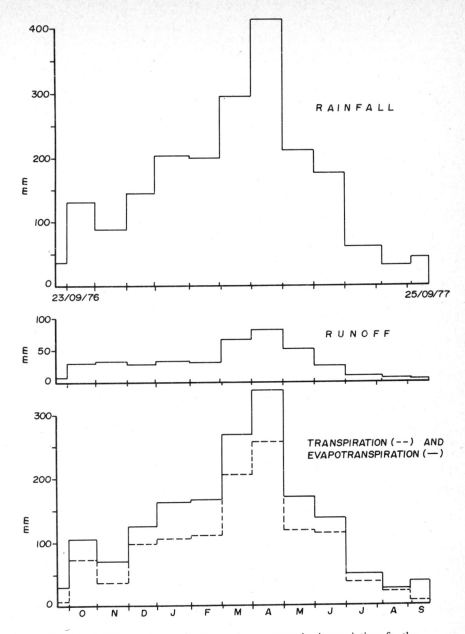

Fig. 11 Rainfall, runoff, transpiration and evapotranspiration variations for the period 23 Sep 76 to 25 Sep 77, of the 'Barro Branco' watershed (not: $I = E - T$)

Table 3 Water balance results for the model basin during the period 2 February 1980 to 10 February 1981.

Observation	Total (mm)	Mean average (%)	mm/day
Rainfall (P)*	2088.9	100.0%	–
Interception (I)*	533.9	25.6%	–
Runoff (Q)*	540.7	25.9%	1.4
Transpiration (T)*	1014.3	48.5%	2.77
1548.2	74.1%	4.1	

* measured values
** values calculated using equations (2) and (3)

Table 4 Water balance results for the Barro Branco watershed during the period 23 September 1976 to 25 September 1977

Observation	Total (mm)	Mean average (%)	mm/day
Rainfall (P)*	2075.5	100.0%	–
Interception (I)*	387.7	18.7%	–
Runoff (Q)*	400.4	19.3%	1.1
Transpiration (T)**	1287.4	62.0%	3.5
Evapotranspiration (E)**	1675.1	80.7%	4.6

* measured values
** values calculated using equations (2) and (3)

was 4.1 mm/day. The transpiration value of 48.5% was also very close to that observed by Jordan (1981). Using the tritium method, Jordan and Heuveldop (1981) obtained much higher values, of the order of 59% precipitation. However, transpiration and evapotranspiration values found for Barro Branco watershed, when compared with those in Table 2, can be considered overestimated while runoff was underestimated. Pereira (1962, 1967) obtained runoff values of the order of 17 and 20% precipitation for the tropical region of East Africa, while Odum (1968) registered values of 29% for the El Verde region in Puerto Rico.

It should be pointed out that most of the data in Table 2 has been obtained empirically. It can be seen from Figures 10 and 11 that transpiration and evapotranspiration rates depend in practice on total rainfall, involving a relatively rapid process, i.e. trees with superficial root systems quickly remove the water that penetrates the soil.

Results and discussion

Table 3 shows data of the water balance for the model basin, while Table 4 shows data for the Barro Branco watershed. It should be noted, however, that interception and transpiration in this type of forest involve extremely large quantities of water when compared to other regions of the world. The mass of water that returns to the atmosphere as water vapour represents a high recycling rate (Salati *et al.* 1979; Lettau *et al.* 1979), playing an essential role in the maintenance of the water balance of the present ecosystem. Deforestation would certainly influence the increase in runoff, causing erosion of *igarapé* beds and increasing removal of sediment and organic matter and other possible damage.

In general, the most marked variations between the values shown in Table 4 and the results of the present work can be ascribed partly to the different methods used, but above all to a function of the pluviometric variations, types of vegetation and soils. However, they do indicate the order of magnitude and importance of the water balance components for the region.

Acknowledgements

The author would like to express thanks to Conselho Nacional de Desenvolvimento Científico e Tecnológico, CNPq (National Council for Scientific and Technological Development); Comissão Nacional de Energia Nuclear, CNEN (National Commission for Nuclear Energy); Financiadora de Estudos e Projetos, FINEP (Projects and Studies Funding); and to the Fundação de Amparo a Pesquisa do Estado de São Paulo, FAPESP (Foundation for the Support for Research in State of São Paulo) for their financial support which made it possible to carry out the present research work.

8   The development of the *várzeas* (floodlands) of Brazilian Amazonia

C. J. BARROW

Introduction

Eight nations extend into the Amazon basin: Brazil, Colombia, Venezuela, Ecuador, Peru, Bolivia, Guyana and Surinam. Roughly 3.5 million km² of the basin, a little less than half the total area is Brazilian territory. In 1966 parts of Mato Grosso, Goiás and Maranhão were added to form a 5 million km² Brazilian administrative and development region – *Amazônia Legal* (see Figure 1) – and it is to this region I refer throughout the paper. Although comprising 58 per cent of Brazil's national territory the region has only about 8 per cent of the country's population. Despite numbers having roughly quadrupled during the last thirty years Amazonia is still sparsely populated, the total being eight to ten million, most of whom dwell in riverside settlements, the largest of which are Belém, Manaus and Santarém. Even taking the city populations the average population density for *Amazônia Legal* would only be about 1.4 persons per km². There is, however, an overall population growth rate of 3.5 per cent in Amazonia and the rest of Brazil is experiencing rapid population growth (Pandolfo 1979).

Amazonia remains one of the last terrestrial frontiers, the region retaining the world's greatest contiguous expanse of tropical forest (about 75 per cent of the world total), through which flow rivers of the Amazon system carrying about a fifth of the earth's total surface flow. There are abundant natural resources – some proven, some imagined, much awaiting assessment. In reality the region is only just being resource mapped (much ground verification still needs to be done); and a start has been made in understanding the complex ecosystem. On those shaky foundations increasing development is being based.

Pressures on the environment

Many of the problems faced by Amazonia are familiar elsewhere in the world, indeed the development of other tropical lowland forests (which has generally meant extensive forest destruction) offers grave warnings to Amazonia's developers (some forecast that in 35 years the forests of Amazonia will have gone). There are in excess of 2000 species of fish in Amazonia's rivers, the vegetation is the world's second richest (and the richest, in Malaysia, is rapidly being destroyed). Much of the soil of the basin is poor and is best left alone, at least until a better understanding of

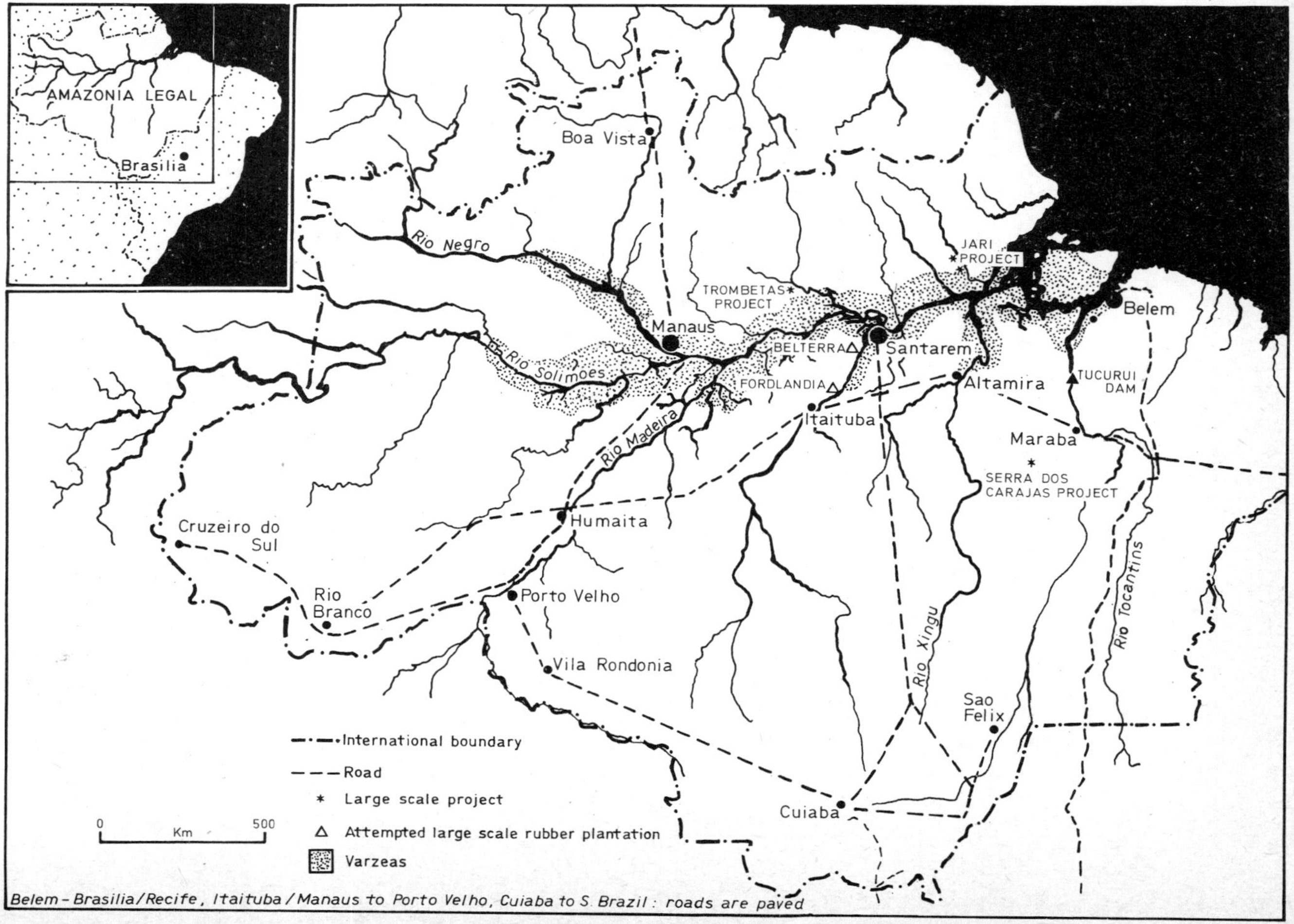
AMAZONIA LEGAL
Brasilia
Boa Vista
Rio Negro
JARI PROJECT
TROMBETAS PROJECT
Manaus
Belem
BELTERRA
Santarem
Rio Solimoes
FORDLANDIA
Altamira
TUCURUI DAM
Itaituba
Maraba
Rio Madeira
SERRA DOS CARAJAS PROJECT
Cruzeiro do Sul
Humaita
Rio Branco
Porto Velho
Rio Xingu
Rio Tocantins
Vila Rondonia
Sao Felix
Cuiaba
International boundary
Road
Large scale project
Attempted large scale rubber plantation
Varzeas
0 Km 500
Belem - Brasilia/Recife, Itaituba/Manaus to Porto Velho, Cuiaba to S. Brazil : roads are paved

Fig. 1 The extent of the Amazon Basin

Amazonian ecology enables its satisfactory exploitation. Successful substitution of agriculture for forest will depend upon ecological knowledge, adoption of appropriate technologies and market conditions all improved far beyond those of today.

The populations of Brazil, Bolivia, Colombia, Ecuador and Venezuela are increasing. Migration has taken place from the Andes into the humid tropical upper Amazon lowlands. In part this is a result of the spread of modern medicine which makes Amazonian settlement safer, and partly pressure on land in the Andes. There has been some migration from Venezuela. Brazil has recently increased efforts to develop mineral, hydroelectric and agricultural resources in Amazonia to earn foreign exchange and reduce the region's dependency on imports (Amazonia is presently a net importer of fuel, food and even rubber).

There are less tangible reasons for Brazil's increased interest in Amazonia: to some extent (not insignificant) there is a drive to establish sovereignty over the sparsely settled basin; development and associated migration also offer a 'safety valve' to relieve socio-economic discontent in the poor, drought-stricken and overpopulated northeast of Brazil. Like the migrations to California during the Depression which provided many poor Americans with hope, so the idea of colonising Amazonia has provided a palliative dream – and for a few *Nordestinos* (Northeasterners) has become the reality of either a better future or failed resettlement.

Most settlement in Amazonia has historically been alongside the rivers (Monteiro nd; Moran 1981). In the late nineteenth century efforts were made to settle a region east of Belém served by the (now defunct) Belém/Bragança railway. The attempt was far from successful, and by the time the railway closed in 1936 about 30 000 km^2 – the 'Bragantina Zone' – had been degraded by poor farming and could support only 8 persons per km^2 on average (Skillings and Tcheyan 1979). Since the 1960s much planned and spontaneous settlement has occurred along the route of newly constructed highways.

Some of the recent literature concerning Amazonian development and conservation has been over-sensationalist and divorced from the realities of life where development will proceed despite protestation from naturalists and others. There is a very real risk that much of Amazonia will suffer the substitution of rich forest by poor, degenerate scrub on such a scale that there will *never* be a chance of re-establishing anything like the original forest.

Sufficient research has accumulated to provide development planners with some valuable guidelines on just how much forest should be conserved, and where it should be conserved. Research on the ecology of oceanic islands has suggested the minimum area needed for conservation – in all probability 10 to 20 per cent of the total forest. Studies of Amazonian prehistory and present wildlife distributions suggest that there are crucial areas that should ideally be set aside as reserves.

Amazonia, along with all of the world suffered quaternary climatic changes – the basin dried and the forest dwindled, probably remaining only in 'forest refugia' (Figure 2). These refugia are both the most secure areas (climatic changes or drainage of surrounding land during development would least affect them) and have the richest selection of wildlife today. Unfortunately much of the development planning of *Amazônia Legal* was finalised before these facts were established. Already four of the refugia are entirely within regions designated by Brazil as 'growth poles' for intensive development.

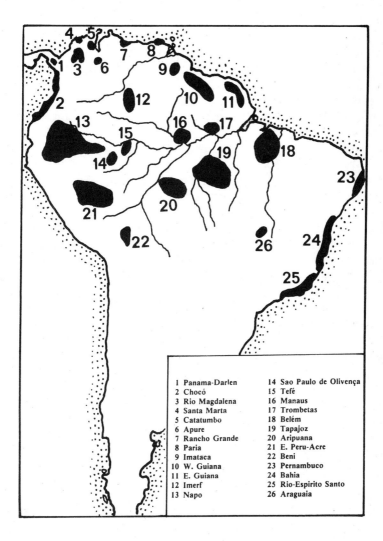

1 Panama-Darlen	14 Sao Paulo de Olivença
2 Chocó	15 Tefé
3 Rio Magdalena	16 Manaus
4 Santa Marta	17 Trombetas
5 Catatumbo	18 Belém
6 Apure	19 Tapajoz
7 Rancho Grande	20 Aripuana
8 Paria	21 E. Peru-Acre
9 Imataca	22 Beni
10 W. Guiana	23 Pernambuco
11 E. Guiana	24 Bahia
12 Imerf	25 Rio-Espirito Santo
13 Napo	26 Araguaía

Fig. 2 Tropical forest refugia

In Africa and Asia forest development has already probably destroyed many refugia – which have been less easy to identify than those in Amazonia.

Dry ground and floodlands

The simplest subdivision of Amazonia is into two broad ecosystems: the *terra firme* or dry ground and the *várzeas*, floodlands which border some reaches of the rivers (Amazonia as a whole is low-lying, falling only about 64 m from the Andes to the Atlantic).

Terra firme

Roughly 98 per cent of Amazonia is *terra firme*. Much of this has poor soil which is very vulnerable to leaching and erosion if cleared of forest cover without *very skilful* management. There tends to be some overgeneralisation that *terra firme* soils are bad but it seems that pockets of good *terra firme* soil do exist, indeed as mapping improves considerable areas may be discovered: already Rondônia state is believed to have considerable areas of fertile soil. However, even the good soils are subject to seasonal unpredictable drought, exacerbated because the soils are generally free-draining, although the annual rainfall is almost everywhere over 3000 mm per annum. When not afflicted by drought heavy rainfall removes nutrients necessitating the input of expensive fertiliser. The cycling of nutrients in tropical forests is 'tight': most are locked up in vegetation itself or in a very thin humus layer (and the forest species have various adaptations to compete for the little there is) – burning and soil erosion after clearance of forest soon destroy most of the nutrients.

Settlers in Amazonia have too often been ill-prepared to face the unfamiliar environment, indeed many adapt by re-migrating so that they never really get a 'feel' for the *terra firme* environment (Moran 1981).

About 14 000 km of trans-Amazon highways have been driven through the forests since the 1960s and have focused planners' attention on the *terra firme*. (Their construction has also consumed vast sums of money; however, strategic arguments are strongly held in Brazilian government planning circles and these have often over-ridden other considerations.) The settlers who follow the roads into the forest rarely produce more than meagre and ephemeral crops of manihot, dryland rice or maize (3 to 4 years at best), in effect they practise shifting cultivation (Skillings and Tcheyan 1979; Johnson 1978; van Wambeke 1978). Cattle ranching exhausts the pasture after a similar period of time. As a result of such developments scrubland (*capoeira*) is estimated to be spreading at around 100 000 hectares per annum. Until techniques for sustainable *terra firme* agriculture can be perfected and disseminated (which will demand credit, training, legal protection and improved marketing) despoliation and wastage will continue.[1]

'Planning in the Amazon basin', commented Wambeke (1978) 'has been somewhat distorted by the assumption that soil is always a completely renewable resource and that because land availability is so huge land qualities can in large part be ignored'.

Almost any development strategy would be desirable provided it delayed the clearance of the *terra firme* forests (which generally means the destruction of valuable timber and loss of genetic resources) until sustained-yield *terra firme* agriculture can be developed and disseminated.

Of late researchers, planners and politicians have begun in varying degree to question presently wasteful development of Amazonia: the development of the *cerrado* (savanna and open woodlands to the south and southeast of the Amazonian forests) has been proposed (Goodland and Irwin 1977; Goodland, Irwin and Tillman 1978); rehabilitation of the abandoned *capoeira* lands (possibly using a rotation of crops and leguminous trees which could maintain the soil's fertility) may become possible (Petrick 1978). Another strategy may be the development of *várzeas* (floodlands), although at least one authority is sceptical of whether *várzea* development aione would ease pressures on the *terra firme* forest lands (Katzman 1976).

The *várzeas*

Despite having the longest history of settlement the *várzeas* have enjoyed only marginal attention from planners and developers (Petrick 1978; Katzman 1976). Although only a relatively small fraction of Amazonia's total land area (Figure 1) the *várzeas* do have considerable agricultural potential, enough to satisfy Amazonian demand, and possibly to yield a surplus for export. A comparison of *várzea* and *terra firme* crop production has been published by Meggers (1977 Table 8). Considerable development would have to take place in order to significantly reduce pressure on the *terra firme* forests, which estimates suggest were being cleared for crops or pasture in 1981 at a rate of between 0.1 and 0.4 per cent of Amazonia's total area (Lugo and Brown 1981).

The *várzea* ecosystem

There is some confusion over the terminology applied to Amazonian wetlands. Limnologists and ecologists have recognised three general categories of river according to water quality (IUCN 1975; Sioli 1975b). Whitewater rivers are turbid and rich in suspended sediment (mainly clays) and flow mainly from the Andes (e.g. the rivers Madeira, Solimões, Purús and Juruá). Blackwater rivers drain regions where sandy soils have developed above igneous or metamorphic rocks; intensive leaching it is suggested is responsible for the production of humic compounds which turn the water dark. Blackwater rivers carry little or no suspended clay, indeed they generally are so poor in nutrients as to be unproductive of fish (IUCN 1975), (e.g. the rivers Negro, Tapajós, Juruena, São Manoel, Cururu). Clearwater streams carry little or no material suspended or in solution, and originate from regions of Palaeozoic and Plio-Pleistocene sedimentary rocks (e.g. Rio Xingu) (Stark and Holley 1975; IBGE 1977). While botonists and some ecologists loosely apply *várzea* to almost any seasonally inundated area, limnologists reserve the term for that flooded by whitewater streams. *Várzeas* do form along the lower courses of some other types of river, but they are nowhere near as fully developed. In this paper *várzea* refers to land periodically flooded by sediment-rich (whitewater) rivers.

The seasonal flood of whitewater streams deposits a somewhat variable quality (and quantity) of alluvium. Estimates by INPA suggest that in the lower Amazon accretion may be as high as 8 tonnes per hectare per annum (Petrick 1978 p. 29). Mid and upper Amazonian large, shallow *várzea* lakes may receive 15 cm or more sediment per annum. Given appropriate flood control – a 'polder' system – to encourage deposition and reduce removal of silt there is good potential for reclamation of rich agricultural land, especially in lower Amazonia. Not all *várzea* deposits are fertile, the quality varies, but in general they are better than most *terra firme* soils, and receive a free annual deposition of nutrients. Some *várzea* soils have been found to be suphur-deficient (Wang *et al.* 1976), some have high pH levels (typically pH 5 to 6); such deficiencies are, however, fairly easily corrected by the addition of sulphur and lime. Poor drainage may be more of a problem for the agriculturalist.

The quality and extent of the *várzeas* is still debated: most estimates suggest these are between 64 000 and 128 000 km² (1 to 2 per cent of Amazonia) (Moran 1981b; Sioli 1975a; Wang *et al.* 1976; Wilhelmy 1973). *Várzeas* may extend 20 or even 40 km in width and run for 100 km in length on both sides of Amazonian rivers, with little interruption to the floodland other than tributary channels and lakes – both of which are usually shallow. Figure 3 illustrates the levee-like structure of *várzeas*: faster flood flow near the main river channel prevents deposition of fine

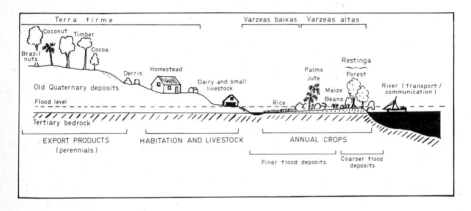

Fig. 3 A *várzea* utilisation scheme, based on proposals made by F. de Camargo in the 1950s. During floods the velocity of the silt-laden water decreases away from the river channel, heavy particles settle first, and furthest from the river where flow is slow fine sediment is deposited – the result is a gently graded levee (vertically exaggerated in the drawing). Coarse soils form the higher *várzea-alta*, and less well drained, softer soils form the lower *várzea-baixa*.

sediment; soils near the mainstream (the higher *várzeas altas*) tend to be coarser, sandy, well drained; the lower *várzeas baixas* are usually composed of fine-grained silts (here the flood was flowing more feebly) – while these may sometimes be rich, they may also suffer from ill-drainage and be easily compacted when cultivated.

In general Amazonian rivers flood in June/July with slight secondary rises in September and January (which may affect some *várzeas baixas*). Generally *várzeas* between Manaus and Belém are inundated from June to November. With tributaries originating in the north, flows are greatest in June and July, lowest in August and from December to March. Between March and April southern tributaries are high, and low from August to October (Sternberg 1975). The flow regime is made more complex by marine tidal hinderance of discharge, which affects the *várzeas* up to Óbidos (some 850 km from the Atlantic). Below the Tapajós confluence, high water due to tidal hindrance occurs in March–May and September (low in November) – flooding due to tidal effects becomes progressively more important compared with floodwater-caused fluctuations towards the sea. Some of the lower Amazon *várzeas* are flooded not only by the 'spring' tides but by more frequent (sometimes monthly) lower tides. Farmers in such *várzeas baixas* can often recognise a predictable cycle of flooding. It should be noted that tides hold up river discharge, rather than result in the penetration inland of salt water; lower Amazon *várzeas* are therefore flooded regularly with fresh water.

In the middle and upper Amazon floods may rise 16 to 20 m above mean river level, in the lower Amazon 5–7 m. Flood levels do vary a little from year to year. Because gradients of *várzeas* are so gentle this causes considerable variation of the areas inundated, some rivers fluctuating more than others (e.g. the Rio Madeira is infamous for this). Such variation makes the mapping of *várzeas* difficult (aerial surveys are also hindered by persistent cloud cover), and means that *várzea* agriculture must always face an element of uncertainty and risk. The areas with the greatest potential for *várzea* development lie along the Solimões/Amazonas proper, the Madeira, Purús, Juruá, lower Marañón, Jarí, lower Xingu, Guamá, lower Tocantins/Araguaia, around the deltaic islands (e.g. Ilha do Marajó) and along the coast north of the Amazon into Guiana.

Floristics

Generally mid and upper Amazonian *várzeas* are forested – such forests having a high biomass but less species diversity than most *terra firme* forests (Prance 1978). In lower Amazonia treeless savanna and grassland is common – beyond narrow belts of gallery forest on the *várzeas-altas* (*restinga* forest). The tree species *Ceiba pentandra*, *Hura crepitans*, *Carapa guianensis*, *Gustavia augusta*, *Couroupita subsessilis* are amongst those typical of *várzea* forests (which tend to have an abundance of leguminous tree species).

Igapó is less diverse in species composition even than the *várzea* forests – flooding for up to 10 months and poor soils often result in stunted trees. In lower Amazonia where tidal influences predominate (Rio Guamá, Tocantins, Xingu and the Ilha do Marajó and coastal lowlands), forest cover typically includes *Allantama lineata, Carapa guianensis, Virola surinamensis, Euterpe lineata* and *E. oleraceae*.

Natural 'grassland' and savanna occurs throughout Amazonia's *várzeas*, but is most extensive in lower Amazonia (especially in the Ilha do Marajó) — such *campos da várzea* cover possibly 20 000 to 25 000 km² (Petrick 1978; Herrera *et al.* 1978) — they are dominated by Cyperaceae spp., and grasses (e.g. *Canarana erecta*) and in drier localities palms (*Mauritia flexuos* and *Euterpe oleraceae*) may be common. The less frequently flooded *campos da várzea* are of great agricultural potential — lower *campos* which may be inundated almost every day have a cover of *Eichhornia azurea* and *Montrichardia alorescens*. Upper and mid-Amazonian *várzeas* may support 'floating meadows' — rafts of vegetation (*matas-de-várzea* or *matupa*) formed by grasses: *Paspalum repens, P. fasciculatum, Panicum spectabile*; *P. amplexicaule*, and other semi-aquatic vegetation (e.g. *Echinocloa polystachia*). Stranded after floods, *matupas* take root and provide excellent pasture for cattle soon after waters recede (Junk 1970). If collected during flooding they may be transplanted to islands or stock pens above high water as forage.

In lower Amazonia mangrove forests (*Rhizophora mangla, Avicenna nitida*, etc) offer less potential for development than *várzeas*.

Várzeas: utilisation

According to Petrick (1978 p. 33) less than 1 per cent of Amazonian *várzeas* are utilised. Yet these lands could be exploited by conventional agricultural practices now available, by small farmers or by larger concerns, and without necessarily needing heavy inputs of expensive fertiliser. Similar environments in south and southeast Asia support intensive small-farmer annual crop production, especially rice (often with little if any import of fertiliser) (Monteiro 1979).

River systems offer the *várzeas* over 80 000 km of maintenance-free communications — bulk transport by ship, as petroleum fuel becomes more expensive, will offer more cost-effective conveyance than roads. Large ocean-going vessels can reach Manaus, vessels of 25 000 tons navigate the Rio Jarí and for many years larger passenger and cargo vessels have plied the greater part of the mainstream and some tributaries.[2] In the *várzeas* supply of protein to settlers (often a problem in *terra firme* settlements) presents little difficulty, fish are abundant and yields could easily be increased by simple fish farming (Junk 1975). The proximity of the river makes crop irrigation much more practicable in the *várzeas* than in *terra firme* developments.

However, against such potential must be weighed the disadvantages of the *várzeas* ecosystem: because Amazonia's wetlands play an important role in moderating extremes of flow, their development, especially the removal of *restinga* and *várzea* forest and drainage or embankment could result in greater flood risk downstream. Amazonia's fisheries are an important source of protein for growing settlements — presently the potential is underutilised and occasional shortages occur, even so some 35 000 tonnes a year are landed in Manaus alone (Johnson 1978). *Várzea* development could not only damage the yield of fisheries, it could also destroy some of the species (1500 alone are known in the vicinity of Manaus) (Johnson 1978), many of which may well be of value to the world if domesticated for intensive pisciculture. Many fish species depend heavily on the floodlands for seasonal feeding grounds or for spawning, and much of the marine ecosystem's nutrients are flushed from the flooded wetlands (Samstag 1981). A number of species are adapted to the shallow *várzea* lakes and would be lost were these reclaimed for agriculture.

So far very little provision has been made for the conservation of *várzeas*, apart from a limited provision in the Tapajós National Park (Barrett 1980). There is a mutual interdependence of every fish and *várzea* plant species, particularly important is the seasonal dissemination of tree seeds by migrating fish (Smithsonian Institution 1980). Ideally as much as possible of the *restinga* forest should be left intact to conserve fish stocks and plant species, provide some moderation of flood flows and help prevent channel erosion (the *restinga* would also offer tourists travelling by boat a 'facade' of 'jungle' rather than a vista of *várzea* rice schemes).

Várzea developments have shown a tendency to use quite a lot of herbicides and pesticides. In Bangladesh riverine fisheries were extensively ruined as a result of agricultural chemicals leaching into the water – it would be only too easy to lose much of the Amazonian genetic potential through such pollution, and tropical pisciculture would be the poorer for it.

The flood regime of the *várzea* has imposed a system of transhumance on traditional agriculture. Cattle ranchers remove their beasts from the *campos-de-várzeas*, either housing them on floating or stilted byres (*marombas*) where for the duration of the flood season they are fed on fodder, or they are pastured in *terra firme* clearings (where pasture is generally poor). In lower Amazonia, if the rancher is rich enough, cattle may be transported by road (the Belém–Brasília highway) to pasture in southern Pará. Whatever the strategy, the flood season brings with it stock losses, falls in milk production, meat quality and availability, and seasonal income fluctuation for the *várzea* farmer (Monteiro 1979; Sternberg 1956).

Flood regime dictates the cropping pattern, determines length of growing season and rotation possibilities. Successful cropping demands that farmers adhere to a suitable agricultural calendar. Extension services now provide Amazonian farmers with simple calendars: see Table 1.

High humidity and frequent rain makes crop drying and storage a problem – however, recently, considerable progress has been made in developing cheap simple solar crop-drying units and better systems of storage for both small- and large-scale producers (Geertz 1963). Inundation does have some beneficial effects, e.g. some pest species are periodically reduced by floodwater.

Initial expenditure on land preparation may be high – dikes, drainage and stump clearance are costly. Small farmers opening forested *várzea* may simply plant

Table 1   Simplified Calendar of Amazonian Arable and Cattle Production

Annual crops	Rice	Beans	Maize	Mandioca	Jute
Prepare soil	Aug/Sept	Aug/Sept	Aug/Sept	July/Sept	July/Sept
Plant	Oct/Nov*	Aug/Sept	Sept/Oct	–	Aug/Nov
Thin	–	–	Oct/Nov	–	Sept/Dec
Insecticide	any time	any time	any time	any time	any time
Disease control	any time	any time	any time	any time	any time
Harvest	Feb/Mch	Oct/Nov	Jan/Feb	Mch/Apr	Feb/Apr

Cattle	
To *várzea* from *terra firme*	March/April/May
From *várzea* to *terra firme*	August/September
Sale of cattle	December/January/February/March/ April/May

Source: Calendario de A tividades Agricolas do Estado Amazonas, (undated – 1981 issue) EMATER-Amazonas, Manaus/EMBRAPA-UEPAE de Manaus.
Calendario de Almdotodas em Bovinocultura do Estado do Amazonas (undated – 1981 issue) EMATER-Amazonas/EMBRAPA-UEPAE de Manaus.
Note: In upper Amazonia – Rio Solimões, April/May.

around stumps – but any attempt at mechanisation necessitates stump clearance. Because fine-grained soils (mainly well away from the river channel) may be easily compacted or may bog down agricultural machinery, equipment such as microtractors must be adapted to *várzea* conditions. Experiments in Belém have proved metal wheels, rather than pneumatic tyres are better – preferably with simple angle-iron treads about 5 cm wide spaced about 30 cm apart to form non-sink wheels approximately 1.5 m in diameter, 1 m in width.[3]

Traditionally the *caboclo* (Amazonian 'creole') farmer has devoted little effort to *várzea* crop production because gathering wild forest products (rubber, Brazil nuts and various woods) brought good prices, while surplus agricultural production brought less profit and was harder to market (Moran 1975 p. 203, 1981). It is not simply that inertia is developed by social and institutional attitudes; the regime lacks the driving forces which operate in Asia: population pressure and land scarcity (Geertz 1963). Intensive permanent cultivation of *várzeas* is only just beginning (having been practised in prehistoric times but having been forgotten) – for the potential to be realised labour shortages must be overcome (primarily through mechanisation); and secondly transportation to markets must be improved (Moran 1975).

Unfortunately small farmers are generally poor risks for investment and marketing difficulties might also undermine profits – so credit for *várzea* development or mechanisation is not easy to get. In mid and lower Amazonia larger landowners (some being multinational corporations) can dominate other cattle ranching or agricultural interests – with landlords frequently away in São Paulo or other cities it is difficult to monitor and control development. Rural credit for micro-tractors or for small farmers to purchase buffaloes for ploughing and haulage must be a priority. Ideally small farmers in upper and mid Amazonia should be aided to produce rice, maize, beans, etc. to help reduce Amazonia's food imports and to generate employment.

The disease risk to *várzea* developers is difficult to predict – cities like Manaus have acceptable health conditions. In the past, rubber plantation workers and immigrant Japanese jute farmers suffered malaria but since the 1930s drugs have greatly improved control. Bilharzia (schistosomiasis) is presently limited in Amazonia to the Fordlândia region (mid Tapajós) but it is present in the northeast of Brazil (notably the São Francisco basin) from where many potentially infected immigrants may originate. Whitewater rivers and clearwater rivers would be most at risk, the blackwaters are probably too acid for the snail vectors. *Tropicorbis* spp. snails are reported from Amazonian *várzeas* (Marlier 1973), but because of low population densities the disease may not become a major threat. Blackfly (*piums*) can cause great discomfort and hinder agricultural work during the wet season in some regions – and may carry river blindness (onchocerciasis). Chagas's disease is a threat to Amazonian settlers – especially if lack of finances prevents regular spraying of dwellings against the reduviid bug vector.

Várzea Crops

Tree crops

Much of the *várzeas* are forested; in all there are perhaps 6 500 000 hectares (Anon. 1978) with a potential yield of timber of about 90 m³/hectare, of which on average 30 m³/hectare is economically exportable (Pandolfo 1979a). There have been studies of timber potential for lumber and pulp, and at least one common *várzea* tree yields tallow and oil suitable for margarine manufacture. The latter, *ucuuba-de-várzea* (*virola surinamensis*), could be incorporated into a cropping system with annual crops like jute or beans (Rodrigues 1972; Pires and Kourym 1959; IDESP 1972). Exploitation of *várzea* forests has so far been mainly limited to lumbering although the Jarí paper pulp mill adds *Mangula* wood from the *várzeas* to plantation-grown softwood.[4] The wetter parts of the *várzeas-altas* and better-drained parts of *várzeas-baixas* have considerable potential for palm cultivation – dênde, the oil palm *Eleaieus guinensis*, is increasingly grown. Malaysia already has expertise, good stock and good communications; Amazonia might be better occupied in the long term by seeking and perfecting alternative palms from among its many wild *várzea* species. Goodland *et al.* (1978) list a number of potentially useful *várzea* plants, including 15 palm species. Already palmetto, coconut, and açai palm (*Euterpe oleraceae*) are exploited; also rubber (which originated in Amazonia's *várzeas*) and cocoa are cultivated in Amazonia. *Hevea brasiliensis*, and other less well known tree crops are well-suited to, or actually originate from *várzea* forests. Like dênde, rubber production using *Hevea* has been highly developed in southeast Asia – efforts might be better devoted to developing alternative species of latex-producing trees from wild stock native to Amazonia and untried elsewhere. Such tree crops would be especially valuable if grown as shade trees for annual crops or perennial crops like cocoa.

Annual crops

Early in the history of Amazonian development sugar and cocoa were important. However, it was upon the profits of rubber that cities like Manaus and Belém grew up. Rubber shows little sign of regaining its nineteenth and early twentieth century success, and of today's more important *várzea* crops, rice and jute, the latter is hardly prospering.

Irrigated (paddy) rice probably has the greatest potential in the foreseeable future – natural *várzea* conditions are very favourable.[5] 30 cm or so of water is naturally present for much of the year in the *várzeas-altas* and diking can create suitable growing conditions in lower *várzeas-baixas*. As yet there has been no attempt to introduce tall-growing 'flood rice' species like those used in floodlands of Bangladesh, Burma and Thailand – such rices might open up even greater areas for paddy cultivation with little need for embankment. Somewhat sporadic research and plantings have over the years improved rice varieties and techniques and have demonstrated in Pará and Amapá most attractive yields under small-farmer cultivation. Along the Rio Guamá (Pará State) three crops per annum yielding a total of 18 metric tons per hectare is possible; experimental plots in *várzeas* near Manaus (in the *municípios* of Itacoatiara, Boca do Acre and Manacapuru) are reputed to yield 5000 to 7000 kg/hectare (Malafaia, Rosas and Silva 1969; Alvim 1977).

Only one large-scale attempt at rice production using modern techniques currently operates in Amazonia – the Jarí rice scheme managed by São Raimundo Agricultura Industria S.A., and reputedly comprising at least 4000 hectares of rice 'polders' which are cropped using sophisticated techniques – sowing pre-germinated seed and applying fertiliser and pesticide from aircraft, strategies similar to those used in South Carolina, USA. Yields are now reputedly 10–12 tonnes per hectare (from 2 crops per annum), however there is considerable doubt whether the scheme is at present economically viable (the Jarí estates have recently been sold). A conservative estimate of the future rice potential of the Amazonian *várzeas* – assuming no marked improvement in current techniques and varieties – is at least 1 000 000 hectares (Alvim 1977), yielding 3900 kg per hectare per annum, although higher yields have been forecast (given use of fertiliser) – e.g. 4500 kg per hectare. At present rice yields from the *terra firme* are poor, usually less than 1500 kg per hectare with yields lasting only one or two years before soil exhaustion. Indeed, *terra firme* rice production is probably the cause of more Amazonian forest clearance than any other crop. Rice statistics for Amazonia rarely distinguish dryland and *várzea*-produced rice, but the indications are that over the last 25 years *várzea* rice seems to have contributed only roughly 13–14 per cent of total rice production. *Várzea* rice farmers presently seem to use little if any fertiliser, and sow in seed beds transplanting at 20 to 25 days as floodwater subsides (fast-growing

Asian varieties able to withstand rising water could usefully extend the growing season); there is very little mechanisation, little weeding and little use of improved seeds. Increased *terra firme* rice production or production in other parts of Brazil could depress regional market prices, making small-scale rice production unattractive. Compared with similar seasonally flooded lowlands in south and southeast Asia two things are apparent; firstly, little of the *várzea's* potential is yet realised, secondly even yields of 3500 kg per hectare (a rather conservative figure for *várzea* production) compares well with the Ganges/Brahmaputra coastal lowlands (1300 kg per hectare), Irrawaddy Delta, Burma (2000 kg per hectare) or Chao Phya Delta, Thailand (1900 kg per hectare) (Petrick 1978).

Jute (*Corchorus capsularis*) is the second most important *várzea* crop – introduced in the mid-1930s by Japanese immigrant settlers (Kaoru Tanaka 1957). Production boomed after 1943 when President Getúlio Vargas prohibited the import of Indian jute into Brazil (the Brazilian coffee industry is a large consumer for sacking for coffee beans) and after 1947 when the partition between India and Pakistan, which left the mills in Pakistan (now Bangladesh) but the jute fields in India, disrupted the near-monopoly India had long enjoyed in jute production. The 'boom' (during which Brazil was self-sufficient in jute) lasted roughly from 1955 to 1965 and much production came from Japanese small farmers between Parintins and Itacoatiara (Amazonia State). Most jute is still grown by small farmers, on 3–4 ha plots with no mechanisation or use of fertilisers, but it rarely provides them with an adequate income and production has stagnated since 1965. A variety of factors has contributed to this decline. Increasing competition from synthetics and from jute substitute – malva (*Pavonia malocaphylla*) and uacuna (*Urena lobata*) – resulted, at least in part because jute farmers could not meet growing demand for coffee sack manufacture after 1965. Poor yields, poor-quality fibre due to careless retting and storage and unfavourable marketing have also been to blame – one firm (Sul Industria Texisis) is reputed to have a virtual monopoly in jute processing in Brazil (personal communication with a government official, Manaus, 1981).

Jute yields average 1400–1600 kg per hectare (120–135 days growing season). With two crops per annum total harvest may reach 3900 kg per hectare per annum – one crop on the *várzeas-altas* and later one on the *várzeas-baixas* as floodwaters fall. Present production is variously cited between 48 000 and 50 000 tonnes per annum (during the boom probably much higher) – possibly 100 000 people are now employed in jute production (EMBRAPA Belém, personal communication 1981). Jute is generally grown with maize between Belém and Santarém, nearer Manaus jute and *malva* may be grown. On average jute farmers hold only 1.8 hectares of land (Petrick 1978) – introduction of cooperative organisations of smallholders is likely to be an important factor in determining the future of jute production. Malva is grown only on the *várzeas-altas* or on *terra firme* (as is uacuna) where it flourishes on sandy poor-quality soils yielding up to 2000–5000 kg per hectare (EMBRATER/EMBRAPA 1980). Much has been written upon the problems and characteristics of small-farm jute production in Amazonia; there is therefore some data base for agricultural improvement schemes to draw upon (Miyazaki and Morio 1958; Libonati 1958; Junqueira 1972).

Other *várzea* crops offer great future potential but are presently little exploited. Sugar, once an important crop, could yield about 200 tonnes per hectare – but small-farm production generally yields only 100–150 tonnes per hectare. Like manioc (*Manihot esculenta*), sugar could be a feedstock for alcohol production; Brazil is presently pursuing a programme of alcohol substitution for petrol for automobiles and demand for sugar will very likely rise.

Groundnuts, soya, romie, chick peas, maize, tobacco, beans, cowpea, sesame, melons and tropical fruits are grown by *várzea* farmers. Amazonia imports beans from other states, yet yields from the *várzeas* can be easily 1000–1300 kg per hectare (compared with 500 kg per hectare on average and 800 at best for *terra firme* production), and could realistically be improved to 1500 kg per hectare. One difficulty is that beans of the *Phaseollus* genera are much imported, but do not thrive on the *várzeas*; beans of the *Vigna* genera do and could easily be grown in rotation with jute (EMBRATER/EMBRAPA 1980). Maize may be grown with jute, yielding 3500–4500 kg per hectare per annum. Short-growing-season cassava is increasingly cultivated in upper and mid Amazonia.

Livestock

In upper and mid Amazonia the main and two subsidiary inundations provides locally reasonable *várzea* pastures. Because the *várzeas-altas* flood only once a year and time of inundation is more predictable, they offer the greatest arable potential – the *várzeas-baixas*, with greater flood risk, do offer livestock grazing potential, so in theory at least *várzea* arable and livestock production should be compatible. The wet season (April–July) transhumance disrupts milk yield and meat supply to cities like Belém and Manaus. Grazing becomes a problem in the flood season, one that could be solved by either making greater use of aquatic vegetation (Junk 1979), or by arable farmers supplying fodder in the form of crop residues. EMBRAPA has examined mixed milk and meat production – the latter on the *terra firme* using *holando* × *zebu* cattle and bulbinos – small buffalo (Teixeira 1980a). Both solutions could help integrate arable and livestock farming: aquatic weeds are very productive and could be useful as a mulch or compost for arable farmers as well as for fodder (Junk 1979); if cattle concentrated in wet-season *marombas* or small enclosures were fed on crop residue, arable farmers in return could utilise the accumulated manure. Presently grazing efficiency is low throughout Amazonia – the stocking density for cattle is about 1 animal per 3 hectares, on 'improved' pastures the carrying capacity is generally about 1 head per hectare per year.

There are probably over 2 000 000 head of cattle in Amazonia – possibly half of these on the Ilha do Marajó, a 1970 estimate of the island's herds was about

560 000 *crioula* × *zebu* cattle (anon. 1980). Water buffalo are steadily increasing in importance and recent estimates suggest there are 400 000 head in Amazonia: 200 000 in the Ilha do Marajó, where in addition to meat and milk production and motive power for farmers they provide a significant tourist attraction (Anon. 1980). The buffalo (*'mediterraneo'* × *murrah* for milking and *'mediterraneo'* × *jaffarabadi* for meat production) were originally introduced to Marajó in the 1890s from Italy but have only recently increased as a result of successful crossing with Indian stock in the 1950s and 1960s (after stock import restrictions were relaxed). Buffalo are better adapted to the wet *várzeas* and can graze semi-submerged land, resist disease better than cattle, are better draught and work animals, and yield more and richer milk (average of 950 litres per head per annum). Stocking density for buffalo may be as good as 1 head per hectare and considerable efforts have been made (centred on Belém) to promote buffalo, especially new, small-sized varieties (bulbinos), improve stock, and provide credit and infrastructure for meat and dairy production. Poor infrastructure makes milk marketing difficult even in Manaus – 'rustic cheese' production may offer a partial solution (Teixeira 1980a). The buffalo may well be a better investment than the micro-tractor for small rice farmers.

The potential for fish farming in *várzea* lakes and waterways has been stressed by several authors (Welcomme 1979). Other animals may well have great potential: ducks, possibly species of river turtle (e.g. *Podocnemis expansa*), the tapir (*Tapirus terrestris*) and various large rodents (already hunted as game in Amazonia). If 'ranched' one or more of these – the capybara (*Hydrochaerus hydrochaerus*), agouti (*Agouti paca*), or cavy could well give good yields of meat and cause far less environmental damage than cattle ranching (Vasey 1979). Already there has been some success in capybara 'ranching' in Venezuela (Ojasti 1980), and the beast will feed happily alongside cattle on plants the cattle do not graze (Junk 1979).

Várzea development strategies

Traditionally *várzea* small farmers follow one or more of the following strategies:
- (a) rubber gathering and food crop production;   ⎫ especially
- (b) açai palm gathering and food crop production;   ⎪ between
- (c) jute growing in the wet season, maize in the dry season; ⎬ Manaus and
- (d) cattle ranching.   ⎭ Santarém

Before and during the Second World War attempts were made to establish plantation system production, notably of rubber, in Amazonia. Labour problems and other factors confounded those efforts. Soon after the war Felisberto Cardoso de Camargo put forward proposals for Amazonian development, based on his studies of the structure and function of the *várzea* and other Amazonian ecosystems (Camargo 1948, 1949, 1958). De Carmargo noted the problems of *terra firme* development and partly as a result of limnological research in the 1950s argued the potential of the *várzeas*. He felt they were Amazonia's most stable ecosystems – above all they received an annual supply of nutrients. Therefore de Camargo proposed *várzeas* be utilised for annual-crop production (with a little cattle ranching integrated), the *terra firme* should be used for perennial (bush and tree) crops and forestry with some limited clearance for wet-season cattle grazing by *várzea* herds. See Figure 3.

The Ganges and other Asian floodlands have long produced rice with little loss of nutrients – with annual flood-silt deposition. Why not, de Camargo proposed, construct simple 'rice polders' in Lower Amazonia. Figure 3 is based upon his proposals for the Rio Guamá near Belém – which with little adaptation would function in many mid or upper Amazonian *várzeas*. Twenty years after de Camargo's proposals some progress has been made in their promotion – in 1975 a prominent Amazonian limnologist felt:

> The scheme is especially appropriate and effective for the cultivation of the *várzeas* in the lower (estuarine) region of the Amazon. Above all it has a role to play in the development of rice cultivation (Junk 1980). [Translation by CJB].

De Camargo's proposals have been increasingly explored (Sioli 1980b; Lima 1956), mainly in lower Amazonia – unfortunately *várzea* rice production is hindered by: (decreasingly) a poor data base, high costs of transport and labour, scarcity of technical, managerial and entrepreneurial talent and frequently confused land tenure (Monteiro nd).

Only projects or small farms that are especially productive will recover the high investment outlay necessary in Amazonia. For large schemes like the Jarí project an economic rate of return of 15 per cent may be the minimum for viability (Skilling and Tcheyan 1979).

Considerable progress has been made, especially in lower Amazonia, in developing rice production techniques. The various small-farm strategies of rice production are listed in Table 2.

Fertiliser trials have been carried out to try to establish by what degree annual nutrient receipts (flood silt) reduces the need for costly artificial fertiliser input (Lopes, Cruz and Kass 1973), and various tillage, stubble burning and herbicide usage strategies have been examined (EMBRAPA 1976).

Recently the state government of Pará published a programme of national *várzea* development – Provarzeas Pará (Governo do Estado do Pará 1981).[6] The programme concentrates on rice production in lower Amazonia (middle Amazon of Pará State, lower Amazon Furos, Campos de Marajó, lower Tocantins, Salgado coastal lowlands, Bragança region, Viseu region: in all some 8 252 000 hectares of *várzea* are suitable for rice). Between 1981 and 1985 some 15 000 hectares of rice will be established. There would appear to be similar potential for Amazonas State (roughly 80 000 ha of which 10 000 will probably be developed in 1981–85).

With few exceptions crops cultivated in Amazonia's *várzeas* are intolerant of

Table 2 Várzea Small-farm Rice Production Strategies

Strategy	Area practised	Yields	Technique	Advantages	Disadvantages	Rice variety
1a. Natural system (tidal flooding)	Bragança region, lower Tocantins, Rio Guamá, Rio Caeté, Ilha do Marajó, Furos region, Viseu, Salgado, Belém–lower Rio Xingu.	2.6 to 5.2 tonnes/hectare (3900–5100 kg/hectare). In some tidal areas 2 crops per annum are not possible because salts are not washed away during dry season.	'Polders' formed by building simple earth bunds. Simple flood gates control tides (which flood 'polders' once every 5–6 days.) Rice is planted, not seeded.	No pumping needed. Minor weed problems. Manual bunding creates employment for rural people. No heavy use of herbicides.	Only rice withstands frequent flooding (no other crops yet developed). Dry season problems of salt accumulation. Drainage may be needed.	'Bella Patna' x 'Dawn' (100 days).
1b. Semi-controlled system	Rio Caeté, Bragança Viseu, Furos, Lower Tocantins (Higher parts of várzeas-altas of várzeas-baixas).	Unknown	Simple dykes to retain rather than control water. Flooding by high spring tides of March/April or September (not short 5–6 day cycle). Rice planted not seeded.	No pumping needed. Crops other than rice can be grown.	Weeds can be a problem. Herbicide use may be necessary. Silt accumulation. Drainage may be needed.	'Bella Patna' x 'Dawn' or 'Washabo' or 'Cica-4' or 'Alupe'.
2. Pump-irrigation	Areas mentioned above – but high *várzeas-altas* and in particular in Ilha do Marajó and NE rará are possibilities (already 77% of Pará State irrigated rice is produced on such land).	2.0 tonnes/hectare – 3.8 tonnes/hectare. 3 crops per annum possible. see Table 1	Diesel pump irrigation – using simple distribution channels (water raised only a few metres). Rice planted not seeded.	3 crops per annum Ideal for local cooperative production.	Pumps necessary Drainage control necessary. Weed problems. Herbicide used.	'Bella Patna' x 'Dawn' or 'Bella Patna' x 'Acorni', (100) days, or 'Apura'.

Source: Chaves *et al.* 1979; Lopes *et al.* 1973; EMBRAPA 1976; EMBRATER/EMBRAPA/IDESP 1979)
Notes: Bella Patna x Dawn is reputedly the best species for the *várzea* small farmer. Growing season given in parenthesis: e.g. (100 days)

flooding, thus the sowing and planting is restricted and flooding all too often damages crops. There is great need for flood-resistant crops which could reduce the risk of crop loss and open up wider areas of *várzea*, and by extending growing seasons enable two or more crops per annum. Aquatic macrophytes have potential – naturally about 90 per cent of Amazonia's standing crop of wild aquatic plants is lost during low water periods. Harvesting could utilise some of that biomass without too much effect on the environment: either to provide forage or to form compost for arable crops. Junk suggested two plants *Impomoe aquatica* and *Neptunia oleracea* as having great potential (Junk 1979).

Deepwater ('flood rice'), e.g. Broadcast Aman, is grown in Asia – typically in waters that rise 1 to 3 metres during growth. It demands little or no fertiliser (typically yields 1.3 to 2.5 tonnes per hectare), and might enable the development of considerable areas of presently unproductive *várzea* (Clay *et al.* 1978; Bangladesh Rice Research Institute 1975; Clay 1978; Harwood 1979). However, there seems to have been little or no interest in such rice varieties in Amazonia so far. Petrick noted that *várzea* rice production suffers from strong competition at present from other parts of Brazil, and while Amazonia's experimental yields can be high, small farmers risk market price slumps if there is overproduction of rice outside Amazonia. Thus the key to small farmers' increasing their rice cultivation lies in state aid, in Petrick's words the potential of the *várzea* 'would have to be demonstrated and secured for him [the small farmer] institutionally' (Petrick 1978 p. 35).

Any *várzea* development strategy should include provision for small farmers. The development of such a strategy might be aided by study in the following three areas:

(a) Identify how people, plants, etc. interact (this will require analysis of farming systems presently operating).

(b) Identify inefficiencies in the practice of present farming systems.

(c) Define changes in traditional farming system(s) that lead to increased productivity, ideally degrading the natural ecosystems as little as possible, and providing sustained yields. Broad guidelines for the development of the American humid tropics have already been published by the IUCN (1975) and should – as far as possible – be incorporated into *várzea* development strategies.

Already in Amazonia, hydroelectric development has begun (e.g. the Tucuruí project on the Tocantins). Brazil intends to develop Amazonia's resources and the key to that development is likely to be hydropower – to power mineral extraction, ore processing, agro-industry and railways. Rivers, like the Tocantins, which have considerable range of flow may be moderated by hydroelectric installations and may have the silt loads important for *várzea* formation altered. Before *várzea* development plans are formulated for any Amazonian tributary, consideration should be made of the potential impact of hydroelectric development. Luckily whitewater rivers, by virtue of their silt loads are unlikely to be attractive for hydroelectric generation, neither is the mainstream Solimões/Amazon likely to be affected.

Conclusion

The *várzea* ecosystem of Amazonia offers some considerable opportunities, particularly for annual crop production, compared with the *terra firme*: there is considerable river transport potential, protein is readily available for settlers, costly fertiliser imports are not as necessary for *várzea* soils, above all farming techniques at present available will easily work in *várzea* conditions. The environment is well suited to rice production, also there should be considerable potential for producing small-volume, high-value export crops (e.g. palmetto, avocado, palm oils, chicale, exotic fruits for export, pyrethrum). Of possible food crops, beans and maize production could easily be expanded to help reduce present food imports to Belém, Manaus and other cities. Yields of most crops are at present well below potential – floating 'flood rice' or 'mangrove rice' may have great potential which should be explored as present cultivation is restricted to flood-recession strategies or pump-irrigation. Increasing rice production now seems primarily a problem of planning, education and extension of credit and marketing facilities. Techniques suitable for *várzea* conditions are available: already on the Araguaia a large project is being established.

There is considerable conservatism and inertia, not only amongst the small farmers but among cattle ranchers: vested interests in cattle ranching might well hinder arable and livestock improvement and integration. Water buffalo in particular have great potential for meat and milk and to aid small farmers in cultivating arable crops. Pasturage of *várzeas-altas* could be improved with grasses like *Brachiaria humidicola* and the sedge *Echinochloa pyramidalis*, and greater use could be made of aquatic vegetation.

Disadvantages which might prove difficult to overcome are mainly socio-economic, but there are dangers from unpredictability of flooding and *várzea* farmers in some regions may somehow have to accept a risk of losing crops 1 year in 4. Excessive herbicide and pesticide usage is a real short-to-medium term danger. It is vital that pesticide and herbicide use should be reviewed, controlled and pollution levels monitored. Apart from being a doubtfully effective means of weed control in the *long term*, herbicide poisoning threatens fish species with tremendous future potential.

In the longer term, lack of an overall strategy for *várzea* development might be a problem. *Várzea* development should proceed, but every effort should be made to prepare overall plans which include *adequate* conservation of *várzea* forest and grasslands – wherever possible the *restinga* forests fringing the rivers should be left.

Notes

1 A limited number of immigrant Japanese farmers have had some success with sustained agricultural production on *terra firme* soils, notably the Cooperative Agricola Mista de Tomé-Açu (Pará State).
2 Road construction investments may well have been better spent were they used for developing *várzea* agriculture and improving river communications rather than building highways which constantly get damaged by heavy rainfalls.
3 Personal observation of author at EMBRAPA-Belém in August 1981 on experiments with Japanese Toyota hand-guided micro-tractors: the metal wheels do not sink and the angle-iron supports the tractor and simultaneously effectively helps cultivate the soil.
4 *Pinus*, *Gmelina* and *Eucalyptus* – personal field research, August 1981.
5 There is a native rice *Oryza perennis* – but the potential of this species does not appear to have been satisfactorily investigated.
6 Under the Programa Nacional para o Aproveitamento de Várzeas Irrigáveis (National Programme for the Use of Irrigated Lowlands) 28 Brazilian states including Amazonian states plan to develop wetlands.

9 The increased importance of ethnobotany and underexploited plants in a changing Amazon

GHILLEAN T. PRANCE

Introduction

It is not necessary to present in detail to this audience the gloomy details about the alarming rate at which the Amazon forest is being destroyed together with the indigenous population and the native species of plants and animals. The basic facts speak for themselves. A population of perhaps 5 million pre-Columbian Amazon Indians has been reduced to less than half a million and many tribes are extinct. Looking at today's Amazon scene does not encourage optimism about the fate of the smaller tribal groups that remain. The large development projects such as the Tucuruí dam, the Carajás iron deposits and the colonisation of Rondônia are all taking their toll on Indian groups. This type of development is obviously important and essential to the economy of the Amazonian nations. However, often while locating the activities of such large development projects, the impact on the local indigenous populations is not considered or not given enough weight before the final decisions are made.

The activities of private individuals insufficiently controlled by the government such as the projects of gold mines or ranchers are even worse. As recently as 1980 a bush pilot in Altamira was telling me how ranchers wanted him to make a flight to drop fire bombs on the houses of the Kayapó-Gorotire Indians. It is not my intention to recount details of these and other evidences which I see in Amazonia threatening the Indian population. Details have been cited in many places, for example, Goodland and Irwin (1975a), Ramos (1981), Ribeiro (1970) and Vidal (1982). Ribeiro (1970) indicated that at least 87 Brazilian Indian groups have become extinct this century, a rate of more than one per year, and details of forest destruction and species loss were summarised well in Myers (1980). The loss of even a single tribe is the loss of an entire body of knowledge built over many centuries of contact with the local environment. It is the loss of a unique part of the human character, of a perspective on relationships, creation and environment that can never be duplicated.

The loss of these people is a great tragedy in itself. As a botanist, I am also grieved by the loss of a treasury of information about useful plants through acculturation and the extinction of Indian groups. During visits to 17 different tribal groups of

Indians in Brazil, the Guianas and Peru, I have seen the extraordinary variety of plants they use (see for example Prance 1972). I never cease to be amazed by the different plant uses encountered as one moves from one tribe to another. Unfortunately, this means that with each tribe that becomes extinct, botanical information unique to that group is lost. Today some Amazonian tribes still remain whose culture is reasonably intact. The purpose of this paper is to show why it is important to gather from the Neotropical Indians as much botanical and ecological information as possible before it is permanently lost.

Indians as a source of botanical information

It is no coincidence that 11 of the 36 underexploited tropical plants with promising economic value highlighted by a National Academy of Science Report (1975) are plants which have been used by South American Indians for many generations, e.g. peach palm (*Bactris gasipaes* H.B.K.) and uvilla (*Pourouma cecropiifolia* Mart.) Many of the other plants in the same report are used by native peoples in other parts of the tropics. The Indians have accumulated a vast store of knowledge about many plants useful as foods, medicines, fibres, building materials, narcotics, poisons, contraceptives, and numerous other uses. In the limited space here I will give just a few examples of some interesting plants which I have studied that are well known to the Indians, and then give some of the compelling reasons for further study of Indian plant uses.

Guaraná (*Paullinia cupana* H.B.K. var. *sorbilis* (Mart.) Ducke, Sapindaceae)
Guaraná (Plate 1, after p. 132) is a fascinating plant that has been known to the Indians for many hundreds of years as a useful stimulant. The chronicles of Padre Betendorf written in 1669 (published in 1910, p. 36, from Cavalcante 1979) state 'The Andirozas (of Central Brazilian Amazon) have in their forest a fruit which they call Guaraná. They dry it and grind it and then make it into a cake which white men think of as their gold. The Indians scrape a powder from the cake into a gourd full of water and drink it. It gives them great strength and they can go out hunting for a whole day without becoming hungry, and they also use it to treat fevers, headaches and cramps.' (from Cavalcante, 1979).

Guaraná was described botanically by Humboldt, Bompland and Kunth (1882) from material which they collected in the Orinoco region of Venezuela. In addition to providing the scientific name *Paullinia cupana* and its original description they made the following observation: 'The seeds of this plant are mixed with cassava and wrapped in palm or musaceous leaves and submerged in water by the Indians. In a state of putrefaction the water becomes a yellow color and tastes bitter and they dilute this with more water and drink it.'

The exact method of preparation of guaraná varies from one Indian group to another, but it was obviously an important stimulant and perhaps also a source of various micronutrients especially for the tribes in central Amazonia around what is now the town of Maués. The products of guaraná have become an important part of the western culture in Amazonia and today guaraná, in the form of a carbonated drink, is the most popular soda throughout the region. The product reaches the market in sticks similar to those prepared by the Indians, in powder and in liquid extract. In 1978, in the Brazilian state of Amazonas, 70.4 tons of sticks, 52.8 tons of powder and 158.4 tons of liquid extract were produced. It has therefore become an important industry. Guaraná is also marketed in Japan and North America and demand now far exceeds production.

The guaraná has long been a sacred plant to the Indians. The Maués Indian legend tells of a couple who produced a wonder child. Through his influence the tribe prospered. He settled disputes, cured sicknesses and was adored by the people. One day the evil spirit Jurupari found the child protector of the tribe climbing a tree to pick a fruit. The spirit turned himself into a snake, and bit the child who then died. The Indians found the child on the ground as if he was asleep with a serene expression and open eyes. When the people were gathered in the village to mourn the child's death a ray of lightning fell from the sky. The child's mother broke their stunned silence and announced that the god Tupã had now decided to console them. They planted the eyes of the child in the soil and from one of them grew the sacred plant which would always help the Maués tribe by killing hunger, and curing sickness, from the other eye grew guaranárana or wild guaraná. The elders of the tribe guarded the seedling until it grew into the guaraná plant.

The legend, the Indian ethnobotany, and the modern industrialisation are all an important part of the story of the guaraná plant. In addition to botanical data about plants it is most important to gather the legends and details about their cultivation and ecology in order to understand their importance to the tribe.

Edible fungi

One of the most fascinating ethnobotanical studies that I have made is of the Yanomamo Indians' use of edible fungi (Plate 2, after p. 132). Unlike most Amazonian Indians who eat few or no fungi, the Yanomamo eat many different species. Prance (1972, 1973) reported four species of fungi used by the Yanomamo of the Serra do Surucucus region, and Fidalgo and Prance (1976) reported no fewer than 21 species in use by the Sanama group of Yanomamo at Auaris in Roraima Territory, Brazil. More recently a study of the Xirianá group of Yanomamo at Tototobi (Prance, in preparation) also reveleaed that they use at least 15 species of fungi as a regular part of their diet. At Tototobi some of the species were the same as those reported at Auaris such as *Favolus brasiliensis* (Fr.) Fr., and *Lentinus crinitas* (L. ex Fr.) Fr., and others are different. The identification of the Tototobi collections is not yet complete, but shows that the Xirianá also eat members of two families Polyporaceae and Agaricaceae, mainly the former family.

It is most interesting that the Yanomamo have specialised in the use of fungi whereas most other tribes have not (Fidalgo, 1965). However, there are other aspects of interest beside the basic catalogue of the species that they eat. For example, the first time I visited these Indians I was unaware that they used fungi, the reason being that all our ethnobotanical informants were male. The job of gathering fungi and consequently the bulk about their names, uses, flavours, etc. is known only to the women. It is most important to ascertain who has what information. Is it confined to one sex, an age group, the family of the chief or the shaman?

A second interesting aspect of Yanomamo ethnomycology is the source of their edible fungi. The fungi are especially important because as well as occurring in the forest, they are accidentally, or incidentally, cultivated by the Indians in their cassava (*Manihot*) plantations. This 'incidential' or 'accidental' cultivation is the result of various contributing climatic and cultural factors. The *Manihot* plantations are prepared by the ancient, typical slash-and-burn methods. After the area has been burnt over, no clearing is done by the Indians; the field remains full of stumps, fallen trunks, pieces of half-burnt and rotting wood. This debris under the local weather conditions provides an ideal habitat for development of wood-rotting fungi. When the *Manihot* is at an early stage of its growth the fungi are most plentiful. This indicates that the charred, decomposing logs have their peak fungus production less than a year after being cut and burned. This peak, however, lasts for several months and occurrs well before the time when *Manihot* is harvested. The Indians gather the fungi as needed for food, but do not appear to be making any conscious effort to cultivate them further for added food supply. However, the growth of fungi on rotting logs and tree stumps continues even after the fields have been abandoned. This is then one of the many plants that is harvested from the fallow fields in active regeneration to forest.

Other ethnobotanical examples

Many other examples could be given of interesting plants that the Indians use. For example, the moraceous tree *Pourouma cecropiifolia* Mart. produces a grape-like cluster of fruit (Plate 3, after p. 132) which has long been used by the Indians of the upper Amazon near Iquitos in Peru where it is called 'uvilla'. The Bora and Huitoto Indians cultivate *Pourouma*. It is a delicious tasting fruit and trees from seeds recently introduced to Manaus in Brazil have begun to produce fruit. It was introduced to the local population of Manaus and the agricultural market by scientists of the National Amazon Research Institute (INPA). The first week they gave away fruit clusters of 'mapati', as it is called in Brazil, the stand was overrun by enthusiastic tasters. The next week it was easy to sell the fruits. Plans are now being made to introduce it more widely into the markets of Amazonia.

An interesting source of carbohydrate that may rival the cassava plant is a species of *Cissus* in the Vitaceae, *C. gongylodes* (Plate 4, after p. 132). This plant is a fast-growing vine with an edible sturdy stem. Chemical analysis shows that it is rich in vitamins and minerals (Kerr *et al.* 1978). This plant called 'cupa' by the Indians is used by several groups of Kayapó Indians in the south of Pará State in Brazil. This is a crop that has not been introduced outside the Indian cultivation.

The cotyledons of the large fruits of *Acioa edulis* Prance (Chrysobalanaceae) are full of oil. This plant is now cultivated by Brazilians in many small towns and

Plate 1 The guaraná, *Paullinia cupana* var. *sorbilis*, one of the most promising of all underexploited Amazonian plants

Plate 2 One of the edible fungi used by the Yanomamo Indians at Tototobi

Plate 3 (above) The grape-like fruit cluster of *Pourouma cecropiifolia*, the uvilla, a fruit much used by the Indians of the upper Amazon that is becoming more utilised throughout the Amazon region

Plate 4 (left) *Cissus gongylodes*, a fast-growing vine the stems of which are an important source of carbohydrate for the Kayapó Indians

Plate 5 Makú Indians fishing with poison from *Euphorbia cotinifolia.* They are beating stacks of the vine so that the plant juices fall into the stream and poison fish for over 100 metres downstream

Plate 7 View of secondary forest with its characteristic tree, *Cecropia*. This type of forest in its regenerative phase also yields many plants of importance to the Indians

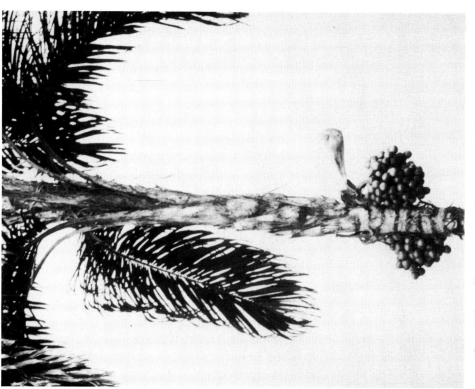

Plate 6 The pejibaye or pupunha palm, *Guilielma gasipaes*, an important food source for many Indian tribes

Plate 8 Deni Indian bringing in a load of beku vine, *Curarea tecunarum*, which they use as a contraceptive

Plate 9 Four-year-old transitional field (*kapúuwa*). Residual manioc in the foreground; uvilla tree to the right; a macambo branch juts out top left

Plate 10 Coppicing macambo in 1-year-old swidden

Plate 11 Six-year-old orchard fallow. Uvilla and peach palm are present. Note open, well lit floor

villages such as Tefé, Cbari and Codajás along the Solimões river. It is used in the manufacture of soap and to produce a comestible oil. These fruits have been used by Indians such as the Jarawara for many years, and the Brazilians have learned to use it from the Indians.

I well remember setting out with the Makú Indians of the upper Rio Uneiuxi on one of the occasional fish-poisoning expeditions. The Makú use at least six different fish poisons (see Prance 1972). On this particular trip they were using the stems of the leguminous liana *Lonchocarpus unrucu* Killip and Smith. However, they carried no food at all for the four-day trip. This was not because they were using a 'hunger-killer' like guaraná, but because of their absolute confidence that they could find food in the forest from plants and hunting. This proved to be correct and we were well sustained by edible fruit, palm heart, the heart of a species of *Heliconia*, honey from wild bees, and of course an abundance of fish from the fish-poisoning expedition. The Indians are so familiar with their environment that they do not need to carry bulky supplies that we always take on expeditions.

These examples are enough to show that among the myriad of plants the Indians have learned to use there must be many more of which we are not yet aware that could be important to all people.

Indians as plant breeders: selection of crops

It is interesting that at the time of the discovery of America by Columbus agriculture was well advanced. Far from being dependent only on wild species the Indians already had many crops in cultivation and had developed an array of cultivars including varieties of corn, peppers, potatoes and various other crop plants. In lowland Amazonia, any tribe that grows *Manihot* has many varieties. For example, the Jamamadi, an Arawak group I visited in the Purús river region of Brazil had at least 17 cultivars of *Manihot* and the nearby Paumari Indians had 12.

The Indians have a very specific use for each variety. Apart from the basic separation between sweet and bitter cassava, the Jamamadi have varieties for growing on the non-flooded *terra firme* and others for the floodplain or *varzeá* forest. The *várzea* varieties tend to be fast growing and can be harvested before inundation. Some varieties are better for one method of preparation of flour and others for the dry *farinha* or water *farinha*. The Sanama group of Yanomamo Indians I studied at Auaris, in Roraima Territory, Brazil, also have different varieties of cassava, all of which are grown on *terra firme*. When a new field is planted they have a careful plantation plan with several different cultivars: some quick-yielding varieties (six months), some that are ready for harvesting after a year, and others that take longer to mature. Instead of storing surplus prepared food they have thus planned the continuous availability of their cassava flour for an extended period rather than for one bulk harvest. Since *Manihot* is propagated vegetatively from cuttings, it is particularly easy for them to manage the plantation, and to obtain a uniform crop of the desired variety.

Many other plants used by the lowland Amazon Indians have numerous cultivars (Plate 6, after p. 132). The Yanomamo have an extraordinary number of varieties of bananas (sweet, cooking or plantain types). The peach palm (*Bactris gasipaes* HBK) is quite varied. The fruit abiu (*Pouteria caimito* (R. & S.) Radlk.) exists in a large number of forms, some of which now weigh many times more than the wild varieties from which they must have originated.

The lowland Indians have domesticated a large number of plants. They are aware that to produce large fruits, they must plant the seeds of the largest of their crop. They have selected crops to adapt to their needs for year-round food, to cope with the flood season of the rivers, and to produce various different components of their nutrient requirements. Through ethnobotanical studies of the remaining tribes it is essential to record this much neglected aspect of the Indians' adaptation to their environments. These studies can illuminate many different aspects of the ecology of the region, and provide useful information for future management plans of the region.

The Indians as ecologists

One of the most striking facts of any Amazonian ethnobotanical study is the Indians' deep sense of responsibility for the management of their environment. In addition to the general information about new useful plants and plant selection, they have much information about the way to live in the forests. The Indian sense of ecology is in marked contrast to much of the recent development schemes for Amazonia by western civilisation. Today's Amazon is marked by an alarming rate of deforestation, the breakdown of the delicate nutrient cycle, extreme soil erosion and soil compaction, greater flooding (Gentry and López-Parodi 1980), and the overhunting of many animals and fish.

It is now thought that the Amazon region sustained a surprisingly large Indian population of five million around 1500 at the beginning of the exploration of the Americas. Large tribes such as the Tapajós and the Omagua Indians lived beside the rivers (Meggers 1971). They had a subsistence system so well adapted to the *várzea* region that they could sustain large towns, yet these cultures were completely destroyed within 150 years of the arrival of the Europeans. The riverside was the basis of the existence of the large populations of Indians. They were able to sustain themselves through a careful management of their environment, perfectly adapted to the annual cycle of the rise and fall of the river level. The main features of this adaptation are the cultivation of fast-growing varieties of plants on the fertile floodplain, and good storage techniques for their meat, fish and agricultural products.

In contrast, modern people have gone to the *terra firme* and organised colonisation schemes along the Transamazon Highway based on upland rice culture which failed, or they have felled vast tracts of forest for cattle ranches. All the energy tied up in the trees is usually burned rather than used, yielding pollution rather than profit, and a species-rich forest containing 450 large trees per hectare with over 150 different species represented is replaced by one cow per hectare! Meat still remains a major import for Brazil in spite of the amount of Amazonian forest that has been sacrificed for pasture. The failure of many of these development projects points out the need for alternatives based on sound ecological principles. An obvious source of new information is the Indian population. Much information especially about the management of the *várzea* has already been lost, and there is an urgent need for ecological studies of the Indian remnant. This is a part of ethnobotany that has been scarcely developed. Ecological information is often apparent in the Indians' taxonomy of vegetation types, in their agricultural methods, their use of different cultivars, and in their tribal ceremonies. The various taboos that exist in each tribe need to be studied, not only from an anthropological viewpoint, but also from the aspect of what they teach us about the environment. There are even Indians aware of the dangers of overpopulation. Both the Deni and Karitiana Indians use the contraceptive plant *Curarea tecunarum* (see Prance 1972) and are aware of the need to limit the population of each village. (Plates 7 and 8, after p. 132).

Posey (1982h) outlined the importance of secondary forests to the Indians. The 'abandoned fields' are in fact yielding many useful products for the Indians as well as acting as game preserves.

The changing of the Amazon today is unfortunately based largely on unsound ecological principles. Its development has followed the thrust of western culture to mine the resources as if they have no limit, to destroy the soils mercilessly because there is more towards the frontier, to cut down the forests because they are perceived as a threat and an impediment, and to increase the population without any thoughts of the consequences. In marked contrast the Indians have adapted to the environment and thrive in the surrounds of the forest. They do not overhunt, do not overextend the soil or cause species to become extinct.

Ethnobotanical studies can gather the information as to how to manage the environment. They have therefore become much more important, and they must be accelerated. The future of the Amazon region, if it is to have one, must be based on the development of sustainable systems and not on destruction of all the natural resources of the region. The ethnobotany of the future will have a strong ecological slant. It should study such things as the use of the floodplain, the use of secondary forest resources, the abundance of different cultivars in each tribe and the various customs and legends attached to plants. Some of the results of such studies will be integrated into the sustained-yield systems of the future.

Conclusion

This appeal for accelerated ethnobotanical work should not conclude without a word of caution about the potential impact of ethnobotanists themselves on intact indigenous populations. It is extremely difficult to carry out effective research in this field without influencing the Indians in some way. It is important to remember that the Indians actually have little to gain from this type of study, but a lot to lose through acculturation. Therefore ethnobotanical studies must be carefully screened and mounted with great care and sensitivity for the Indians' welfare.

Acknowledgments

Fieldwork in Amazonian Brazil was carried out with the support of the National Science Foundation which is gratefully acknowledged. I am grateful to the Instituto Nacional de Pesquisas da Amazônia in Manaus and the Museu Paraense Emílio Goeldi for continuous support of my field projects, and to Michael Balick and Douglas Daly for reading an earlier draft of this manuscript.

10 Indigenous agroforestry in the Peruvian Amazon: Bora Indian management of swidden fallows

WILLIAM M. DENEVAN, JOHN M. TREACY,
JANIS B. ALCORN, CHRISTINE PADOCH,
JULIE DENSLOW, SALVADOR FLORES PAITAN

Introduction

In recent years students of Amazonia have emphasised that some of the most successful food-producing adaptations to the rainforest habitat have been those of the indigenous tribes, and that consequently we have much to learn from these 'ecosystem' people. 'Refined over millennia, Amazon Indian agriculture preserves the soils and the ecosystem ... If the knowledge of indigenous peoples can be integrated with modern technological know-how, then a new path for ecologically sound development of the Amazon will have been found' (Posey, 1982 p. 18, 1983 p. 225). For similar statements for other tropical regions see, for example, Nigh and Nations 1980; Clarke 1977; Eckholm 1982 pp. 34–35; and Klee 1980. In particular, Indian cultivation is characterised by multiple cropping (intraspecific and interspecific) and interaction with natural vegetation.

Attention has been directed to several forms of traditional management of tropical forest resources: (1) the diverse, multistoreyed swidden (shifting cultivation field) which protects the soil and allows for habitat recovery under long fallow (e.g. Conklin, 1957; Harris 1971); (2) the house garden, or dooryard garden, also diverse and multistoreyed, but with a large complement of tree crops and with soil additives from household garbage, ash, and manure (e.g. Covich and Nickerson 1966); and (3) the planting, protection, and harvesting of trailside and compsite vegetation ('nomadic agriculture' or 'forest fields'), involving wild, semi-domesticated, and domesticated plants (e.g. Posey 1982, 1983 pp. 241–3). A related type of plant management is the manipulation and utilisation of swidden fallows, a form of agroforestry, involving a combination of annual crops, perennial tree crops, and natural forest regrowth.

Swidden-fallow management is apparently widespread among Amazon tribes, and some *caboclo* (local mestizo) farmers and rarely among *colono* (colonist) farmers. However, it has received little attention; brief mentions include Denevan (1971 pp. 508–9) for the Campa in eastern Peru; Posey (1982, 1983 pp. 244–5) for the Kayapó in central Brazil; Basso (1973 pp. 34–5) for the Kalapalo in central Brazil; Eden (1980) for the Andoke and Witoto in the Colombian Amazon; Smole (1976 pp. 152–6) for the Yanoama (Yanomamo) of southern Venezuela; Harris (1971 pp. 487, 489) for the Waika in southern Venezuela and Torres Espinoza (1980) for the Shuar in eastern Ecuador. Some observers have assumed that all that is involved is a return to abandoned swiddens to search for residual crops left from the former cultivation, but indications are that actual management is involved, including planting and protection as well as utilisation of certain useful wild plants that appear at various stages of fallow succession.

The purpose of this paper is to examine the swidden fallows of an Amazon native group, the Bora of eastern Peru, with the objective of demonstrating how fields are gradually abandoned. This contrasts with most studies of shifting cultivation which focus on why fields are abandoned, and which present a sharp distinction between the field (swidden) and the abandoned field (fallow). For the Bora there is no clear transition between swidden and fallow, but rather a continuum from a swidden dominated by cultivated plants to an old fallow composed entirely of natural vegetation. Thirty-five years or more may be required before the latter condition prevails. Abandonment is not a moment in time but rather a process over time.

Agroforestry is currently receiving considerable attention as a potentially stable and ecologically viable form of tropical forest land use (King and Chandler 1978; Hecht 1982a; Budowski 1981; Salas 1979; Hart 1980; Spurgeon 1980). One of the major recommendations of the recent U.S. National Research Council (1982 pp. 4, 5, 146) report on tropical development is that the agroforestry systems of indigenous people should be studied and recorded before such knowledge is lost. We believe that certain features of Bora swidden-fallow management can be incorporated into systematic models of tropical agroforestry systems. Indeed, an examination of Bora land use indicates that 'agroforestry' is new in name only to native groups in the Amazon. Under denser populations in the past (Denevan 1976), large areas of Amazon forest may actually have been stages of productive swidden fallows. Whole biotic components were largely selected and managed, a condition Nigh and Nations (1980) call 'intermediate disturbance', and which Gordon (1969) calls an 'orchard–garden–thicket' or 'tree garden'.

The research area

Field work was undertaken from July to December 1981 in the Bora settlement of Brillo Nuevo on the Yaguasyacu river, an affluent of the Ampiyacu river (between the Napo and Putumayo) which joins the Amazon at Pebas 120 km northeast of Iquitos. The climax vegetation of the area is humid tropical forest. The closest meteorological station to Pebas is Francisco de Orellana, 75 km distant, where an annual average of 2757 mm of precipitation was recorded (1964–72). There is a distinct seasonal distribution, with rains peaking from December to May and abating from June through November, but with the driest month (August) still having 133 mm. Temperatures average around 26 °C throughout the year

(ONERN, 1976 p. 37). Brillo Nuevo is situated beside an oxbow lake formed by the Yaguasyacu. The area is a hilly, dissected fluvial terrace interlaced with numerous seasonal streams. The soils are primarily deep Ultisols (paleudults). They include red and yellow clay soils, red and brown sandy soils, and a grey soil in depressions. The Bora prefer to farm the clay soils and red sandy soils (Gasché 1979).

There are 43 families living in the settlement. All are descendants of tribal groups brought to the Ampiyacu from the Igaraparaná–Caquetá region of Colombia following Peru's loss of a border war with that country in 1934. They were resettled on land eventually granted to them by the Peruvian government and to which they retain community title. (The study was undertaken at Brillo Nuevo, rather than with a community long established in its habitat, because of previous unpublished agroforestry research there by project member Salvador Flores.) The Bora are gradually being assimilated into Peruvian society through missionaries, commerce, and access to Pebas, Iquitos, and Pucallpa. Bora villagers speak Spanish, wear manufactured clothing, and market handicraft items and lumber. Bora subsistence, however, retains many of its traditional elements, with a reliance on swidden agriculture, house gardens, fallow management, high forest collecting, hunting, and fishing. Previous accounts of the Peruvian and Colombian Bora include Whiffen (1915), Jiménez (1933), Forde (1934), Girard (1958), Gasché (1980), and Guyot (1971, 1974, 1975a, b).

Background: Bora shifting cultivation

A brief survey of Bora agriculture was conducted to grasp the fundamental dynamics of the system, and to understand how cultivation techniques might influence fallow-field character and management. Various aspects of cropping – spacing, zonation within fields (*chacras* in Peru), and the schedules of planting, harvesting, and weeding – are examined below. Together, these affect the eventual structure and composition of the fallows (*purmas* in Peru). Almost the entire area of village land is in some stage of secondary forest due to shifting cultivation since the Bora arrived here 50 years ago. However, stands of old, mature forest are within 20 minutes walking distance.

Family fields are dispersed throughout the forest surrounding the communal *maloca* (residence of the village ceremonial head). Fields are often closely clustered because farmers find it convenient to visit several on one trip. Most plots are accessible within 15 minutes on foot from the *maloca*; others are across the Yaguasyacu and are reached by dugout canoe. Both primary and secondary forest are cleared for gardens. Primary forest sites are recognised as more fertile, while secondary forest (fallow) is closer at hand and more easily felled. The oldest clearly identified fallow is about 35 years of age. There is botanical evidence, however, of secondary forest over 40 years of age. (Presence of buried and surface potshards indicates previous occupation of the area at unknown times, by unknown Indian farmers.)

The Bora say that a minimum of ten years of fallowing is needed before a plot can be cut and planted anew. Most swiddens, however, appear to be prepared from fallows 20 years of age or older. For the Bora, one indicator of a fallow ready to be felled and cropped is a lack of shrubby growth near ground level.

Most fields are cut and burned during the months of least rain; however a field can be prepared any time the weather permits. Field sizes range from a fourth of a hectare to one hectare. Axes and machetes are the only tools used for felling the forest. Cutting is often accomplished within hours by community work teams, but individual families can cut a field over a period of several days. Often small hills are chosen as field sites, the highest part of the hill becoming the centre of the field. Fallen vegetation is allowed to dry for two or three weeks before burning. Selective cutting, a common management technique of swidden farmers, is practised by the Bora. Valuable timber species, such as tropical cedar, are routinely spared during clearing, and various palms and other useful trees are commonly left in or on the edges of newly cleared fields.

The Bora plant a wide variety of crops (see Table 1); however the main staple is manioc. Some 22 varieties of sweet and bitter manioc are known by the Bora, and a newly planted field bristles with manioc cuttings spaced 50 to 80 centimetres apart. The Bora intersperse pineapples, fruit trees, and minor annual crops amongst the manioc. Both seeds and seedlings of trees are planted. Minimum spacing for fruit trees is said to be between 1 and 2 metres. However, as the planting period may extend over several weeks, farmers forget from day to day where tree seeds are already planted and often place seeds closer together inadvertently. Consequently, a few planted trees end up growing virtually side by side.

Some crops are aggregated within the field. Fruit trees are commonly clustered on high land, topography permitting. Areas away from field boundaries, or near trails, also appear to be preferred sites for these trees. Patches from 1 to 2 metres square are made into planting beds for tubers on sites selected according to ash distribution or local soil variations. The Bora recognise various soil types, based upon texture and colour. Coca is almost always planted in well tended rows near trails and field entryways.

Peanuts, grown in second or third-year fields, are planted using a special management technique. In a small area from which manioc has recently been harvested, soil (previously loosened by manioc growth and root decay) is gathered and packed into several dozen mounds measuring from about 0.5 to 1 metre square. Ashes brought to the fields from home cooking fires are mixed in with the soil as fertiliser. Between six and a dozen shelled peanuts, previously soaked overnight in a solution of basil to prevent ant predation, are planted in the mounds. From two to four cuttings of sweet manioc are placed laterally into the sides of the mounds.

Bora names for swidden stages are based upon a field's capacity to produce manioc. A field containing the first, most productive planting of manioc is called an *úmihe*. As an *úmihe* is gradually harvested and replanted, it becomes a *kapúuwa*,

Table 1   Common Bora cultivated and protected economic plants
(Names tentatively matched with scientific names from Soukup 1970 pending final plant identifications.)

Common name (English; Peruvian)	Bora name	Scientific name	Use (see code)	
*Annatto; Achiote	–	*Bixa orellana*	H, U	
*Annona; Anona	Tacááhe	*Annona* sp.	F	
*Assai; Huasaí	Tóólliujɨ	*Euterpe* sp.		F, C
*Avocado; Palta	–	*Persea americana*	F	
*Balsa; Topa	Hiíñujuícyo	*Ochroma lagopus*	U	
*Banana; Manzana, Guineo	Ujúoh	*Musa* sp.	F, U	
*Barbasco	Mujcúrriwa	*Lonchocarpus* sp.		U
Basil; Albahaca	–	*Ocimum* sp.		F, U
*Breadfruit; Pandilla, Arbol de Pan	Nájhe	*Artocarpus incisa*	F	
*Cashapona	Iíwajyu	*Iriartea* sp.		C
*Cashew; Cashu, Marañón	Anáájɨhe	*Anacardium occidentale*	F	
*Cedar (tropical); Cedro	–	*Cedrela odorata*	C	
*Chambira	Nɨɨjɨhe	*Astrocaryum chambira*	C, H	
Chili pepper; Ají	–	*Capsicum* sp.		F
Citron; Citrón	–	*Citrus medica*	F	
*Coca	Iípi	*Erythroxylon coca*	M	
*Cocona	Roolahé	*Solanum* sp.		F
Cocoyam; Huitina	Hóónawa	*Xanthosoma* sp.		F
*Copal; Copalhuallo	Míijillehe	*Hymenaea courbaril*	F, C	
Cotton; Algodón	–	*Gossypium barbadense*	M	
Cowpea; Chiclayo	–	*Vigna unguiculata*	F	
*Cumala	Allíunéhe, Cúúruco	*Iriartea* sp. or *Virola* sp.	C	
Dale-dale	Cúúnijcye	*Calathea allouia*	F	
*Genipa, Huito	–	*Genipa americana*	H	
*Guava; Pacay	Tútsehe, Ajɨvahe	*Ingha* sp.	F	
*Guayaba	–	*Psidium* sp.		F
Huaca	Hawuámihe	*Clibadium* sp.		U
*Huacra pona	–	*Iriartea* sp.		C
*Huamansamana	Méneko	*Jacaranda* sp.		C
*Huicungo	Tsitsábah	*Astrocaryum huicungo*	C	
Lemon; Limón	–	*Citrus limon*	F	
*Llanchama	Páácámɨco	?	H	
*Macambo	Aáhe	*Theobroma bicolor*	F, U	
Maize; Maíz	–	*Zea mays*	F	
Mamey	–	*Mammea* sp.		F
Manioc; Yuca	Aániwa	*Manihot esculenta*	F	
*Mauritia, Moriche; Aguaje	Iñéjhe	*Mauritia flexuosa*	F, U	
Orange; Naranja	–	*Citrus sinensis*	F	
*Papaya	–	*Carica papaya*	F	
*Peach palm, Pejibaye; Pifuayo	Méme	*Guilielma gasipaes*	F, U	
Peanut; Maní	Mátsájcahe	*Arachis hypogaea*	F	
Pineapple; Piña	Kutsya	*Ananas comosus*	F	
*Plantain; Platano	–	*Musa* sp.		F
Rice; Arroz	–	*Oryza sativa*	F	
Shapaja	–	*Scheelea* sp.		C
*Shimbillo	–	*Inga* sp.		F
Soursop; Guanábana	–	*Annona muricata*	F	
*Star Apple; Caimito	Mutsɨtsehe	*Chrysophyllum cainito*	F	
Sugar Cane; Caña	–	*Saccharum officinarum*	F	
Sweet Potato: Camote	Cáátuu	*Ipomoea batatas*	F	
Tangarine; Tangerina	–	*Citrus reticulata*	F	
Tobacco; Tabaco	–	*Nicotinana tabacum*	M	
Tree Gourd; Pati	–	*Crescentia cujete*	U	
*Umari	Nímuhe	*Poraqueiba sericea*	F	
Ungurabe	–	*Jessenia batana*	F	

Table 1 Continued

Common name (English; Peruvian)	Bora name	Scientific name	Use (see code)	
*Uvilla	Báácohe	*Pourouma cecropiaefolia*	F	
Yam; Sacha-papa	–	*Dioscorea* sp.		F
*Yarina	Tokeíipah	*Phytelephas macrocarpa*	C	

* Appears in fallows

Use code
F: Food
C: Construction or thatching
A: Handicrafts and dyes
U: Utilitarian
M: Medicinal and drugs

the term for a field yielding less productive secondary replantings of manioc. The Bora consider two replantings of manioc the maximum possible. When manioc is no longer replanted the field is termed a *jƗa*, which is roughly equivalent to fallow field or *purma*.

Initial crop zonation influences subsequent management options and the pattern of forest regeneration. First, clustering fruit trees in the field centre or in areas of access allows them to be easily harvested and weeded as the field matures. Second, heavily distrubed or weeded areas, particularly the coca and peanut zones, will frequently only support sparse, grassy secondary growth. This may be due to local soil exhaustion or compaction, plant allelopathic effects, removal of seedlings of secondary species during intense cultivation, or some combination of these. (See Uhl *et al.* 1981 for a discussion of microhabitat preferences of secondary seedlings in the Amazon.)

The crop composition of Bora fields can vary widely. Some fields have an apparent low diversity index, planted only with manioc, pineapple, and corn (mainly for poultry), and perhaps a few scattered bananas. Others are rich in species and numbers and feature complex zonation. While a range of options is to be expected in any swidden system (Denevan 1971), the two extremes seem to be common in Bora swiddens. A similar duality is noted by Harris (1971) for tribes in the Orinoco region of Venezuela, where fields seem to be either primarily monocropped with staples or polycropped with abundant subsidiary plants. In many of these cases the crop composition in any one field may in part be determined by what a farmer has available from other fields in various stages of development. Since a Bora family may have six or more fields of different ages and crop mixtures, diversity between fields fulfils the same function of assuring a supply of varied crops as does diversity within a single field. Another significant point regarding crops is that simplified fields receive few visits after two or three years of harvests, while diversified fields have longer-lasting utility in the fallow stage.

Bora swidden fallows

A series of fields was selected to examine vegetation structures and the process of abandonment. This paper examines plots of 3, 5, 6, 9 and 19 years of age from date of cutting. Each field was measured to determine its approximate size, and the owners were interviewed to record cropping histories and to help inventory plants found within the fields. The vegetation was sampled using the line-intercept method. In each field, zones of vegetation were identified. These included plant communities in areas occasionally weeded and areas of unweeded secondary vegetation. Each zone was sampled by extending two 10 m long intercepts into the zone from randomly determined points. Plants along the lines were collected and identified by their Bora names. In addition, Bora informants identified useful plants.

The plots are not strictly comparable in terms of relief or soil type, or planting histories. However, finding a series of fields with identical histories and characteristics is impossible in practice. None the less, a dynamic model of abandonment is revealed by comparing vegetation patterns in the different aged plots.

The swidden fallows described below reflect a strategy of managed succession designed to solve a shifting cultivator's dilemma of how to maintain field production in the twilight of the cropping cycle, while at the same time permitting forest regeneration. Abandonment is similar to Manners's (1981 p. 360) evaluation of the swidden cropping cycle, which he describes as a 'successional series partly regulated by human populations on the one hand, and ecological processes on the other'. A *kapúuwa* is chosen to head the sequence here because it represents a stage when human management is still relatively intense and forest regeneration is only just beginning.

Transitional field: 3 years old (*Kapúuwa*)

Figure 1 is a representation of an enriched Bora swidden, cut from 30-year-old *purma*, located not far from the settlement centre. The field has developed multiple canopies, features complex zonation, and contains at least 20 cultigens. Guava, uvilla, macambo, and peach palm are the dominant tree species, all measuring between 3 and 4 metres in height. The trees provide a 30 per cent field cover, but have not reached their peak yielding periods. Fruit-tree density in general is greatest near the southern end along the trail. The understorey of manioc is sparse because tree roots and shade prevent replanted manioc from fully developing, as illustrated in Plate 9 (after p. 132) for a 4-year-old field. A small peanut patch, also containing chili pepper and other minor crop plants, is located near the northwest corner. Bananas are more or less clustered on the southwest downslope corner. The field is surrounded on three sides by 3-year-old forest and on the south by newer fields less than one year old.

The *kapúuwa* is a changing mosaic of vegetation reflecting Bora management techniques. Weeding, harvesting, and replanting manioc are performed in one small area at a time, producing a pattern of different aged stands of both manioc and associated secondary growth within the field. Weeds are often pulled out by the roots. In Figure 1 the pineapple zone on the left is weeded and the one in the centre is

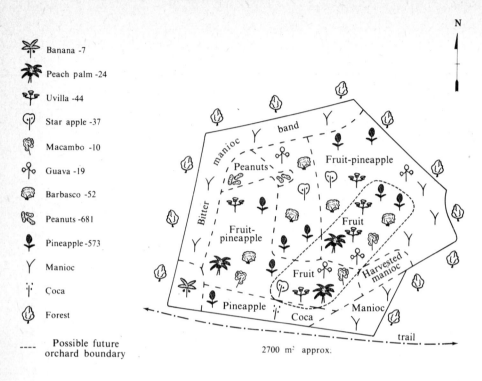

Banana -7
Peach palm -24
Uvilla -44
Star apple -37
Macambo -10
Guava -19
Barbasco -52
Peanuts -681
Pineapple -573
Manioc
Coca
Forest
---- Possible future orchard boundary

2700 m² approx.

N

Fig. 1 Map of 3-year-old transitional field (*kapúuwa*)

unweeded. Selective weeding, another widespread swidden technique, is practised by the Bora. Seedlings of useful tree species are often spared; however it is not axiomatic that all are left untouched.

In fields at this stage, tree coppicing is readily observed (Plate 10, after p. 132). Some of the fruit trees in the field may be coppicing trunks of trees planted in the field when it was a *chacra* 30 years before. *Inga* species, useful as soil nitrogen fixers, are persistent coppicers, so abundant that they are nevertheless dispatched with machetes as annoyances. Others, such as copal, resprout and are protected. This tree grows slowly, reaching harvestable age (for edible fruits) within some 20 years. A bonus of useful coppicers appears to be one advantage in clearing *purma* for new fields.

Because the field is periodically weeded, secondary growth makes little headway except for invasion at the edges where fallen trees were not burned during field preparation. Some two or three metres of unweeded field perimeter have been ceded

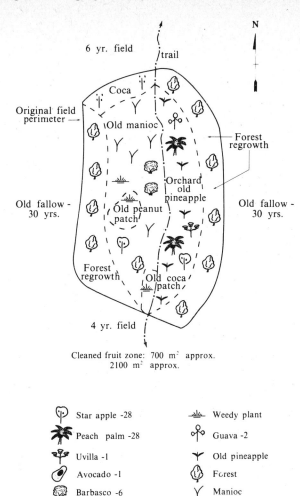

Fig. 2 Map of 5-year-old transitional fruit orchard (*kapúuwa*)

to the encroaching forest. The growth primarily consists of fast-spreading vines and thin saplings.

Transitional fruit field: 5 years old (*kapúuwa*)

Some of the processes outlined above were noted in this field, also cut from a 30-year-old *purma* (Figure 2), but at a later stage of development. The field contains a manioc *kapúuwa* zone; however the unharvested manioc plants were small. As cuttings are routinely thrust into the earth after harvesting the roots, manioc can continue to grow without forming much below-ground material. Manioc is also a persistent plant; cuttings merely thrown aside will occasionally take root. Twelve other cultigens were originally planted, of which six were still clearly harvestable: coca, star apple, peach palm, uvilla, avocado, and barbasco.

Zonation resulting from management is evident. The large coca patch is well weeded and maintained. A small coca patch is abandoned and empty, as is a peanut patch. Secondary growth in both these abandoned areas is limited to short grasses, low herbs, and occasional seedlings of pioneer forest trees. A fruit zone extends the length of the field along the trail. The understorey consists of a viney thicket mixed with low herbs growing amongst old pineapples and stray spindly manioc stems. This thicket forms an intermittent subcanopy 1.5 m in height. The overstorey is primarily comprised of equal numbers of well spaced, productive star apples (3 to 5 m in height) and peach palm (8 to 10 m in height).

Secondary vegetation has swallowed about a third of the original plot. The regrowth zone contains trees 10 to 15 m in height and measuring from 8 to 15 cm in diameter. *Cecropia*, *Jacaranda* and *Inga* are common. The trees and abundant upper-storey vines form a 100 per cent canopy. The forest floor is a dense tangle of herbs, including abundant *Melastomataceae*, *Piperceae*, and *Araceae*; palms are few.

In this *kapúuwa*, pineapples, fruit trees, and other minor plants deemed useful are maintained. The pineapples may be harvested for up to five years; thereafter the fruits produced are small and bitter tasting. Visits to the field follow the ripening schedules of the fruits, although visits for hunting also occur periodically. The main activity besides harvesting fruit is weeding. Coca is weeded every three months; the fruit trees and pineapples receive a slash weeding by machete every three to four months.

The field's owner identified many useful plants, both in the weedy orchard and *kapúuwa* zones and in the reforested perimeter. Most immediately harvestable species are vines and low herbs. These include utilitarian vines and ceremonial plants not now used by the Bora, including reeds, once used to make decorative noseplugs and flutes, and plants yielding body paints. Other useful, but not yet harvestable species were construction and other woods in the seedling stage.

The reforested zone contained a great number of species. Thirty-four plants appeared on two 10 m transects, 13 of which were considered useful. Six were construction woods; four provided materials for weaving and dyeing baskets; and three were firewoods.

Most of the useful forest species in this fallow will not be harvestable for 10 to 30 years. Rapidly growing construction woods are harvestable, but they are so plentiful around Brillo Nuevo they receive no special care. The Bora casually harvest useful herbaceous plants as needed.

Orchard fallow: 6 years old (jía)

This orchard fallow is mapped in Figure 3 and illustrated in Plate 11 (after p. 132). Cut from primary forest, it is astride a sloping hill surrounded by newer fields on three sides.

The field consists of two general vegetation communities: a residual fruit orchard occupying about one sixth of the original cleared area, and abundant secondary growth surrounding the orchard. The original field was planted with over 26 crops, some of which are tree species now surviving within the orchard. Star apple is the most numerous planted species, and these trees measure 3 to 5 m in height. A

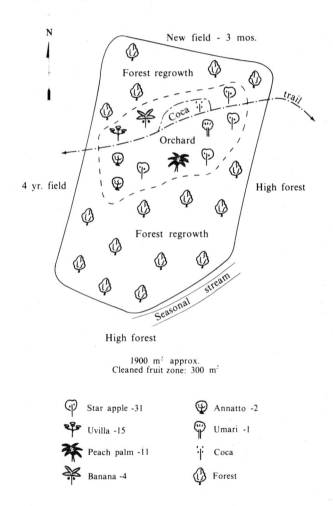

Fig. 3 Map of 6-year-old orchard fallow

canopy is formed by uvilla (5 to 8 m in height) and peach palm (10 to 13 m in height). Several 18 m tall *Cecropia* trees dominate the orchard area. The orchard has a 70 per cent canopy and is well lit by sun splash. Regular weeding has resulted in an open floor of grassy vegetation covered with slashed mulch. Harvesting fruit in such *purma* orchards is a casual pastime. The Bora use poles equipped with vine loops on the ends to ensnare and pluck fruit-laden racemes from high branches. Coca, however, has suffered from shading and harvesting is reduced. Cuttings are removed for replanting in nearby new fields. There is little evidence of manioc besides occasional stubble debris.

Growth surrounding the orchard is topped by 25 m tall *Cecropia* trees towering over dense stands of 10 to 15 m high trees and saplings. A thick, shrub understorey mixed with abundant short saplings and palm sprouts occupies the entire subcanopy regrowth zone. The forest floor has accumulated a thin layer of leaf litter, and no grasses are present. An array of useful spontaneously appearing species similar to those in the 5-year-old field were present in this field.

Orchard fallow: 9 years old (*Jÿa*)
This *purma* (Figure 4), cut from high forest, demonstrates how long a managed orchard-fallow succession can be maintained. The orchard zone is small and

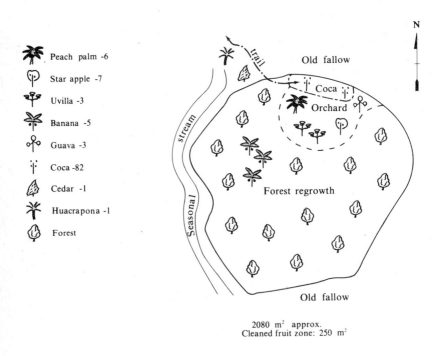

Peach palm -6
Star apple -7
Uvilla -3
Banana -5
Guava -3
Coca -82
Cedar -1
Huacrapona -1
Forest

N

Old fallow
Coca
Orchard
Forest regrowth
Old fallow

trail
stream
Seasonal

2080 m² approx.
Cleaned fruit zone: 250 m²

Fig. 4 Map of 9-year-old orchard fallow

cultivated trees are few; however, a vigorously growing unshaded coca patch remains. The patch contains 82 evenly spaced, well tended bushes. Coca is clearly the most valuable crop available here. The owner visits the field on a regular basis to harvest the leaves, and on those occasions may refresh himself with uvilla, guava, and star apple foraged from the residual orchard.

The secondary regrowth is a woody thicket, 10 to 15 m in height, with many vines and substorey shrubs. Several useful trees including cedar were on the field's perimeter. Because this field is a downriver site, soils and topography differ from the upland sites nearer the settlement zone. The downriver sites are less well drained, and thus the secondary communities differ from the other fallows studied.

Forest fallow: 19 years old (*Jía*)

This older forest fallow (Figure 5) was surveyed for useful tree species. The original *chacra* was cut from mature forest and, according to the owner, planted with at least 11 species, including several varieties of fruit trees.

The forest displayed clear stratification. Low vegetation consisted of herbaceous plants, including ferns, measuring 30 cm to 1 m in height. Above is a second stratum of thin, straight saplings, 5 to 6 m high, including many palms. Seventy-five per cent of the canopy was provided by trees 15 to 18 m in height, while emergent *Cecropia* and huamansamana, both 25 m tall, filled out the canopy. The forest floor was 40 per cent covered in leaf litter and walking was unhindered, except in small thicket-filled gaps caused by falling trees.

All individual trees measuring 15 cm in circumference within a transect 10 m wide and 102 m long (length of the field) were tallied. Some 233 trees belonging to 82 species were counted. Over half the trees were single occurrences.

Our informants identified 22 useful trees in the transect, fitting into the following categories:

  (a)   Construction materials: 11 species, 25 individuals, including 2 varieties (3 individuals) of highly valued cumala; 13 huicungo palms, used for general thatching, were also present.
  (b)   Medicinals: 4 species, 4 individuals (not yet identified).
  (c)   Food: 2 species, 11 individuals, consisting of 8 macambos and 3 assai palms bearing edible fruits.
  (d)   Artisan material: 1 individual, a dye-bearing tree (not yet identified).
  (e)   Utilitarian: 4 individuals, 4 species. These included 3 palms from which salt is distilled, and 1 tree from which pitch is extracted and used to seal canoe hulls (all not yet identified).

In addition there were at least two other species of trees from which edible grubs are harvested. The only apparent survivors of the prior swidden were the macambos, which were clustered within the transect 60 metres downslope. These are harvested sporadically.

None of the above trees, all of which are common, appeared to receive individual attention. The cumalas are not yet harvestable, nor will they be for about a decade.

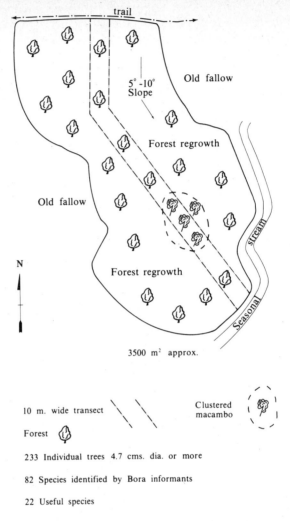

Fig. 5 Map of 19-year-old forest fallow

This old fallow apparently receives few visits for collection purposes, but hunting trips and grub foraging are frequent.

The process of abandonment: analysis

The Bora recognise that two ecological processes, soil depletion and secondary succession, must be confronted. The Bora acknowledge that manioc is not sufficiently productive to merit harvest after three or four years, mainly because of soil depletion, but also because of weed invasion. Abandonment of fields planted almost entirely in manioc occurs within the space of a year. However, if fields are polycropped with trees, weeds may be the major obstacle to extended field use. Management shifts from replanting manioc to dealing with encroaching secondary vegetation threatening tree crops. With periodic weeding, trees can remain productive for several years before disappearing into the secondary forest, often succumbing to the effects of shading and competition for nutrients.

A number of tree species planted in Bora fields are, however, adapted to growing in dense secondary forests. Umarí and macambo are common cultivated trees found in old *purmas*, either growing alone or in groups. These survivors of swidden orchards are valued components of Bora fallows. At 20 or 30 years of age most fruit trees cannot be easily harvested; however the Bora occasionally gather the fallen fruits. A valuable function of fallen fruit is that they attract game animals. It is rare to find an umari fruit on the forest floor without tooth marks of a majás (*Cuniculus paca*) or other browser. For this reason older *purmas* are good hunting grounds.

The process of abandonment and forest regeneration clearly has a spatial aspect. While successionary processes are complex (Uhl *et al.* 1981), there is a tendency towards a pattern of centripetal forest regrowth which might be explained largely as a result of the history of weeding. Harvesting and weeding of manioc holds regrowth at bay. Once a manioc zone is abandoned, terrain is surrendered to the forest and the field shrinks in size.

Abandonment is also related to how harvesting proceeds sequentially from grain-producing annuals (rice and maize) to root crops and pineapples to fruit trees and spontaneously appearing utilitarian trees and vines.

Table 2 shows the succession of harvestable plants in Bora fields and fallows. While the Bora recognise many useful fallow plants, many go unharvested and are essentially neglected. The main reason for this is that high forest, from where sturdy construction woods and vines are harvested, is still a short walk away. At present most plants used for handicrafts, for example, are taken from high forest. Nevertheless, as the high forest frontier becomes more depleted and distant, secondary growth species become more important. There is evidence that this is occurring. The Bora have recently become interested in planting hardwoods and useful palms in swiddens and in fallowed fields.

Phased abandonment: implications for agroforestry

There are similarities between complex swidden systems and agroforestry systems (Hecht 1982a). Agroforestry combines the production of trees and other crops on the same unit of land (King and Chandler 1978), a strategy essentially identical to swidden-fallow management. Both systems rely on the succession of tree crops following the harvests of short-term cultigens.

Viewed in this fashion, Bora agriculture converts to an agroforestry system during the early stages of forest fallow. The enriched swidden to fallow sequence

Table 2 *Succession of harvestable plants in Bora fields and fallows*

Stage	Planted harvestable	Spontaneous harvestable
High forest	None	Numerous high-forest construction, medicinal, utilitarian, handicraft, and food plants available.
Newly planted field (*úmihe*); 0–3 months	All species developing	Dry firewood from unburnt trees for hot fires.
New field (*úmihe*); 3–9 months	Corn, rice, cowpeas	Various useful early successional species.
Mature field (*úmihe*); 9 months to 2 years	Manioc, some tubers, bananas, cocona, and other quick maturing crops	Abandoned edge zone has some useful vines, herbs.
Transitional field (*kapúuwa*); 1 to 4 or 5 years	Replanted manioc, pineapples, peanuts, coca, *Inga*, star apple, uvilla, avocado, cashew, barbasco, peppers, tubers. Trapped game.	Useful medicinals, utilitarian plants within field and on edges. Seedlings of useful trees appear. Abandoned edges yield straight, tall softwoods. *Ochroma lagopus* common.
Transitional fruit field (*kapúuwa*); 4–6 years	Peach palm, banana, uvilla, star apple, *Inga*, annatto, coca, some tubers. Propagules of pineapple and other crops. Hunted and trapped game.	Abundant regrowth in field. Many useful soft construction woods and firewoods. Palms appear, including *Astrocaryum*. Many vines, useful understorey aroids.
Orchard fallow (*Jía*); 6–12 years	Peach palm, some uvilla, macambo. Propagules; hunted game.	Useful plants as above, self-seeding *Inga*.
Forest fallow (*Jía*); 12–30 years	Macambo, umarí, pandilla, copalhuallo	Self-seeding macambo, umarí. High forest successional species appearing. Early successional species in gaps. Some useful hardwoods becoming harvestable, e.g. cumala. Many large palms: huicungo, chambira, assaí, ungurabe.
Old fallow; high forest	Umarí, macambo	Same as high forest above. Full maturity not reached until 50 years or more.

closely resembles the natural succession analogue approach to tropical agroforestry outlined by Hart (1980; also Uhl 1983 pp. 78–9). Hart suggests that select cultigens be placed in the niches normally occupied by common early successional species. The analogue plants would have growth structures and resource requirements similar to those of their weedy counterparts. Thus, rice or maize replaces early annual species, bananas replace wide-leafed *Heliconia*, and late-appearing tree crops mimic early successional tree species. Whether by accident or design, the Bora seem to follow this approach. Bananas do well in low shady areas, where *Heliconia* plants are also common. The most obvious example is uvilla which matches its ubiquitous cousin, the *Cecropia*. Guava is also in the same genus as its semi-domesticated analogue, the shimbillo (*Inga* sp.). Further research may reveal other similarities between naturally appearing species and cultigens which could be incorporated into swidden agroforestry-type models.

Another feature of Bora swiddens that could be useful in agroforestry design is the use of space. Bora tree clustering according to local topographical conditions suggests that slope and terrain should be considered when planning agroforestry plots. More important, slowly abandoning ground to secondary forest may be sound strategy for tropical farming. There is no reason to think that agroforestry plots should have 100 per cent planted standing biomass. Managed forest regrowth could provide useful products, as well as canopy cover for the soil and a source of stored nutrients for when the forest is cleared to begin the swidden and agroforestry cycle anew.

Swidden-fallow agroforestry, enriched with tree crops planted in areas of forest regrowth, could approximate the 'tree-garden' model of silviculture which may have been a pre-Columbian agricultural adaptation in the Caribbean lowlands of Colombia, Central America, and the Maya region (Gordon 1969). This thicket model involves a combination of overstorey fruit trees and subcanopy woody shrubs, interspersed with open areas of swiddens of maize, bananas, manioc, and other crops. Systematic swidden-fallow agroforestry would have a fruit orchard core, or series of cores, but these would be embraced by areas of regenerated forest. The forest, in turn, could be enriched by a variety of useful analogue species able to compete in the viny subcanopy, or later on as canopy species (fruit, timber) in high-forest fallow. Timber species would be appropriate late-fallow enrichment trees. Over a large area, swidden-fallow agroforestry would resemble Gordon's image. It would be more a thicket and less a plantation. Furthermore, the growth rate of managed successions may be as fast or faster than natural successions (Uhl 1983 p. 79).

Swidden-fallow products

The cumulative dietary contribution of fruits and nuts, even when harvested casually, may be significant. Certainly they provide a continuing (seasonal) variety of minerals, fats, and vitamins to tropical diets dominated by roots and tubers rich in carbohydrates. Some trees, moreover, can provide major staples. The peach palm, very important to the Bora for its fruit and heart, can compete with maize as a nutritious food (Hunter 1969; Johannessen 1966). In addition, plant products useful for beverages, condiments, construction, tools, drugs, and medicines are of more than minor importance to village societies and economies.

As with major and minor natural forest products, those in swidden fallows frequently reach markets beyond the village, at regional, national and international levels. Even remote traditional cultivators are willing and able to respond to market opportunities for forest products and manage those products accordingly. Pelzer (1978 p. 286) argues that a large percentage of the rubber, black pepper, copra, coffee, and benzoin harvested for cash in southeast Asia comes from smallholder swiddens through intercropping 'in what is ordinarily thought of as the "fallow" period of the swiddens'. The ultimate success of agroforestry systems will depend on such cash cropping.

For isolated communities such as Brillo Nuevo, cash cropping of forest products is problematic. Tropical cedar and other timber trees can be floated downriver to market. One can only be impressed by Boras planting or protecting tropical cedar seedlings in their swiddens and fallows, anticipating a substantial cash return for their children 30 years later. The use of swidden-fallow products, such as palm and liana fibres, tree bark, and dyes, for the manufacture of handicraft items can bring an income to Bora households. The considerable tourist and export trade in the Iquitos area provides an outlet for traditional items such as hammocks, bags, baskets, bowls, or ornaments. On the other hand, the marketing of perishable food items does constitute a difficult problem for remote villages such as Brillo Nuevo, especially in view of the poorly developed processing and marketing facilities in the region. Toasted macambo nuts, a Bora delicacy, could have market potential. Palms such as *Jessenia* and *Mauritia*, potential sources of edible oils (Balick 1982), are common in Amazon forests and could be integrated into agroforestry models.

The history of the Amazon has been one of commercial harvesting of forest products (quinine, copal, sarsaparilla, barbasco, palm heart, Brazil nuts, rubber, timber). Much of that history involved the destruction of important resources by unwise harvesting practices and the economic and social exploitation of indigenous peoples. Sustainable and equitable procedures are possible, and trade in forest products can be enhanced by incorporating forest species of commercial value into agroforestry systems. Such commercial orientation would, of course, necessitate not only the development of specific agroforestry designs and techniques, but also appropriate processing, transportation, credit, and marketing facilities. The economic possibilities for Amazonian plants are vast (Myers 1983). An argument might well be made that the potential value of marketable production from sustained-yield agroforestry plots, including swidden fallows, can be significantly greater per year per hectare than that from cattle ranching or shifting cultivation.

Conclusions

The Bora process of swidden abandonment is in reality a conversion of a short-term cropping system into a longer-term agroforestry system. The main conclusion regarding abandonment and fallow management are summarised as follows:

(a) Fallowing is multipurpose. The secondary forest is not only nutrient storage for future cropping, but an important niche for secondary crops and useful spontaneously appearing plants. We identified 131 different useful species in Bora fallows. We propose that an appropriate designation be established to account for enriched fallows, a characteristic which may be common in tropical swidden systems. The term 'orchard fallow' could be used to describe the structural and functional aspects of traditional agroforestry. In a subsequent 'forest-fallow' stage, economic plants are still present but are more dispersed, fewer in number, and less managed.

(b) Viewed properly, a swidden site is never completely abandoned as a resource zone. Secondary harvests of fruits, spontaneously appearing species, and even animals continue until the forest is removed for further cropping.

(c) There exists an identifiable sequence from original forest with some economic plants present, to a swidden with numerous individual economic plants present, to an orchard fallow or agroforestry phase combining managed economic plants and natural vegetation, to a forest fallow in which economic plants are fewer but still present in greater numbers than in the original forest. Likewise, there is a corresponding sequence in the proportions of biomass which are cultivated or managed, spontaneous economic, and spontaneous non-economic.

(d) Research is needed on analogue species with growth architectures and nutrient requirements adapted to secondary forest environments.

(e) Swidden-fallow management is not unique to Amazonia. It appears to be widespread in Africa (De Schlippe 1956 pp. 215–16; Dubois 1979) and in the Pacific, including the Philippines (Conklin 1957 pp. 125–6; Oración 1963), New Guinea (Clarke 1971 pp. 82–4; Hyndman 1982), and Micronesia (Yen 1974). It may once have been common in Middle America (Gordon 1969). These systems need to be studied.

(f) Agroforestry drawing on traditional management methods and combining planted species and natural secondary vegetation could be an ecologically appropriate and economically viable alternative to destructive short-fallow shifting cultivation in tropical areas. Such a model would help fulfil the need for sustained production of food and other needed products and simultaneously do minimal damage to a fragile environment.

Acknowledgements

The Bora agroforestry project was funded by the UNESCO Man and the Biosphere Program (MAB), 1981–3, under an agreement with the University of Wisconsin, Madison and the Universidad Nacional de la Amazonía Peruana in Iquitos. We are grateful to Manuel Mibeco, the Bora village leader in Brillo Nuevo, for his cooperation and considerable assistance to our fieldwork. Plant collections, facilitated by the Iquitos herbarium supervised by Franklin Ayala, are still in the process of identification in Madison. Ing. Salvador Flores and his assistants are continuing the project, concentrating on older swidden fallows, as well as managing experimental agroforestry plots at Iquitos.

11 Native and indigenous guidelines for new Amazonian development strategies: understanding biological diversity through ethnoecology

DARRELL A. POSEY

The Amazon Basin of South America has suffered considerable social and ecological damage in recent decades under the guise of development (Moran 1981; Barbira-Schazzocchio 1980 p. iii). The vastness of Amazonia, combined with the erroneous view that it is basically homogeneous in its composition, has resulted in unsuccessful attempts to design development policies for the Basin as a whole (Moran 1980 pp. 6–7). As a result, widespread deforestation has had disastrous effects on soil erosion and nutrient loss (Denevan 1973, 1982; Sioli 1973; UNESCO 1978) with subsequent problems in flooding and water pollution (Schubart 1977; Lovejoy and Schubart 1980 p. 21). Extinction of plant and animal species is occurring at an astonishing rate (Gottleib 1981 p. 23), and general environmental stability, regional rainfall patterns and even the global oxygen–carbon dioxide balance may be jeopardised by the devastation of Amazonian tropical rainforest (Pimentel 1979; Sioli 1980 pp. 233–62).

Destruction of indigenous populations (Ribeiro 1977 p. 238; Ramos 1980 p. 222), unsuccessful colonisation plans (Moran 1981; Smith 1982), and unfavourable land tenure patterns due to the proliferation of large *fazendas* and *agropecuárias* (Hecht 1982a, b) have made the human costs high indeed for Indians and *caboclos* (peasants) of Amazonia.

Limited economic success of projects likewise points to the necessity of radically different strategies of development. If ecologically sound development policies are ever to emerge for the benefit of all segments of Amazonian society, then the biological heterogeneity of the vast region must be understood.

Indigenous and folk societies of the Amazon offer new strategies and solutions to the dilemma of Amazonian development (Posey 1982d; Posey *et al*, in press a, b, c; Francelino de Silva *et al*, in press). Indigenous ecological knowledge has evolved over millennia of adaptation to Amazonian environments. Aboriginal populations were much more dense than generally assumed (cf. Denevan 1976; Smith 1980). Thus indigenous subsistence strategies are more relevant to modern population needs than realised (Posey 1982d, in press). *Caboclo* societies have likewise incorporated Indian knowledge into their own resource models and are valuable living sources for ethnoecologists.

Indigenous and traditional *caboclo* societies are rapidly disappearing. Consequently there is urgency in collecting ethnoecological data from as many Amazonian societies as possible to increase the understanding of tropical ecological diversity. This understanding should then form the guidelines for new Amazonian development strategies. The following avenues of investigation built upon indigenous folk examples are suggested.

Ecological zones and resource units

A great obstacle to the Western understanding of Amazonia has been the tendency to generalise about its ecology and ignore its highly variable 'ecological zones' (Moran 1981). The Kayapó Indians of Brazil see their environment in an expanded series of 'ecological zones'. Kayapó village sites are purposefully selected to be near a variety of these eco-zones. The distinct advantage is that Kayapó villages are in the midst of maximum species diversity because each zone provides natural products and attracts different game species during different seasons (Bamberger 1967; Posey 1979a). Location of the Kayapó village of Gorotire and the surrounding diversity of ecological zones is represented in Figure 1.

Each ecological zone has associated with it specific plants and animals. The Kayapó have a well-developed knowledge of animal behaviour and know which plants are associated with particular animals. In turn, plant types are associated with soil types. Each ecological zone, therefore, is an integrated system of interactions between plants, animals, the earth – and, of course, the Kayapó. Table 1 summarises selected systemic relationships in the ecological zone called *bà-ràràrà* (forest with intermittent openings and penetration of sunlight).

Concentrations of specific resources characterise certain ecological zones for the Kayapó. These concentrations perceptually reduce the heterogeneity of the forest to known 'resource islands' that can be periodically exploited for specific products and purposes. Figure 2 is modified from a map drawn by a Kayapó informant and indicates 'resource islands' along a trail connecting the village of Kubẽnkrãkêin and the abandoned site of Pykatôti.

Caboclos in the Lake Coari region along the Rio Solimões (Amazonas) have also been shown to have extensive knowledge of ecological zonation in the region. Figure 3 represents the Coari region with folk biogeographical knowledge encoded in 40 named 'resource units'. Specific ecological zones are recognised by a characteristic resource unit or combination of units. Ecological zones, therefore, show an overall ecological uniformity and predictability of natural resource locations. Table 2 is a glossary of these 40 units, each of which is numbered and can be located by corresponding number on Figure 3.

Coari *caboclos* also classify their ecological world by vertical levels. Figure 4

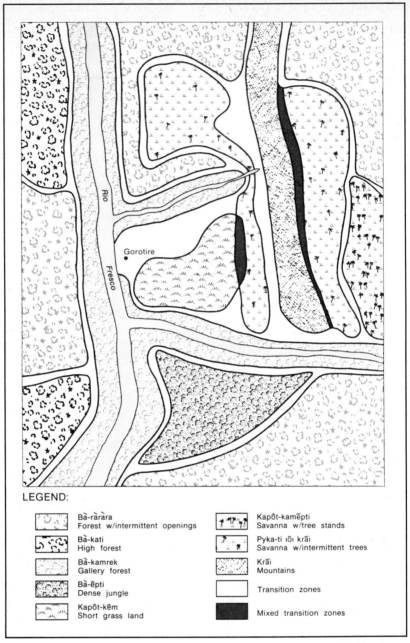

LEGEND:

	Bà-ràràra Forest w/intermittent openings		Kapôt-kamēpti Savanna w/tree stands
	Bà-kati High forest		Pyka-ti ιôι krãi Savanna w/intermittent trees
	Bà-kamrek Gallery forest		Krãi Mountains
	Bà-êpti Dense jungle		Transition zones
	Kapôt-kêm Short grass land		Mixed transition zones

Fig. 1 Ecological zones surrounding the village of Gorotire as perceived by the Kayapó

Table 1 Selected soil–plant–animal relationships in the selected ecozone (Bà-raràrà)[a]

Preferred soil[b]	Particular animal association[c]	Plants associated with zone	Use of plant — Man	Use of plant — Animal	Kayapó name
1, 2	A, B, C, D, E	Humeria balsamifera (Aubl.) St. Hil.	eat fruit	eat fruit	bà-rerek
1, 2	F	Psidium guyanese Pers.	eat fruit	eat fruit & leaves	kamokàtytx
3	F	Zingiberaceae	use root for tea; smoke leaves	eat leaves	madn-tu
3		Paschieria sp.	use for paint		pita-teka
2, 3		Catasetum sp.	medicinal		pitu
2, 3	C, F	Bignoniaceae	medicinal	eat leaves	ngra-kanê
1, 2, 3	C, D	Cissampelos sp.	fish bait	eat fruit	tep-kanê
1	A, B, C, D	Piperaceae	fish bait	eat fruit	màkrê-kanê
3		Amasonia sp.	prophylaxis		pidjô-rà
1	A, B, C, D	Oenocarpus distichus Mart.	eat fruit	eat fruit	kamêrê (baca-ba)
1, 2, 3	H	Macrostaychia sp.		?	kukrymyka
1, 3	F	Myrcia sp.	use wood	eat leaves; eat roots	kàryre
1, 2	A, C, D, F	Monotagma sp.	grind leaves; eat oots	eat fruit & leaves	kônôkô
1, 3	H, F	Cecropia leucocoma Miq.	eat fruit	eat fruit	atwyra 'ô'
2		Polypodiaceae	medicinal		tôn-kanê
2	F	Clarisia ilicifolia (Spreng.) Lang. & Rossb.	medicinal	eat leaves	pidgô-niré
2, 3		Centrosema carajasense Cavalc.	fish poison		akrô
2,,3	C, D, F	Cassia hoffmanseggii ex. Benth.	Mart.medicinal	eat fruit & leaves	pidjô-kakrit

[a]Identifications of plants made by Dr Susanna Hecht, Department of Geography, UCLA.

[b]Soil types: 1 = black (pyka-tyk), 2 = red (pyka-kamrek), 3 = yellow (pyka-tî).

[c]Animals: A = white-lipped peccary (porção), B = white paca (paca branch), C = agouti (cutia branca), D = tortise (jaboti), E = red paca (paca vermelha), F = red agouti (cutia vermelha), G = deer (veado), H = tapir (anta).

Animals:
white-lipped peccary (porção)
2 red (pyka-kamrek)
3 yellow (pyka-tî)
tortoise (jaboti)
red paca (paca vermelha)
red agouti (cutia vermelha)
deer (veado)
tapir (anta)

Soil types:
1 black (pyka-tyk)
white paca (paca branca)
agouti (cutia branca)

Source: Identifications made by Dr Susan Hecht, Department of Geography, UCLA

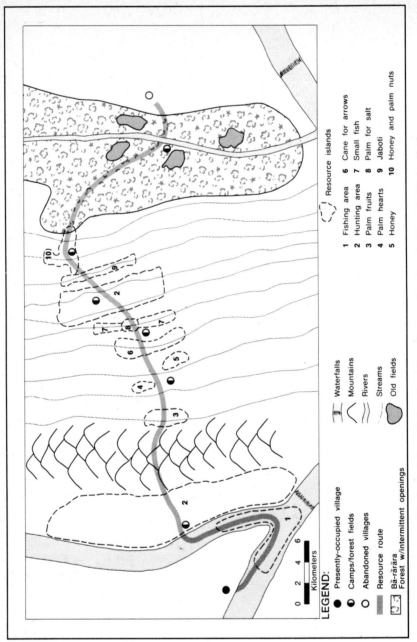

LEGEND:

● Presently-occupied village
◑ Camps/forest fields
○ Abandoned villages
▬ Resource route
▨ Bá-rárára
Forest w/intermittent openings

〰 Waterfalls
Λ Mountains
)) Rivers
))) Streams
▨ Old fields

⬭ Resource islands

1 Fishing area   6 Cane for arrows
2 Hunting area   7 Small fish
3 Palm fruits   8 Palm for salt
4 Palm hearts   9 Jaboti
5 Honey   10 Honey and palm nuts

Kilometers
0 2 4 6

Fig. 2 Trek from Kuben-kra-kéin village to abandoned village site (Pyka-tô-ti) showing resource islands and campsites associated with forest fields

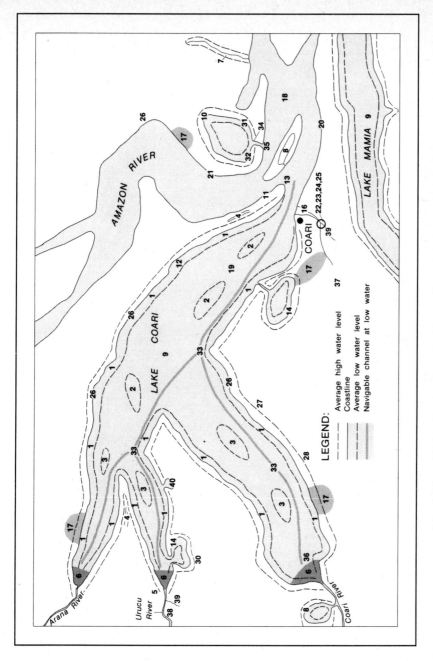

Fig. 3 Map of Lake Coari region showing resource unit locations (see Table 2 for a glossary of these units), and high (dashes) and low (dots) water levels, as perceived by a *caboclo* of the area

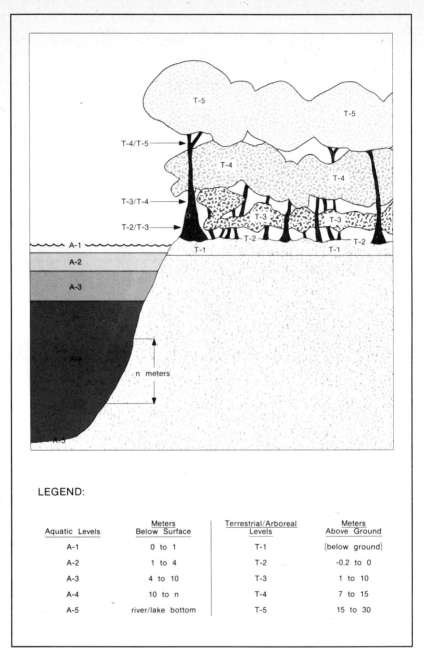

LEGEND:

Aquatic Levels	Meters Below Surface		Terrestrial/Arboreal Levels	Meters Above Ground
A-1	0 to 1		T-1	(below ground)
A-2	1 to 4		T-2	-0.2 to 0
A-3	4 to 10		T-3	1 to 10
A-4	10 to n		T-4	7 to 15
A-5	river/lake bottom		T-5	15 to 30

Fig. 4 An example of aquatic and terrestrial/arboreal vertical levels from an Amazon river *várzea* ecological zone near Coari

Table 2   *Glossary of resource units appearing on map; as defined by a* caboclo *of the Lake Coari region*

1 *praia branca* – dry season, white sandy beaches of Lake Coari where birds and turtles lay their eggs
2 *praia suja* – dry season, wet or muddy beaches where a great number of birds feed
3 *praia verde* – dry season beaches, covered in short vegetation, where birds feed on weeds and insects
4 *restinga* – natural river levees, usually covered in forest, and not inundated during the dry season
5 *charco* – swamp area found within the *várzea* ecological zone
6 *chavascal* – transition area between rivers draining into Lake Coari and the lake itself, characterised by low vegetation which is mostly inundated during the rainy season and which during the dry season forms a labyrinth of dead-end river-like branches, *ressacas*, *poços*, and *pocinhos* surrounded by large areas of muddy land
7 *igapó* – forest area which is flooded during the height of the rainy season
8 *laguinho* – small lake connected to the river by a narrow stream during the rainy season, and only accessible by land during the dry season
9 *lago grande* – large lake, such as Lake Coari or Lake Mamiá
10 *lago* – lake connected to the river by a passage navigable by canoe or small boat
11 *costa* – margin (bank) of the Amazon river
12 *enseada* – gulf-like section of a large lake, usually characterised by calm waters
13 *encontro das águas* – point where the Lake Coari water system flows into the Amazon river
14 *poço grande* – deep section in a sharp turn of a smaller river, characteristic of the sinuosity of these rivers
15 *ressaca* – lake-like formation connected to a small river
16 *igarapé* – a blackwater stream flowing from deep in the forest to a river
17 *castanhal* – the *terra firme* forest where the castanheiras (*bertholletia excelsa*) are located
18 *águas fundas brancas* – deep whitewaters of the Amazon, where the piraibas (*Brachyplatystoma* spp) are caught
19 *águas fundas pretas* – deepwater areas of Lake Coari, associated with scarcity of resource except when in close proximity to the banks of the lake
20 *barreiras* – high vertical banks of the Amazon river, characterised by swift currents and an abundance of clay varieties
21 *embaubal* – section of the *várzea* where embaúba trees (*Cecropia* spp) are predominant
22 *buritizal* – a concentration of buriti palms (*Mauritia flexuosa*)
23 *jauarizal* – a concentration of jauari trees (*Astrocaryum jauari*) usually at critical zones during periods of medium water level
24 *açaizal* – a concentration of açai trees (*Euterpe edulis*) in the *terra firme*
25 *bacabal* – a concentration of bacaba trees (*Oenocarpus distichus*) along *igarapés*
26 *aratizal* – a concentration of arati (?) bushes at the critical zone during periods of medium water level
27 *capoeira alta* – an abandoned garden site more than ten years old
28 *capoeira baixa* – an abandoned garden site approximately five years old
29 *baixio* – shallow section of the Amazon river opposite the channel side, characterised by the predominance of oeirana trees (*Salix martiana*)
30 *tabocal* – a concentration of green-and-yellow bamboo (*Guadua* spp) in the high *várzea*
31 *canaranal* – a floating meadow dominated by canarana (*Panicum spectabile*), commonly used as cattle fodder
32 *muriruzal* – a floating meadow dominated by muriru (numerous species, see Smith 1981 p. 14), providing food for both fish and turtles
33 *canal seco* – navigable channel in the lake during low water
34 *boca de cima* (*lago*) – point where a lake narrows into a stream before entering a river
35 *boca de baixo* (*rio*) – point where the water from a lake flows into a river
36 *matupazal* – a floating meadow dominated by matupá (?)
37 *roçado novo* – a recently planted slash-and-burn garden site
38 *roçado velho* – a slash-and-burn garden site which is still being systematically utilised
39 *igarapezinho* – a clearwater rivulet which provides drinking water, also called a *fonte*
40 *pocinho* – a small lake which does not dry up during periods of low water, usually located near *ressacas* and *chavascals*, and where fish are easy to catch by hand

shows the ten vertical levels recognised by the *caboclos*. These are divided into terrestial/arboreal levels (T 1–5) and aquatic levels (A 1–5):

Terrestial/arboreal levels:

T–1: area below ground level, where most burrowing animals and large roots/tubers are found.

T–2: ground level to approximately 20 cm below, where organic matter is concentrated and the plant/animal communities associated with the superficial root zone are located.

T–3: understorey (1–10 m above ground), which predominates in *capoeira* or 'open forest'. This is the area of smaller trees and shrubs and is attractive to many birds and mammals; when this zone exists, hunting is good.

T–4: middle canopy (7–15 m above ground), which occurs in most mature forests and is the principal zone for arboreal mammals and large birds (such as parrots.)

T–5: high canopy (more than 15 m above ground), which characterises the *terra firme* high forest. This is known to have arboreal mammals and birds, but hunting them is difficult because of the height. Forests with T–5 zones are more useful for their forest products, including *castanha* (nuts) and honey.

Aquatic levels:

A–1: surface level (0–1 m below surface), where water-surface insects and top-feeding fish, as well as water snakes, are found.

A–2: upper level (1–4 m below surface), where the greatest number of fish and eels can be caught.

A–3: middle level (4–10 m) is less productive, but hosts some fish species.

A–4: lower level (various depths from A–3 to bottom) is the least productive zone.

A–5: river (lake) bottom, which is rich in bottom-feeding fish and sting-ray species.

Classification of vertical micro-environmental levels by *cabclos* has as its basis a functional component: where to find certain natural resources. Each aquatic level, for example, is noted for certain species of fish, turtles, snakes or aquatic plants. Likewise each terrestrial/arboreal level has varying concentrations of mammal, bird, and insect resources. There are also 'transitional corridors' which are relatively open spaces between terrestrial/arboreal levels and are the spaces most observed by *caboclos* searching for animal movement. These are perhaps best thought of as vertical hunting zones. (For a discussion of these zones and related natural resources, see Posey *et al.* in press c.)

Indian and *caboclo* knowledge of ecological relationships within and between natural categories extends far beyond those summarised herein. This evidence, however, is sufficient to substantiate the intricacy of information available from folk and indigenous sources about ecological zones and natural resource distribution.

The forest/field continuum

One of the most important forest ecological zones for the Kayapó Indians is a type of forest opening called *bà-ràràrà* that is produced by large trees that fall in the tropical forest due to storms or antiquity. Light is thereby permitted to penetrate through the opening to the forest floor and allows the proliferation of small plants in the natural reforestation sequence. These plants provide the Kayapó with a variety of fruits, nuts, and medicinal plants. Furthermore, the low, bushy vegetation attracts and provides food for a myriad of birds and mammals hunted by the Indians. Thus *bà-ràràrà* is a type of naturally produced 'resource island' in a relatively sparse forest.

The Indians replicate this process by felling large trees in the forest to raid *Meliponid* nests. This provides a double bonus for the Kayapó: bees' honey and wax for food and artifacts, and the legacy of an area that will not only provide a variety of useful plants, but will also stimulate game populations.

Agricultural fields are likewise seen as larger man-made versions of *bà-ràràrà*. Fields are carved out of the forest and planted with a variety of crops. The crops bear produce for several years,[1] but even after principal plantation production ceases, old fields remain rich resource areas. The Kayapó are known to periodically visit sites up to 40 years after initial clearing to harvest a large inventory of wild plants (Posey 1982a, d). A representative list of major plants collected from old fields and their uses appears in Table 3(a). Table 3(b) is a list of fruit trees planted by the Kayapó in old fields for food and to attract game.

Because of the attractiveness of old field sites to wildlife populations, the Kayapó purposefully disperse their fields great distances from their villages. Kayapó men hunt in old field areas while the women tend adjacent new field sites. Improved hunting yields make longer hunting treks less necessary and thin wildlife populations sufficiently to reduce damage to crops under cultivation.

For the Kayapó, therefore, no clearcut demarcation between field and forest exists. Rather the more general reforestation process is reflected by a continuum between undisturbed and disturbed forest.

The distinction between domesticated and wild plants and animals is likewise ill-defined. It could be argued that systematic utilisation of plants and animals by intentional manipulation of old fields is a type of semi-domestication. There are more formidable examples, however, to support the utility of a folk classification system that looks at the 'transitional' qualities of natural processes rather than presumed neat categories. Consider the following:

'Nomadic agriculture'

Kayapó taxonomy shows a propensity for *not* classifying the natural world into neatly defined categories, but rather relies heavily on 'graded' categories of transition (Posey 1981b, 1982c). The distinction between domesticated and wild plants is an excellent example of how categories blend one into the other.

During hunting treks,[2] Kayapó men may be away from the village two to four weeks. They carry little food with them, relying instead on natural 'islands of resources' along the established forest trails, as previously described. The Kayapó

Table 3 Partial list of gathered food plants of the Kayapó*

Kayapó	Portuguese	Scientific	Seasonality	Part(s) eaten
pidjo-rã	açai	*Euterpe oleracea*	June–November	Fruit; heart
norã	bacaba	*Oenocarpus distichus*	September–December	Fruit; leaves[1]
kubenkrã	cacaubraba	*Theobroma speciosa*	December–January	Fruit
pidjõko	cajá	*Spondias lutea excelsa*	March–May	Drupe
pidjõ-ti	Castanha do Pará	*Bertholletia excelsa*	December–March	Nut
nejaka	cupuaçu	*Theobroma grandiflorum*	December–March	Fruit
ronkã	babaçu	*Orbygnia speciosa*	All year	Nut; leaves[1]
pidjo-bã	frutão	*Pouteria pariry*	December–March	Fruit
pidjo-tyk	genipapo	*Genipa americana*	All year	Fruit[3]; leaves[2]
rõtu	nàjá	*Maximilliana regia*	August–February	Fruit
pidjo-bãti	piqui	*Caryocar villosum*	December–February	Drupe
pidjõ-kamrek	uxi	*Endopleura uchi*	November–March	Drupe
Idjy-kryre	fruta de campo	*Psidium guianensis*	January–February	Flower
pitu	orchidia de campo	*Catasetum* sp.	January–March	False bulb
kryry-re	biro	*Monotagima* sp.	All year	Tuber
konoko	ingá	*Myrcia* sp.	August–October	Fruit
mõyt	jatoba		July	Fruit
pidjõ kakut		*Cassia hoffmanseggii*	January–April	Fruit
bàdjum		*Psidium* sp.	July–August	Fruit

*Note: Identifications based on Cavalcante (1972, 1974)
[1]Leaves used for making salt
[2]Leaves dried and smoked
[3]Fruit eaten and used as base for body paint

Table 3B   Tree species planted by the Kayapó Indians

Scientific name	Portuguese name	Kayapó name	Planted for — Food	Planted for — Other uses	Attract — Game	Attract — Fish
Alibertia eduis A. Rich.	marmelada (lisa)	motu	X		X	
Alibertia sp.	marmelada do campo	roi-krãri	X		X	
Anonna crassiflora Mart.	araticum	ongrê	X			
Artocarpus intergrifolia L.f.	jaca	jaca	X			
Astrocaryum tucuma Mart.	tucum (2 varieties)	roi-ti (mrã)	X	salt		
Astrocaryum vulgare Mart.	tucumã	woti	X	oil		
Bertholletia excelsa Humb. & Bonpl.	castana do Pará	pïyfɛ̃	X			
Bixa orellana L.	urucú (4 varieties)	pïïkumrenx / pïïpoiti / pïïkrãre / pïïjabiê		body paint		
Byrsonima crassifolia H. B. K.	muruci	kutenk	X			
Caryocar villosum (Aubl.) Pers.	piqui (3 varieties)	prïkáti / prïkrãti / prïkumrenx	X		X	
Citrus aurantifolia (Christm.) Swingle	lima	pidgõ ngrã ngrã	X			
Citrus limonia Osbeck.	limão	pidgõ poi re	X			
Coffea arabica	café	kapê	X			
Cordia sp.	cereja Kayapó	kudja redjõ	X		X	
Endopleura uchi	uxi	kremp	X			
Eugenia jambus L.	jambo	pidjõ nore	X		X	
Euterpe oleraceae Mart.	açaí (2 varieties)	kamere kàk (makere kàk ti)	X		X	
Genipa americana L.	genipapo (2 varieties)	mroti, mrotire	X	body paint		
Hancornia speciosa Gomez	mangaba	pi-ô-tire	X		X	
Hymenaea courbaril L.	jatobá	moi (moix)	X		X	
Inga sp.	inga (6 varieties)	kohnjô-kô (jaka, kryre, poire, tire, ngrãngra, tyk)	X			
Lecythis usitata Ledoux	sapucaia	kromu	X			
Lecythis usitata Miers, var. parensis (Ducke) Knuth	sapokaia	pïytêkrêti	X			
Mangifera indica L.	manga	kuben poi re	X			
Manilkara huberi (Ducke) Stand.	massaranduba	krwya no kamrek	X		X	X
Mauritia martiana Spruce	buritirana	ngrwa ràre	X			
Mauritia vinifera Mart.	buriti	ngrwa	X			
Maximiliana regia Mart.	inajá	rikre	X	salt		
Orbignia piassaba	piaçaba	ngra djàre	X			

Table 3B Continued

Scientific name	Portuguese name	Kayapó name	Planted for		Attract	
			Food	Other uses	Game	Fish
Oenocarpus bacaba Mart.	bacabá	*kamere*	X		X	
Orgygnia martiana	babassu	*rõ*	X	oil, salt		
Parinari montana Aubl.	pariri	*kamô*	X		X	
Persea americana Mill.	abacate	*kaprã*	X			
Platonia insignis Mart.	bacuri	*pĩ panhê ka tire*	X		X	
Pourouma cecropiaefolia Mart.	inbauba	*atwyrà krã krê*	X		X	
Pouteria macrophylla (Lam.) Eyma	tuturubã	*kamokô*	X		X	
Psidium guayava L.	goiaba	*pidjô kamrek*	X			
Ravenata guyanensis	banana brava	*tytyti djõ*	X			
Rollinia mucosa Baill.	biribá	*biri*	X			
Solanum paniculatum (L.)	jurubeba	*miêchet ti*	X		X	
Spondia lutea L.	cajá		X			
Spondias lutea L. (*S. mombim* L.)	taperaba	*bàrere-krã-kryre*	X			
Theobroma cacao L.	cacau	*kuben krã ti*	X		X	
Theobroma grandiflorum K. Schum.	cupuaçu	*bàri-djõ*	X			X

Identifications based upon Cavalcante (1972, 1974, 1979) from comparisons with common names of the region; systematic specimen collection is now under way.

have a vast network (thousands of kilometres) of trails interlacing villages, hunting grounds, gardens, old fields, and natural resource islands. Food supplies are hardly left to chance. To further ensure food supplies, the Kayapó create 'forest fields' of semi-domesticated plants that are collected during the day's travels along trails and hunting reconnoitres into the forest. The plants are then replanted near established forest campsites.

There are at least 54 species of plants used by the Kayapó in these forest fields.[2] All grow naturally in *bà-ràràrà* (forest with intermittent openings and penetration of sunlight), which the Kayapó see as a ntural counterpart of their human-made fields. Replanting is done (usually after defaecation) in transitional ecological zones adjacent to campsites. Figure 2 indicates the route of a trek taken in 1978 to the ancient Kayapó village of Pyka-tô-ti (cf. Posey 1979d). The map (based on a drawing by a Kayapó informant) shows natural 'resource islands' as well as 'forest fields' created by the Kayapó. Elsewhere (Posey 1982a, d) I have described this system of ecological exploitation as 'nomadic agriculture' to emphasise the special adaptation of forest fields to the semi-nomadic system of the Kayapó.

The tendency of Western science to analyse only those data that fit into neat categories tends to underestimate or miss entirely the importance of transitional categories of ecological exploitation. This transitional system is probably much more widespread in Amazonia than expected and underlines the inadequacies of existing subsistence typologies and carrying-capacity theories.

Manipulated animal species

Another area of 'transitional' knowledge for the Kayapó is that of semi-domesticated animals. These are perhaps best called 'manipulated species' to emphasise the Indians' intentional manipulation of animal behaviour.

The larvae of beetles of the families *Scarabaeidae* and *Buprestidae*, for example, are utilised by various tribes in the lowland tropics (Chagnon 1968; Posey 1978, 1980). The adult beetle lays eggs in the refuse of dead banana plants and old palm trees. The Indians intentionally stack the remains of banana and palm plants near villages, fields, and campsites to attract the adult beetles. After some months (depending on species and region, as well as season of the year), the eggs develop into large grubs that are tasty and nutritious (Chagnon 1968). Indians know the life cycle of the beetle and can predict when to collect the mature grubs.

The Kayapó recognise 54 folk species of stingless bees (*Meliponidae*) and 2 folk species of stinging bees (both subspecies of *Apis mellifera*). All these species are classified by distinctive honeys and waxes (Posey 1981a, 1982b, c). Honey is a prized food, while beeswaxes are used as treatments for burns, cures for diseases, disinfectants of wounds, and adhesives for artifacts.

Six species of stingless bees are 'kept' by the Kayapó (see Table 4). The Indians know that if a portion of the brood comb with the queen bee is returned to the tree after the honey is taken, certain species of bees will return to re-establish the colony. Thus hives of these six species can be raided seasonally (cf. Posey 1983a).

Table 4   *Semi-domesticated (manipulated) species of Apidae utilised by the Kayapó*

Kayapó name	Scientific name
[1]Ngài-pêrê-ỳ	*Apis mellifera*
[1,2]Ngài-ñy-tyk-ti	*Melipona seminigra cf. pernigra* (Moure & Kerr)
[1,2]Ngài-kumrenx (mehn-krak-krak-ti)	*Melipona rufiventris flavolineata* (Friese)
[1]Ngài-re	*Melipona compressipes cf. fasciculata* (Sm.) or *afinis* Moure Ms.
[1]mykrwàt	*Frieseomelitta* sp.
[1,2]udjỳ	*Trigona amlthea* (Olivier)
[1,2]kukraire	*Trigona dallatorreana* Friese
[3]mehnôrâ-kamrek	*Trigona cilipes pellucida* (Ckll.)
[3]mehnôrã-tyk	*Scaura longula* (Lep.)

[1]These species are systematically raided in subsequent seasons.
[2]Those species whose nests are taken to the village.
[3]Those species that are encouraged to build nests in dry posts in the houses.

Nests of two other species (again see Table 4) are gathered in the forest and brought with the complete bee swarm back to the village.[4] The nests are then mounted on a housetop and guarded until the Indians feel the time is optimal to take the honey (cf. Posey 1983b).

The Kayapó also know two species of bees (*Trigona cilipes* and *Scrura longula*) that prefer to nest in dry logs in open areas. These species often colonise the dried timbers of Kayapó houses and their nests are left undisturbed until honey production is maximal.

Two other stingless bee species are intentionally attracted to Kayapó fields. The Kayapó either dig a hole in their field clearings, or utilise a hole already dug by an armadillo. Into this hole they put rotting logs. One species (*Trigona fluviventris guinae*) prefers to nest in earthen walls; the other (*Trigona fuscipennis*) nests in rotten logs. Bees are thereby attracted to the fields and are associated with increased crop yield, although no conscious concept of pollination *per se* exists.

Agriculture

Domesticated plant inventories of indigenous populations in Amazonia are extensive, yet their potential for consumption and industrial use is poorly evaluated and largely ignored by development planners. An exemplary list of some major cultivars is provided in Table 5.

Some of the aboriginal domesticates are well-known and form an impressive list of New World inventions (Ucko and Dimbleby 1969). Many other cultivars remain unknown, or if known, are seldom utilised in Western agriculture (cf. Kerr *et al.* 1978). *Cupá* (*Cissus gongylodes*), for example, is an ancient cultigen of the Kayapó. It has only recently been shown to be nutritionally significant and offer potential for large-scale exploitation in Amazonia (Kerr *et al.* 1978).

Numerous Amazonian domesticates demonstrate economic potential for

Table 5   *Commonly cultivated food plants of Amazonia (based principally upon Lowie 1948 pp. 3–5 and Denevan 1974 p. 101)*

English common name	Scientific name	English common name	Scientific name
	Tubers	Peach palm	*Guilielma gasipaes*
Arracacha	*Arracaha xanthorrhiza*	Mangabeira	*Hancornia speciosa*
Achira	*Canna edulis*	Inga	*Inga* spp.
Dali-dali	*Calathea allouia*	Lucuma	*Lucuma obovata*
Cupá	*Cissus* sp.	Mango	*Mangifera indica*
Taro	*Colocasia antiquorum*	Plantain	*Musa paradisiaca*
Taro	*Colocasia esculenta*	Banana	*Musa sapientum*
Yam	*Dioscorea alata*	Granadilla	*Passiflora ligularus*
Yam	*Dioscorea trifida*	Avocado	*Persea americana*
Sweet potato	*Ipomoea batatas*	Guava	*Psidium guajava*
Manioc	*Manihot esculenta* Crantz	Sicana	*Sicana odorifera*
Arrowroot	*Maranta arundinacea*	Frutas de lobo	*Solanum lycocarpum*
Potato	*Solanum tuberosum*	Pepino	*Solanum muricatum*
Tani	*Xanthosoma sagittifolium*	Cocona	*Solanum guitoense*
		Topiro	*Solanum topiro*
	Fruits	Cacao	*Theobroma cacao*
Bacaiuva palm	*Acrocomia* sp.		
Cashew	*Anacardium occidentale*		Seeds
Pineapple	*Ananas comosus*	Groundnut	*Arachis hypogaea*
Pineapple	*Ananas sativus*	Pigeon pea	*Cajanus indicus*
Chili pepper	*Capsicum* spp.	Jack bean	*Canavalia ensiformis*
Papaya	*Carica papaya*	Hyacinth bean	*Dolichos lablab*
Piqui	*Cayocar brasiliensis*	?	*Lagenaria* sp.
Star apple	*Chrysophyllum caimito*	Yam bean	*pachyrhizus erosus*
Watermelon	*Citrullus vulgaris*	Lima bean	*Phaseolus lunatus*
Lemon	*Citrus limon*	Kidney bean	*Phaseolus vulgaris*
Orange	*Citrus* sp.	Castor bean	*Ricinus communis*
Coffee	*Coffea* sp.	Corn	*Zea mays*
Turmeric	*Curucuma longa*		
Squash	*Cucurbita maxima*		Others
Surinam cherry	*Eugenia unifora*	Sugar cane	*Saccharum officinarium*

large-scale exploitation (Williams 1960; NAS 1975). Indigenous uses of these plants include more than just foodstuffs; plants are frequently used as medicines, insect repellants, dyes, and raw materials for production (cf. Posey *et al.* in press a).

Indigenous varieties of cultivars attest to the great diversity of genetic stock and afford the opportunity for scientific experimentation in crop adaptations to various tropical soils and environmental factors (Kerr and Clement 1980; Posey *et al.* in press a, b).

Preservation of biological diversity is the key to tropical adaptation. Yet the Western approach has been to eliminate complexity and impose a limited and controlled range of specific monocultures. This approach has not only been ineffective, but has endangered the greatest of Amazonian riches, its genetic diversity (Gottlieb 1981).

Justification for the imposition of Western agricultural methods has traditionally been that shifting cultivation systems of the indigenous populations are primitive and inefficient. Scientists now recognise, however, that the range of indigenous agricultural systems is more complicated and, generally, better adapted to tropical conditions than was previously assumed (Lovejoy and Schubart 1980; Dickinson 1972; Geertz 1963; Frechione 1981).

Indigenous agriculture depends heavily upon native plants which demonstrate an adaptation to localised climatic conditions (Alvim 1972, 1980). They have also been found to be more efficient in their utilisation of micronutrients and less dependent upon nutrients considered essential for good soil fertility in the mid-latitudes (Hecht 1982a).

Indigenous agricultural systems generally result in positive soil-conservation effects. Aboriginal systems minimise the time that soils are exposed to the destructive impact of direct sunlight and tropical rains (Goodland and Irwin 1975; Vickers 1976, 1980). Vegetative cover is maintained at various heights to deflect the impact of tropical rainfall and provide sufficient shade, thus helping to prevent rapid erosion and leaching (Goodland and Irwin 1975; Goodland *et al.* 1978; Schubart 1977).

The Kayapó fell trees for their fields in such a way as to provide planting corridors between masses of debris. A portion of their tuberous crops is actually planted (in these corridors) before the burn. Firing is carefully controlled to provide a 'cool burn' that does not destroy the root systems of the developing cultigens (cf. Posey 1982a). When the first rains come after the burn, young root systems maximise uptake of dissolved ash nutrients. The remainder of the crop is then planted in the other areas of the field (see Figure 5).

This is simply one way in which the Kayapó fine-tune their agriculture to the environment. They also utilise various planting patterns to coincide with localised soil types. Thus specific cultigens are planted in soils in which they are known to produce best. Kayapó fields may even have sizeable monocultural zones of manioc, corn or rice between the usual interspersed species (maximum recorded size is 0.7 ha). Kayapó agriculture has been shown to be a very efficient and environmentally sound management system (Posey and Hecht in preparation).

The Yekuana of Venezuela likewise utilise a variety of planting patterns to match cultivars with soils, drainage patterns, and microclimatic features (Frechione 1981). Considerable 'microzonal' planting has been reported for the Yekuana (Frechione 1981 p. 54) and Yanomamo (Smole 1976) in which monocultures predominate (see Figures 6, 7). Thus in various indigenous agricultural systems monocropping is possible, but only when matched to micro-environmental conditions and limited to zones within fields.

Indigenous horticulturalists usually rely on small, dispersed field openings. Field dispersal contributes to the maintenance of the ecosystem and the success of native horticulture. Spatial dispersal minimises the epizootic growth of insect pests and plant diseases (Pimentel and Goodman 1979; Stocks 1980; Posey 1979a, 1982a), thus minimising the need for expensive and environmentally dangerous pesticides. As previously mentioned, field dispersal also stimulates wildlife populations (Gross 1975; Ross 1978; Linares 1976; Hames 1979).

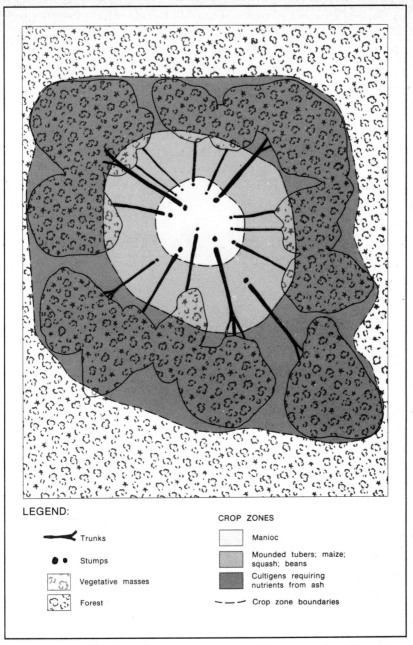

LEGEND:

——◂ Trunks

● ● Stumps

Vegetative masses

Forest

CROP ZONES

Manioc

Mounded tubers; maize;
squash; beans

Cultigens requiring
nutrients from ash

— - — Crop zone boundaries

Fig. 5 Overhead view showing ideal pattern of felling trees for a Kayapó
garden and the major crop zones within the garden

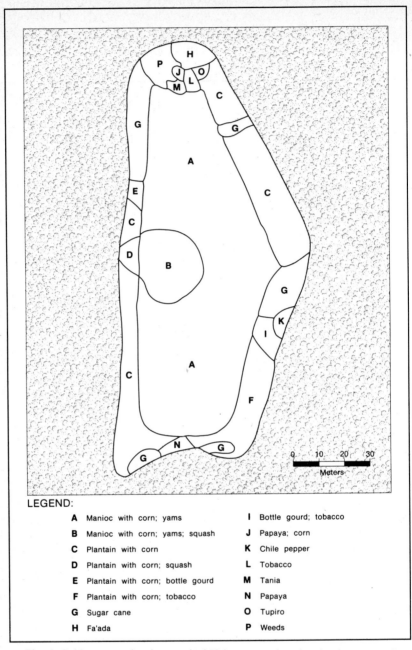

LEGEND:

A Manioc with corn; yams
B Manioc with corn; yams; squash
C Plantain with corn
D Plantain with corn; squash
E Plantain with corn; bottle gourd
F Plantain with corn; tobacco
G Sugar cane
H Fa'ada

I Bottle gourd; tobacco
J Papaya; corn
K Chile pepper
L Tobacco
M Tania
N Papaya
O Tupiro
P Weeds

Fig. 6 Cultigen zonation in a typical Yekuana garden showing interspersed monozonal planting (based on Frechione 1981, p. 70)

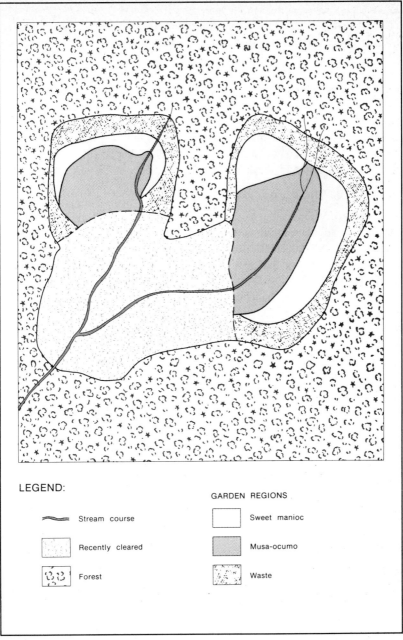

LEGEND:

GARDEN REGIONS

~~	Stream course	☐	Sweet manioc
☐	Recently cleared	▨	Musa-ocumo
☐	Forest	☐	Waste

Fig. 7 Yanomamo garden showing micro-environmental planting and monozonal cropping (based on SMole 1976, pp. 130–1)

Perhaps most important, indigenous agricultural systems always include 'natural corridors' between field sites. The natural corridors form valuable ecological refuges for plant and animal species (Gómez-Pompa *et al.* 1972; Lovejoy and Schubart 1980). Species are not only protected from extinction but are reserved close at hand for re-establishment in old fields.

Tropical forest cultivators can produce surpluses through shifting cultivation with a minimal amount of labour expended, but they generally lack the necessary economic and political stimuli to do so (Allen and Tizon 1973; Carneiro 1961 p. 54). Recent emphasis on continuous crop rotation with heavy reliance on expensive fertilisers and pesticides (e.g., Sánchez *et al.* 1982) further threatens the viability of traditional agriculture and the self-sufficient farmer.

Aquacultures and game farms

One of the most promising strategies of aboriginal resource utilisation with potential for large-scale development is aquaculture, or systems of water-resource management (Goodland 1980 p. 14). Indigenous populations in Amazonia make use of numerous species of fish, reptiles, and water mammals, as well as riverine and lacustrine vegetation.

Fish provide substantial portions of protein for most indigenous groups (Ross 1978; Sternberg 1973). Fish have high quantities of essential amino acids (Bell and Canterbury 1976) and are superior to meat animals in terms of feed/protein conversion ratios as illustrated in Table 6.

Table 6   Feed conversion ratios (from Ackefors and Rosen 1979)

	Dry weight feed: live weight	Dry weight feed: shredded weight (flesh)
Cow	7.5:1	12.6:1
Pig	3.25:1	4.2:1
Chicken	2.25:1	3.0:1
Rainbow trout	1.5:1	1.8:1

Turtles are also efficient in meat/protein production (Smith 1974 p. 85). Turtle meat is a delicacy in many parts of the world, and would be a highly exportable and valuable commodity. Since aboriginal times, Indians have corralled turtle breeding groups for year-round cropping (Sternberg 1973 p. 258; Smith 1974 p. 85).

Caimans (various species, see Smith 1981 p. 180) may prove important in large-scale aquaculture because they too can be bred in captivity (Montague 1981 pp. 21, 28). Raised in a symbiotic relationship with fish species, they increase the latter's harvestable levels under controlled situations (Fittkau 1973; Smith 1981 p. 180).

The manatee (*Trichechus inunguis*) can also be managed to produce meat while at the same time contributing to the larger aquaculture system by keeping waterways clear of vegetation and releasing large amounts of nutrients into the water to stimulate primary fish production (Spurgeon 1974 p. 239; Myers 1979 p. 178; Smith 1981 p. 185).

Lacustrine and riverine vegetation has been used in various ways by indigenous groups in the Amazon and shows great potential for inclusion in a highly productive aquaculture. Water hyacinth (*Eichhornia crassipes*) purifies water (a third of a hectare can purify one ton of sewage per day) and filters out toxic heavy metals (Myers 1979). A variety of other water plants that form familiar 'floating meadows' generate as much as seven tons of biomass per hectare per day (Myers 1979 p. 78). These are used by the indigenous and *caboclo* populations for fertiliser, feeds for domesticated animals, and fuel (Posey *et al.* in press a, b, c; Francelino de Silva *et al.* in press).

In the past two decades, growing commercial exploitation of water resources has resulted in a drastic decrease in traditional resource commodities, including common fish species. Uncontrolled commercial exploitation will only further add to local social and economic hardships while accelerating ecological destruction. Integrated management systems based on indigenous knowledge and use of water resources, however, can provide sustained productivity using local labour with minimal capital input.

The same principles of integrated management could be applied to forest resources. The Kayapó have already been shown to manage large areas of forest interspersed with old fields to harvest plant products and game. Their strategies depend upon understanding the natural reforestation sequence and the ways to replicate it, 'resource islands' in the forest, and knowledge of animal behaviour including preferences for specific plants, fruits, nuts, etc.

Game animals are efficient in use of available food, with high protein-to-fat ratios and resistance to diseases (Sternberg 1973; Surujbally 1977; de Voss 1977). Thus cropping of game animals could be combined with plantations of trees bearing fruit favoured by the animals in an integrated management system (Smith 1977). This 'game farm' strategy has been suggested as a viable system for sustained Amazonian development (Goodland 1980; Goodland and Bookman 1977; Goodland, Irwin and Tillman 1978; Vasey 1979; Smith 1977).

Belief system, myth, and tribal rituals

Each indigenous culture has a 'belief system' that functions to establish a relationship between humans and the environment. Myth has been demonstrated to encode highly symbolic information about important social and environmental relationships (Posey 1981b, 1982c, d). A Kayapó myth about ants, for example, reveals information about a biological 'coevolutionary complex' (cf. Gilbert and Raven 1975) that relates ants, manioc, beans, and maize to Kayapó gardeners.[5] Such complexes are essential to understanding ecological communities yet are generally complicated and difficult to assess scientifically. Myth has not seriously been studied as a transmitter of encoded ecological knowledge. This example, however, provides evidence to necessitate a serious approach to myth analysis for biological information and ecosystemic relationships.

Cycles of rituals and ceremonies have been shown to function as regulators of natural resources in some societies (Rappaport 1967, 1971). It is still difficult, however, to demonstrate direct relationships between social systems and ecological resource management. Attempts have been made to relate food taboos with resource protection (e.g. McDonald 1977; Ross 1978) and to correlate ritual cycles with natural seasonality (Reichel-Dolmatoff 1976) in the Amazon.

The Kayapó belief system is based upon a ubiquitous belief in energy balance (Posey 1982e) similar to that described for the Desana Indians (Reichel-Dolmatoff 1978). All living objects are endowed with this universal energy and, therefore, all life is to be revered and protected.

The Kayapó have specific rituals before and after each trek to hunt or collect plants in order to placate those spirits that will be dispossessed from their physical forms through death. The annual ecological cycles are likewise ritually punctuated to mark the maize and manioc seasons. Other festivals celebrate the hunting 'seasons' for land turtle, tapir, anteater, and other game animals.

Each Kayapó ceremony requires a specific array of natural objects for the completion of the associated ritual (a particular type of feather, plant or beeswax, for example). This requires an organised trek to procure the needed materials, which leads the Kayapó to different 'resource islands' over a vast area. Since needed materials vary with each ritual, the ritual cycle causes the Kayapó to systematically exploit different ecological zones associated with diverse 'resource islands'.

Without the natural ritual cycle, life would cease to perpetuate itself for the Kayapó. All ceremonies and rituals that are essential for the transformation of life-giving energy are controlled by tribal elders, chiefs, and shamans. Thus ecological management is given utmost priority.

The Kayapó theory of illness also operates on a concept of energy balance. Sickness results when this balance is destroyed by overkilling or overcollecting plants and animals or through eating taboo foods. Refusal to participate in necessary rituals and ceremonies can also destroy the healthy balance; thus each individual has an intimate state of maintaining 'ecological' health.

Concluding remarks

Large-scale development projects for the Amazon region have generally resulted in lack of ecological, economic, and social success. Recent emphasis on extended monocropping based upon heavy fertiliser and pesticide usage threatens to accelerate the demise of native peoples of the Amazon, who cannot afford such expenses. Development that does not provide benefits for all Amazonian peoples can no longer be tolerated, not even in the name of soil science and efficiency of production.

Systematic study of indigenous and folk systems of knowledge about Amazonian ecosystems can, however, serve as the basis for new strategies of development that are ecologically sound, yet productive and profitable for all segments of society. Integrated management systems of agriculture, aquaculture, and the cropping of wild and semi-domesticated plants, mammals, fish, reptiles, birds, and insects can be commercially productive, yet preserve the genetic diversity of Amazonia and its potential for commodities of nutritional, medicinal, and industrial value.

The international scientific community urgently needs to cooperate with governments of Amazonian countries to investigate the biological diversity of the Amazon Basin through ethnoecological research. Special emphasis should be given to the study of:

1 Folk ecological zones and their complexity – e.g. the floral, faunal, edaphic and climatic associations within zones as perceived by indigenous populations.
2 Forms of shifting, diversified field agriculture – e.g. the special adaptations of native plants, the function of vegetative cover and importance of spatial distribution of crops within fields for pest or weed control.
3 Monocropped 'microzones' in diversified fields and their potential for large-scale mechanised agriculture.
4 Manipulation of semi-domesticated plants and animals in 'old fields' and 'resource concentrations'.
5 'Natural corridors' and their role in the preservation of biological diversity and facilitation of reforestation.
6 Sustained-yield aquaculture focused upon the integrated and controlled cropping of riverine and lacustrine flora and fauna.
7 Large-scale management of animals and forests to develop 'forest-game reserves'.

Perhaps the most exciting aspects of ethnoecological research are the possibilities to test the practical application of indigenous and folk knowledge. Programmes like those we have proposed at the Laboratória de Etnobiologia, Universidade Federal do Maranhão (São Luís, Maranhão) would bring together folk and Indian 'experts' on agriculture, water resources, and local environments to devise their own experimental crop/water/forest-management systems.

Similar research programmes are needed where native plants can be tested scientifically as to their suitability for large-scale production; 'game farm' and aquaculture strategies can be evaluated; effects of field distribution and crop dispersal can be measured. An opportunity to test the role of 'natural corridors' in the preservation of ecological diversity and pest control is needed, as well as experimentation with microzonal monocropping combined with dispersed fields, natural corridors and crop rotation.

There are many new approaches to the dilemma of Amazonian development that can be based on folk knowledge. This knowledge is readily available, but only to those scientists who are willing to accept that there are other experts on the Amazon and learn from them. Any truly successful development in the Amazon must not only provide for the needs of the local people, but also incorporate the fundamental requirements for self-sufficiency and independence that characterise indigenous and folk societies.

Acknowledgments

Research for the Kayapó study was funded by the Wenner-Gren Foundation for Anthropological Research and the American Philosophical Society. I would like to thank the following people for their helpful comments on previous drafts of this paper: Brent Berlin, William Denevan, Robert Goodland, Daniel Gross, John Frechione, Susan Hecht, Warwick Kerr, Emilio Moran, John Peterson, Nigel Smith, Sandy Parker, and Ghillean Prance. Many thanks to Carol Jones for her assistance in typing and proofreading.

This paper was written while I was Visiting Professor, Center for Latin American Studies, University of Pittsburgh, Pittsburgh, Pennsylvania, USA. I would like to thank the CLAS staff for their assistance and encouragement. The quiet inspiration provided by the Carnegie Museum's Powder Mill Nature Reserve while actually writing is also greatly appreciated.

For production of the drawings I would like to thank the Cartographic Production Laboratory, University of Maryland Baltimore County.

Notes

1 Years 1 to 3 are the most productive, although many fields continue to bear for 12 to 15 years. (See Hames 1980 p. 9; Posey 1982a; Smole 1976 pp. 152–6; Basso 1973 pp. 34–5; Bergmann 1974 pp. 147–8; Harris 1972).

2 The Kayapó have relatively stationary villages, but are none the less semi-nomadic, spending four to five months per year away from the main village. Kayapó families often spend weeks at a time in their gardens; women go on frequent gathering trips that may last several days; lineage groups spend one to two months in river camps where the primary activity is gathering Brazil nuts (*Bertholletia excelsa*). Men are the most fond of trekking, spending two to four weeks hunting prior to the major festivals in the ecological cycle (Posey 1979d, 1982 a, d).

3 Identification of plants is currently under way with plans to carry out further research and collection in the Kayapó area. Most are tuberous plants similar to those described by Maybury-Lewis (1974 p. 334) for the Shavante.

4 When the nests are found in the forest or savanna, the Kayapó climb up to the nest and close the opening of the nest with leaves to prevent the bees from escaping.

5 The text of the myth is as follows:
   Why women Paint their Faces with Ant Parts
   The trails of the fire ant (*mrum-kamrek-ti*) are long. They are ferocious (*akrê*) like men. But the little red ant of our fields (*mrumre*) is gentle like women; they are not aggressive (*wajobõre*). Their trails meander like the bean vines on the maize. The little red ant is the relative/friend of the manioc. This is why women use the little red ant to mix with urucu to paint their faces in the maize festival. The little red ant is the

guardian of our fields and is our relative/friend.

The principal theme of this myth is that a certain ant (*mrumre*) is the friend of the fields and the women, who are the cultivators in Kayapó culture. The myth begins to make sense when we understand the coevolutionary comples of maize, beans, manioc and the (*Pogomyrmex*) ant.

Manioc produces an extra-floral nectar that attracts the ants to the young manioc plant. The ants use their mandibles to trim their way to the nectar, cutting away any bean vines that would prevent the new, fragile manioc stems from growing. The twining bean vines are, thus, kept from climbing on the manioc and are left with the maize plants as their natural trellis.

The maize can shoot up undamaged by the bean vines, while the bean plant itself furnishes valuable nitrogen needed by the maize. The ants are, thus, the natural manipulators of nature and facilitate the horticultural activities of the women.

The *mrum-kamrek-ti* has a vicious sting and is used for the men's hunting magic to make man and dogs strong and aggressive in the chase. The *mrumre* does not sting and is, therefore, considered weak (*wajobõre*), but is admired by the women for its industrious and organised activity. It is common for the Kayapó to mix bits of insects into their body paint (mainly with urucu, *Bixa orellana*) in order to acquire the perceived qualities of the insect utilised in the mixture. Thus Kayapó women paint themselves with *mrumre* to be industrious in the fields like the little ant.

SUMMARIES

12 Omagua culture change before 1700

THOMAS P. MYERS

The standard ethnographic accounts of the Omagua are based upon observations made in the middle and late seventeenth century. However, statistics presented by the earliest observer suggest that the Omagua were already in decline before 1639. This paper draws upon data from the Orellana and Orsúa expeditions to build an ethnography of the Omagua in the sixteenth century. It concludes that aboriginal Omagua communities were larger and more complex than the seventeenth century evidence would lead us to believe. It also concludes that the Omagua occupied the area about the mouth of the Napo river from earliest historical times rather than having migrated upstream during the first century of European contact.

13 Obstacles to change in the Amazon during the rubber boom

BARBARA WEINSTEIN

For all the turmoil and activity generated by the upsurge in Amazonian rubber production (1850–1920), the impact of the boom on relations of production and exchange in the region was limited. I will argue that the rubber boom merely intensified existing modes of production and marketing that had dominated economic life in the Amazon since the colonial period. Although the export boom did lead to rapid population growth, settlement of previously remote districts, and the emergence of new local elites in the interior, it produced virtually no major changes in the structure of Amazonian society and economy. I explore the factors that blocked the transformation of the regional economy. One important 'obstacle' was the physical environment itself. The rubber tappers took advantage of the configuration of *Hevea* growth to retain some control over their work rhythms and to combine latex extraction with traditional subsistence activities. Despite their oppressive and precarious conditions, the tappers proved capable of resisting innovations that threatened their last shreds of autonomy. The interest of the powerful middlemen (*aviadores*) in the rubber districts were based on indirect control of productive resources and surplus appropriation through exchange mechanisms. Therefore, they opposed the efforts of outsiders to establish direct control over the rubber fields and to 'rationalise' production – since the latter usually entailed elimination of the middleman. I make a brief comparison of the changes wrought by the rubber trade and those occurring as a result of the current 'boom' in the Amazon. I contend that the rubber trade caused only slight alterations in the long-standing property and productive relations in the Amazon and caused little damage to the regional ecology, whereas present patterns of development seem to be predicated on the wholesale disruption of traditional lifestyles and the widespread devastation of the environment.

14 George Catlin and Frederick Church in South America

JOHN GARDNER

George Catlin and Frederick Edwin Church, two of the most famous nineteenth century North American artists, both travelled and painted in South America. Catlin, in addition, wrote three books which tell of his South American wanderings. Considering the frequent complaints about the scarcity of visual materials illustrating nineteenth-century South America, their works should become better known. In my paper I hope to show slides of all the South American works of both painters. Catlin's paintings of South American Indians exceed in number and equal in importance those he made in the United States. They depict many of the tribes of Venezuela, the Guianas, Amazonia, the Pampa de Sacramento, the Paraná and Uruguay valleys, and the northeastern Argentine Pampas before they were influenced significantly by White contact. Some tribes, such as the Payaguás, have since become extinct, and others, such as the Zurumatis, never were described by anyone else. Catlin's paintings reveal details of Indian decoration, housing, weapons, and lifestyles. His books are vivid accounts of wilderness travel filled with insights and observations of Indian life and customs. Some of Church's greatest landscapes were painted in the Ecuadorean Andes and rainforest. It is doubtful if any other artist has ever captured the grandeur of South American scenery so well as he did.

15 Changes among indigenous Tupi groups of the Tocantins-Xingu region of the Amazon Basin

EXPEDITO ARNAUD

This paper was written as part of the research project 'The Indian and National Expansion'. It concentrates on the following tribes: Akuawa-Asurini (Trocara river, Tocantins); Surui-Mudjetire (Sororosinho river, Tocantins); Parakanan (Pucurui river, Tocantins); Asurini (Piaçaba river, Xingu); and Araweté (Ipixua river, Xingu). The paper contains the following: (a) general aspects of the region, its penetration by frontier activities in extraction, farming and cattle ranching, and the situation caused by the construction of the Itaboca dam on the Tocantins and the Tucuruí hydroelectric dam currently in progress; (b) the nature of the aforementioned Indian tribes, with a comparative sketch of their respective socio-cultural characteristics; (c) their inter- and extra-tribal contacts and the changes that they have suffered and are suffering as a result of these – both in respect of their customs, environment and demography, and the manner in which they are being led towards integration into Brazilian society.

Bibliography

Ackefors, M. and Rosen, Carl Gustaf (1979) Farming aquatic animals. *Ambio* **8**, 132–43

Acuña, Fr. Cristoval de (1859) New Discovery of the Great River of the Amazons. Translated from the Spanish Edition (1641) by Clements R. Markham. In *Expeditions into the Valley of the Amazonas, 1539, 1540, 1639*. Hakluyt Society: London.

Adams, J. A. S., Mantovani, M. S. M., and Lundell, L. L. (1977). Wood versus fossil fuel as a source of excess carbon dioxide in the atmosphere: a preliminary report. *Science* **196**: 54–6.

Allen, W. L. and Tizon, J. H., (1973) Land use patterns among the Campa of the Alto Pachitea, Peru. In Lathrap, D. W. and Douglas, J. (eds.) *Variation in Anthropology: Essays in Honor of John C. McGregor*. Illinois Archaeological Survey: Urbana.

Alvim, P. de T. (1972) Potencial agrícola de Amazônia. *Ciencia e cultura* **24**: 437–43.

——(1975) The lowland tropics of Latin America: resources and environment for agricultural development. In *Symposium on The Potential of the Lowland Tropics, October 13, 1973. Cali*. (pp. 43–61). CIAT., Cali, Colombia (Sept. 1975 series CF–7).

—— (1977) The balance between conservation and utilization in the humid tropics with special reference to Amazonian Brazil. In Prance, G. T. and Elias, T. S. (eds.), *Extinction is Forever*, (pp. 347–52). The New York Botanic Gardens.

—— (1980) Agricultural production potential of the Amazon Region. In Barbira-Scazzocchio, F. (ed.) *Land, People, and Planning in Contemporary Amazônia*, (pp. 27–36). Centre for Latin American Studies, Cambridge University.

—— (1981) A perspective appraisal of perennial crops in the Amazon basin. *Interciencia* **6**(3), 139–45.

AMB (1980) Anuário Mineral Brasileiro – 1980. Brasília, Dept. Nacional de Produção Mineral.

Amoroso, M. C. de M. (1981) Alimentação em um bairro pobre de Manaus, Amazonas. *Acta Amazonica* **11**(3) suplemento: 1–43.

Anon. (1975) Carajás: staggering iron ore reserves in isolated splendor. *Engineering Mining Journal* **176**(11), 145–52.

Anon. (1978) *Carta da Amazônia*, Manaus.

Anon. (1980) Harnessing energy in the Amazon. *Engineering News Record* **204**(2): 24.

ARC (1981) Brazil: A decade of disposition. Newsletter, *Anthropology Resource Center* **5** (3): 2–3.

Arkcoll, D. B. (1979) Nutrient recycling as an alternative to shifting cultivation. *Berlin Science Foundation, Conference on Eco-farming*.

Aspelin, P. L. and Santos, S. C. dos (1981) Indian areas threatened by hydroelectric projects in Brazil. Copenhagen, *IWGIA Doc.* **44**: 201.

Asselin, V. (1982) *Grilagem: Corrupção e Violência em Terras do Carajás*. Ed. Vozes/CPT: Petrópolis.

Avelino de Souza Costa, P. and Silva Araújo Silveira, R. (1980) Environmental impact assessment in Brazil. *UNEP Industry and Environment* **1**: 2–3.

Ayres, J. M. and Best, R. (1979) Estrategias para a conservação da fauna Amazônica. *Acta Amazonica* 9(4): 81–101.

Balick, M. J. (1979) Amazonian oil palms of promise. *Econ. Botany* 33(1): 11–28.

—— (1982) Palmas neotropicales: Nuevas fuentes de aceites comestibles. *Interciencia*, 7: 25–9.

Bamberger, Jean (1967) Environmental and cultural classification: A study of the Northern Cayapó. Ph.D. Dissertation, Harvard University.

Bangladesh Rice Research Institute (1975) *Proceedings of the International Seminar on Deep-Water Rice*, August 21–26, 1974, BRRI, Dacca.

Barbira-Scazzocchio, F. (ed.) (1980) *Land, People and Planning in Contemporary Amazonia.* Cambridge Univ., Centre Latin Amer. Studies.

Barrett, S. W. (1980) Conservation in Amazonia, *Biological Conservation*, 18, 209–35.

Barrow, C. J. (1981) Development of the Brazilian Amazon. *Mazingira* 5/4: 36–47.

Basso, E. B. (1973) *The Kalapalo Indians of Central Brazil.* Holt, Rinehart, and Winston: New York.

Bates, H. W. (1892) *The Naturalist on the River Amazons.* John Murray: London.

Bell, F. W. and E. Ray Canterbury (1976) *Aquaculture for Developing Countries.* Ballinger: Cambridge, Mass.

Benchimol, S. (1981) *Expansão e concentração demográfica na Amazônia legal na década 70/80.* Manaus, Univ. do Amazonas.

Bennema, J. (1975) Soil resources of the tropics with special reference to the well-drained soils of the Brazilian Amazonian forest region. In *International Symposium on Ecophysiology of Tropical Crops, Manaus 25–30 May 1975.* Vol. 1. (pp. 1–47).

Bentley, B. L. (1977) Extrafloral nectaries and protection of pugnacious body bodyguards. *Annual Review of Ecology and Systematics* 8: 407–27.

Bergmann, R. (1974) Shipibo Subsistence in the Upper Amazon Rainforest. Doctoral dissertation, Department of Anthropology, University of Wisconsin, Madison.

Bernhard-Reversat, F. (1975) Nutrients in throughfall and their quantitative importance in rainforest mineral cycles. In Golley, F. and Medina, E. (eds) *Tropical Ecological Systems* (pp. 153–61) Springer: New York.

Bishop, J. P. (1978) The development of a sustained yield tropical agro-ecosystem in the upper Amazon. *Agro-Ecosystems* 4: 459–61.

—— (1982) Agroforestry systems for the humid tropics east of the Andes. In Hecht, S. B. (ed.) *Amazonia: Agriculture and Land-use Research.* (pp. 403–16) (CIAT 1980 Conf.). University of Missouri: Columbia.

Björkström, A. (1979) A model of CO_2 interaction between atmosphere, oceans, and land biota. In Bolin, B., Degens, E. T., Kempe, S., and Ketner, P. (eds.) *The Global Carbon Cycle.* Scientific Committee on Problems of the Environment (SCOPE) No. 13 (pp. 403–57) John Wiley and Sons: New York.

Bluntschli, H. (1921) Die Amazonasniederung als harmonischer Organismus. *Geogr. Zeitung* 27: 49–67.

Bodard, L. (1972) *Green Hell: Massacre of the Brazilian Indians.* Outerbridge and Dienstfrey: New York.

Bolin, B. (1977) Changes of land biota and their importance for the carbon cycle. *Science* 196: 613–15.

Bourne, R. (1978) *Assault on the Amazon.* Victor Gollancz: London.

Brazil, Ministério da Agricultura, Divisão de Pesquisa Pedológica (DNPEA). (1973a) *Levantamento de Reconhecimento dos Solos de uma Área Prioritária na Rodovia Transamazônica entre Altamira e Itaituba.* DNPEA Boletim Tecnico No. 34. Rio de Janeiro.

—— (1973b) *Estudo Expedito dos Solos no Trecho Itaituba-Estreito da Rodovia Transamazônica para Fins de Classificação e Correlação.* DNPEA Boletim Técnico No. 31. Rio de Janeiro.

Brazil, Ministério da Agricultura, Empresa Brasileira de Pesquisa Agropecuária (EMBRAPA) – Instituto de Pesquisas Agropecuárias do Norte (IPEAN). (1974) *Solos da Rodovia Transamazônica: Trecho Itaituba-Rio Branco. Relatório Preliminar.* EMBRAPA–IPEAN, Belém.

Brazil, Ministério da Agricultura, Instituto de Pesquisas Agropecuárias do Norte (IPEAN). (1967) *Contribuição ao Estudo dos Solos de Altamira.* IPEAN Circular No. 10 Belém.

Brazil, Ministério de Minas e Energia, Departamento de Produção Mineral, Projeto RADAMBRASIL. (1973–9) *Levantamento de Recursos Naturais, Vols. 1–18.* Departamento de Produção Mineral, Rio de Janeiro.

Brazil, Presidência da República (1974) *II Plano Nacional de Desenvolvimento (1975–1979).* Brasília.

Brazil, Presidência da República, Secretaria de Planejamento, Fundação Instituto Brasileiro de Geografia e Estatística (IBGE). (1981) *Sinopse Preliminar do Censo Demográfico: IX Recenseamento Geral do Brasil – 1980. Vol. 1* Tomo. 1, No. 1. IBGE, Rio de Janeiro.

Bremner, J. M. and Blackmer, A. M., (1978) Nitrous oxide emission from soils during nitrification of fertilizer nitrogen. *Science* **199**: 295–6.

Brinkmann, W. L. F. and de Nascimento, J. C. (1973) The effect of slash and burn agriculture on plant nutrients in the Tertiary region of Central Amazonia. *Turrialba* **23**(3): 284–90.

Briscoe, C. (1978–9) Improved utilization of tropical forests: silviculture in plantation development: Jari *Coedewigor* **31**: 57–71.

Broecker, W. S. Takahasi, T., Simpson, H. J., and Peng, T. H. (1979) Fate of fossil fuel: carbon dioxide and the global carbon budget. *Science* **206**: 409–18.

Brooks, E., Fuerst, R., Hemming, J. H. and Huxley, F., (1973) *Tribes of the Amazon Basin in Brazil 1972.* C. Knight: London.

Brown, K. S. (1979) *Ecologia geográfica e evolução nas florestas neotropicais.* Campinas, São Paulo, Univ. Estadual de Campinas.

Brown, L. R. (1981a) World food resources and population: the narrowing margin. *Population Bull.* **36**(3): 45.

—— (1981b) *Building a Sustainable Society.* Norton: New York.

Brunig, E. F. (1980) Structure and function of a tropical rainforest in the Amazon MAB-ecosystem project at San Carlos de Río Negro. In Furtado, J. I. (ed.) *Tropical Ecology and Development* (pp. 33–5). Int. Soc. Trop. Ecol. Kuala Lumpur.

Bryson, R. A. and Dittberner, G. J. (1976) A non-equilibrium model of hemispheric mean temperature. *Journal of the Atmospheric Sciences* **33**: 2094–106.

Budowski, G. (1956) Tropical savannas, a sequence of forest felling and repeated burnings. *Turrialba* **6**(1–2): 23–33.

—— (1976) Why save tropical rain forest? Some arguments for campaigning conservationists. *Amazoniana* **4**: 529–38.

—— (1981) The place of agroforestry in managing tropical forests. In Mergen, F. (ed.) *Tropical Forests* (pp. 181–94). Yale School of Forestry: New Haven, Connecticut.

Budweg, F. M. G. (1982) Reservoir planning for Brazilian dams. *Water Power and Dam Construction* **34**(5): 48–9.

Budyko, M. I. (1969) The effect of solar radiation variations on the climate of the earth. *Tellus* **21**: 611–19.

Bunker, S. G. (1980) Forces of destruction in Amazonia. *Environment* **22**(7): 14–43.

—— (1981) The impact of deforestation on peasant communities in the Medio-Amazonas of Brazil. In Sutlive, V. H. *et al.* (eds.) *Deforestation in the Third World*, (pp. 45–60) College of William and Mary, Studies in Third World Socs.: 13: Williamsburg, Virginia.

—— (1982) The state, extractive economies, and the progressive underdevelopment of the Brazilian Amazon. Paper presented at the conference on 'Frontier Expansion in Amazonia', Center for Latin American Studies, University of Florida, Gainesville, Florida. February 8–11, 1982. (ms.).

Calkins, J. (ed.) (1982) *The Role of Solar Ultraviolet Radiation in Marine Ecosystems.* Plenum: New York.

Camargo, F. C. de (1948) Terra e colonização no antigo e novo Quarternário na Zona da Estrada de Ferro de Bragança, Estado do Pará, Brasil. *Bol. Mus. Paraense E. Goeldi, Belém* **10**: 123–47.

—— (1949) Reclamation of the Amazonian flood lands near Belém, *Proc. UN Scientific Conference on Conservation and Utilization of Resources*, 1949, Lake Success, New York, United Nations, pp. 598–602.

—— (1958) Report on the Amazon region, problems of humid tropical regions. In UNESCO, *Humid Tropics Research: Problems of Humid Tropical Regions*, (pp. 11–24) UNESCO: Paris.

Carajazão (1981) Rio de Janeiro, *Relatório Reservado Especial* (August): 4.

Carneiro, C. M. R. (1980) Programa de monitoramento da cobertura florestal do Brasil. Brasília, *IBDF, D. Pq-Serie Tec.* **4**: 31.

Carneiro, Robert L. (1961) Slash-and-burn cultivation among the Kuikuru and its impact for cultural development in the Amazon Basin. In Wilbert, J. (ed.) *The Evolution of Horticultural Systems in Native South America: Causes and Consequences, a Symposium* (pp. 47–67). Antropologica Supplement No. 2: Caracas.

Carvajal, Fr. Gaspar de (1934) *The Discovery of the Amazon according to the Account of Friar Gaspar de Carvajal and other Documents.* H. C. Heaton (ed.) American Geographical Society, Special Publication No. 17: New York.

Carvalho, J. C. de M. (1979) *Considerações sobre o uso da terra na Amazônia brasileira.* Rio, Fund. Bras. Conserv. Natureza.

Caulfield, C. (1982) Brazil, energy and the Amazon. *New Scientist* (28 Oct.): 240–3.

Cavalcante, Paulo (1972) *Frutas Comestíveis da Amazônia*, Vol. 1. Publicações Avulsas do Museu Goeldi: Belém.

—— (1974) *Frutas Comestíveis da Amazônia*, Vol. 2. Publicações Avulsas do Museu Goeldi: Belém.

—— (1979) *Frutos Comestíveis da Amazônia*, Vol. 3. Publicações Avulsas, Museu Paraense Goeldi: Belém, No. 33, 46.

CEQ: Council on Environmental Quality (1981) *Global Energy Futures and the Carbon Dioxide Problem*. Washington DC.

Chagnon, Napoleon (1968) *Yanomamö: The Fierce People*. Holt, Rinehart, and Winston: New York.

Chaves, R. de S., Vieira, L. S., Vieira, M. de N. F. and Santos, P. C. T. C. dos (1979) *Sistemas de Preparo de Solo para Arroz (Oriza sativa) em Área Sistematizada de Várzea*, FCAP-Pará, Servico de Documentação e Informação (presented to XVII Congresso Brasileiro de Ciência do Solo – Manaus, July 1979), Belém.

Clarke, W. C. (1971) *Place and People: An Ecology of a New Guinean Community*. University of California Press: Berkeley.

—— (1976) Maintenance of agriculture and human habitats within the tropical forest ecosystem. *Human Ecology* **4**: 247–59.

——(1977) The structure of permanence: The relevance of self-subsistence communities for world ecosystem management. In Bayliss-Smith, T. P. and Feachem, R. G. (eds.), *Subsistence and Survival* (pp. 363–84) Academic Press: London.

Clausen, A. W. (1981) *Sustainable Development: The Global Imperative*. World Bank (Fairfield Osborne Memorial Lecture) Nov. 12: Washington DC.

Clay, E. J. (1978) Genetic evolution and utilization: deepwater – Yields of deepwater rice in Bangladesh, *International Rice Research Newsletter*, **3**(5): 11–13.

Clay, E. J., Catling, H. D., Hobbs, P. P., Bhuiyan, N. I. and Islam, Z. (1978) *Yield Assessments of Broadcast Amon (Deepwater Rice) in Selected Areas of Bangladesh in 1977*. Bangladesh Rice Research Institute, Agricultural Development Council, Inc.

CNDDA (1975) *A Amazônia Brasileira em Foco (No. 10)*, julio 1974–junho 1975, Rio de Janeiro, pp. 84–94.

Cochrane, T. T. and Sánchez, P. A. (1981) Land resources, soils and their management in the Amazon Region: a state of knowledge report. In Hecht, S. B. (ed.) *Amazonia: Agriculture and Land Use Research* pp. 137–209. Centro Internacional de Agricultura Tropical (CIAT), Cali, Colombia. (CIAT series 03E-3(82)).

Conklin, H. C. 1957. *Hanunóo Agriculture*. FAO: Rome.

Construtora Andrade Gutierrez (1982) *Projeto Tucumã: contribuição ao ciclo de palestras sobre Carajás: CNP_q*. CNP_q.; Brasília. (ms.).

Coomer, J. C. (ed.) (1981) *Quest for a Sustainable Society*. Pergamon: New York.

Covich, A. P. and Nickerson, N. H. (1966) Studies of cultivated plants in Choco dwelling clearings, Darien, Panama. *Economic Botany* **20**: 285–301.

Crutzen, P. J., Heidt, L. E., Drasnec, K. P., Pollock, W. H. and Seiler, W. (1979) Biomass burning as a source of atmospheric gases CO, H_2, N_2O, CH_3Cl, and CO_2. *Nature* 283: 626.

Cunningham, R. K. (1963) The effect of clearing a tropical forest soil. *Journal of Soil Sciences* **14**(2): 334–45.

Dall 'Olio, A., Salati, E., Azevedo, C. T. and Matsui, E. (1979) Modelo de fracionamento isotópico da água na Bacia Amazônica. *Acta Amazonica* **9**(4): 675–87.

Daly, H. E. (1977) *Steady-state Economics*. Freeman: San Francisco.

—— (ed.) (1980) *Economics, Ecology, Ethics*. Freeman: San Francisco.

Dantas, M. (1979) Pastagens da Amazonia Central: ecologia e fauna de solo. *Acta Amazonica* **9**(2): suplemento: 1–54.

Davis, S. (1977) *Victims of the Miracle: Development and the Indians of Brazil*. Cambridge

University Press.

Denevan, W. M. (1973) Development and the imminent demise of the Amazon rain forest. *Professional Geographer* **25**(2): 130–5.

—— (1974) Campa subsistence in the Gran Pajonal, eastern Peru. In Lyon, P. J. (ed.) *Native South Americans* (pp. 92–110). Little, Brown and Company: Boston.

—— (1976) The aboriginal population of Amazonia. In Denevan, W. M. (ed.) *The Native Population of the Americas in 1492* (pp. 205–34) University of Wisconsin Press: Madison.

—— (1980) Swiddens and cattle vs. forest: the imminent demise of the Amazon rainforest reexamined. In Sutlive, V. H., *et al. Deforestation in the Third World* (pp. 25–44) College of William and Mary, Studies in Third World Socs.: Williamsburg, Virginia.

De Oliveira, A. E., Cortez, R., Velthem, L. H., Brabo, M. J., Alves, I., Furtado, L., da Silveira, I. M. and Rodrigues, I. (1979) Antropologia social e a politica florestal para a Amazônia. *Acta Amazonica* **9**(4) suplemento: 191–5.

De Schlippe, P. (1956) *Shifting Cultivation in Africa.* Routledge and Kegan Paul: London.

Dickenson, R. E. (1981) Effects of tropical deforestation on climate. *Studies in Third World Societies* **14**: 411–41.

Dickinson, III, J. C. (1972) Alternatives to monocluture in the humid tropics of Latin America. *Professional Geographer* **24**: 217–22.

Diniz, L., Alves, M. B. M. and Sa, R.-M. da S. (eds.) (1982) *Carajás: Informações Documentais.* Museu Paraense Emílio Goeldi: Belém.

DMET, Departamento Nacional de Meteorologia (1972) *Balanço hídrico do Brasil.*

Dobyns, Henry F. (1966) Estimating aboriginal American population. *Current Anthropology* **7**: 395–416.

Donahue, T. M. (1975) The SST and ozone depletion. *Science* **187**: 1145.

Doren, Lee (1981) Amazon Region Production Possibilities Update, unpublished paper for The Johns Hopkins School of Advanced International Studies.

Dubois, J. (1979) Aspects of agroforestry systems used in Moyombe and Lower Congo (Zaire). In G. de las Salas (ed.) *Workshop: Agro-forestry Systems in Latin America* (pp. 84–90) CATIE: Turrialba.

Dynia, J. F., Moreira, G. N. C. and Bloise, R. M. (1977) Fertilidade de solos da região da Rodovia Transamazônica. II Fixação do fósforo em podzólico vermelho-amarelo e terra roxa estruturada latossólica. *Pesquisa Agropecuária Brasileira* **12**: 75–80.

Eckholm, E. P. (1978) *Disappearing Species: The Social Challenge.* Washington, D.C. Worldwatch Inst. paper 22.

—— (1982) *Down to Earth: Environment and Human Needs.* W. W. Norton: New York.

Eckholme, Erik and Brown, L. R. (1977) *Spreading Deserts: The Hand of Man.* World Watch Paper No. 13. Worldwatch Institute.

Eden, M. J. (1980) A traditional agro-system in the Amazon region of Colombia. In Furtado, J. I. (ed.), *Tropical Ecology and Development* Vol. 1 (pp. 509–14) International Society of Tropical Ecology, Kuala Lumpur.

E.G. (1982) Conservacionistas brasileiros ganham o premio Paul Getty. *Engenharia Sanitaria* **21**(1): 66–7.

Ehrlich, P. R. (1982) Human carrying capacity, extinctions, and nature reserves. *BioScience* **32**(5): 331–3.

Ehrlich, P. R. and Ehrlich, A. H. (1981) *Extinction: The Causes and Consequences of the Disappearance of Species.* Random House: New York.

Ehrlich, P. R., Ehrlich, A. H. and Holdren, J. P. (1977) *Ecoscience: Population, Resources, Environment*: W. H. Freeman: San Francisco.

Eigen, M. (1979) Zeugen der Genesis – Versuch einer Rekonstruktion der Urformen des Lebens aus ihren in den Biomolekülen hinterlassenen Spuren. In *Jahrbuch der Max-Planck-Gesellschaft* (pp. 17–54). Vandenhoeck & Ruprecht: Göttingen.

Eigner, J. (1975) Unshielding the sun: environmental effects. *Environment* **17**(3): 15–25.

Eletronorte (1976) Usina hidreletrica de Tucuruí: projeto básico. Eletronorte: Brasília (Jan): 114.

EMBRAPA (1976) *Sistema de Produção para Arroz em Várzea* (Bragança–Pará), Circular 115, Belém.

EMBRATER/EMBRAPA/IDESP (1979) *Sistema de Produção para Arroz em Várzeas (Microregion 16)*, Belém.

—— (1980a) *Sistemas de Produção Para Feijão (Amazonas)* (revisão), Sistemas de Produção Bulletin (No. 190), Manaus.

EMBRATER/EMBRAPA (1980b) *Sistemas de Produção Para Juta e Malva (Amazonas)*, (revisão), Sistemas de Produção (Bulletin No. 195), Manaus.

E.N.R. (1980) Harnessing energy in the Amazon. *Engineering News Record* **204**(2): 24.

Etkins, R. and Epstein, E. S. (1982) The rise of global mean sea level as an indication of climate change. *Science* **215**: 287–9.

Ewel, J. (1981) Environmental implications of tropical forest utilization. In Mergen, F. (ed.) *Tropical Forests* (pp. 157–67) Yale University Press: New Haven, Connecticut.

Ewel, J. and Conde, L. (1976) *Potential Ecological Impact of Increased Intensity of Tropical Forest Utilization.* USDA Forest Serv.: Madison, Wisconsin, 12–18: 115.

—— (1978) Environmental implications of any-species utilization in the moist tropics. In *Proc. Conf. Improved Utilization of Tropical Forests* (pp. 106–23) Madison, Wisconsin. USDA Forest Service, Forest Products Laboratory.

Falesi, I. C. (1972) *Solos da Rodovia Transamazônica.* Instituto de Pesquisas Agropecuárias do Norte (IPEAN) Boletim Técnico No. 55. Belém.

—— (1976) *A ecosistema de pastagem cultivada.* CPATU: Belém.

Farnworth, E. G. and Golley, F. B. (eds.) (1974) *Fragile Ecosystems: Evaluation of Research and Applications in the Neotropics.* Springer-Verlag: New York.

Fassbender, H. W. (1969) Retención y transformación de fosfatos en 8 latosoles de la Amazonia del Brasil. *Fitotecnia Latinamericana* **6**(1): 1–10.

Fearnside, P. M. (1978) *Estimation of carrying capacity for human populations in a part of the Transamazon Highway colonization area of Brasil.* (Ph.D. dissertation in biological sciences, University of Michigan, Ann Arbor, Michigan). University Microfilms International, Ann Arbor, Michigan.

—— (1979a) The development of the Amazon rainforest: priority problems for the formulation of guidelines. *Interciencia* **4**(6): 338–43.

—— (1979b) Cattle yield prediction for the Transamazon highway of Brazil. *Interciencia* **4**(4): 220–6.

—— (1979c) O processo de desertificação e os riscos de sua ocorrência no Brasil. *Acta Amazônica* **9**(2): 393–401.

—— (1980a) Land use allocation of the Transamazon highway colonists of Brazil and its relation to human carrying capacity. In Barbira-Scazzocchi, F. (ed.) *Land, People and Planning in contemporary Amazonia* (pp. 114–38) Cent. Lat. Amer. Stud: Cambridge University.

—— (1980b) A previsão de perdas de terra atraves de erosão de solo sob varios usos de terra na área de colonização da Rodovia Tansamazônica. *Acta Amazônica* **10**(3): 505–12.

—— (1980c) The prediction of soil erosion losses under various land uses in the transamazon highway colonization area of Brazil. In Furtado, J. I. (ed.) *Tropical Ecology and Development* (pp. 1287–95) Int. Soc. Trop. Ecol.: Kuala Lumpur.

—— (1980d) Os efeitos das pastagens sobre a fertilidade do solo na Amazônia Brasileira: consequencias para a sustentabilidade de produção bovina. *Acta Amazônica* **10**(1): 119–32.

—— (1980e) The effects of cattle pasture on soil fertility in the Brazilian Amazon: consequences for beef production sustainability. *Tropical Ecology* **21**(1): 125–37.

—— (1982) Deforestation in the Brazilian Amazon: how fast is it occurring? *Interciencia* **7**(2): 82–8.

—— (1983a) Stochastic modeling and human carrying capacity estimation: a tool for development planning in Amazonia. In. Moran, E. F. (ed.) *The Dilemma of Amazonian Development* (pp. 279–95) Westview Press: Boulder, Colorado.

—— (1983b) Development alternatives in the Brazilian Amazon: an ecological evaluation. *Interciencia* **8**(2): 65–78.

—— (nd–a) Land clearing behaviour in small farmer settlement schemes in the Brazilian Amazon and its relation to human carrying capacity. Paper presented at the Symposium on the Tropical Rain Forest: Ecology and Resource Management. Leeds, U.K., 14–18 April 1982. (In preparation).

—— (nd–b) Land use trends in the Brazilian Amazon as factors in accelerating deforestation. *Environmental Conservation.* (In press).

—— (nd–c) Agriculture in Amazonia. In Prance, G. T. and Lovejoy, T. E. (eds.) *The Amazon Rain Forest.* Key Environments Series, Pergamon Press: Oxford. (In press).

—— (nd–d) Initial soil quality conditions on the Transamazon Highway of Brazil and their simulation in models for estimating human carrying capacity. *Tropical Ecology.* (In press).

—— (nd–e) *Carrying Capacity for Human Populations: the Colonization of the Brazilian Rainforest.* Burgess: Minneapolis, Minnesota. (To be published).

Fearnside, P. M. and Rankin, J. (1980) Jari and development in the Brazilian Amazon. *Interciencia* **5**(3): 146–56.

—— (1982) Jari and Carajás: the uncertain future of large silvicultural plantations in the Amazon. *Interciencia* **7**(6): 326–8.

Feder, E. (1980) The odious competition between man and animal over agricultural resources in the underdeveloped countries. New York, *SUNY Research Foundation Review* **3**(3): 463–500.

Ferraroni, J. J., Spencer, Clarence A., Hayes, Jack and Suzuki, Mamoru (1981) Prevalence of chloroquine-resistant falciparum malaria in the Brazilian Amazon. *Amer. J. Tropical Med. Hyg.* **30**(3): 526–30.

Ferraz, I. (1982) *Os Índios Gaviões: observações sobre uma situação crítica.* São Paulo, Univ. São Paulo, Dept. Cienc. Soc. (ms).

Fidalgo, O. (1965). Conhecimento micológico dos índios brasileiros. *Rickia* **2**, 1–10.

Fidalgo, O. and Prance, G. T. (1976) The ethnomycology of the Sanama Indians. *Mycologia* **68**, 201–10.

Fittkau, E.-J. (1973) Artenmannigfaltigkeit amazonischer Lebensräume aus ökologischer Sicht. *Amazoniana* **4**: 321–40.

—— (1973) Crocodiles and the nutrient metabolism of Amazonian waters. *Amazoniana* **5**(1): 103–33.

Flohn, H. (1974) Climatic variation and modification of climate: facts and problems. *Applied Sciences and Development* (Institute for Scientific Cooperation, Tübingen, F. R. Germany) **8**: 96–105.

Fonseca, F. V. (1980) Development and operations of the Trombetas bauxite. *Soc. Mining Engineers* 80–144: 6.

Fonseca, O. J. M. (1980) Projeto Tucuruí: CNP_q–INPA/Eletronorte. *Acta Amazônica* **10**(2): 243–44.

Forde, C. D. (1934) The Boro of the western Amazon forest. In Forde, C. D. *Habitat, Economy and Society* (pp. 131–47) Methuen: London.

Fox, D. L., Kamens, R. and Jeffries, H. E. (1975) Stratospheric nitric oxide: measurements during daytime and sunset. *Science* **188**: 1111–13.

Francelino da Silva, L., Frechione, J., Parker, E. and Posey, D. (in press) Resource Exploitation in Amazonia: Ethnoecological Examples from Four Populations.

Franco, N. de. (1981) The superelectrification of Brazil. *IEEE Spectrum*: 57–62.

Franken, W. (1982) Interceptação das precipitações em floresta amazônica de terra firme. *Acta Amazonica* **12**(3) suplemento: 15–22.

Franken, W., Leopoldo, P. R., Matsui, E. and Ribeiro, M. N. G. (1981) Estudo da interceptação da água de chuva em cobertura florestal amazônica do tipo terra firme. *Acta Amazonica* **11** (In press).

Frechione, John (1981) Economic self-development by Yekuana Amerinds in Southern Venezuela. Ph.D. dissertation, University of Pittsburgh.

Freitas, M. de L. D. and Smyrski-Shluger, C. M. (1982) *Brazil's Carajás Iron Ore Project: Environmental Aspects*. Rio de Janeiro, Companhia Vale do Rio Doce.

Furch, K. (1976) Haupt- und Spurenelementgehaltes zentralamzonischer Gewässertypen (Erste Ergebnisse). *Biogeographica* **7**: 27–43.

Furley, P. A. and Leite, L. L. (1983) Land development in the Brazilian Amazon with particular reference to Rondonia and the Ouro Preto colonization project. Department of Geography, University of Edinburgh (ms).

Furtado, J. I. (ed.) (1980) *Tropical Ecology and Development*. Int. Soc. Trop. Ecol.: Kuala Lumpur.

Galati, Eneas, José Marques and Luiz Carlos Molion (1978) Origem e Distribuição das Chuvas na Amazônia *Interciencia*, V. Caracas, **3**, 4, July–August.

Gasché, J. (1979) *Cultivo de corte y quema y evolución del médio forestal en el noroeste del Amazonas: ecología de los sistemas de cultivo indígenas en la selva peruana*. Centre National de la Recherche Scientifique, Paris. Mimeo.

—— (1980) El estudio comparativo de los sistemas de cultivo nativos y su impacto sobre el bosque amazónico. *Consulta científica subregional sobre las actividades de corte y quema en el ecosistema de bosque tropical* (pp. 61–74). Man and the Biosphere Program: Iquitos.

Gazolla, E. A. (1982) Pollution problems in the mining industry in Brazil: the performance of the Companhia Vale do Rio Doce (CVRD). Rio de Janeiro, CVRD, *International Conference on Environment* (Stockholm, April 19–22).

Geertz, C. (1963) *Agricultural Evolution: The Process of Ecological Change in Indonesia*, University of California Press: Berkeley.

Gentry, A. H. and López-Parodi, J. (1980) Deforestation and increased flooding of the Upper Amazon. *Science* **210**: 1354–6.

Gilbert, L. E and Raven, P. H. (eds.) (1975) *Coevolution of Animals and Plants*. University of Texas Press: Austin.

Girard, R. (1958) Los Bora. In Girard, R. *Indios selváticos de la Amazonía peruana* (pp. 85–124) Libro Mex: México.

Giugliano, R., Shrimpton, R., Arkcoll, D. B., Guigliano, L. G. and Petrere Jr., M. (1978) Diagnóstico da realidade alimentar e nutricionial do Estado do Amazonas, 1978. *Acta Amazonica* **8**(2) suplemento 2: 1–54.

Gliessman, S. R. and Amador, A. M. (1980) Ecological aspects of production in traditional agroecosystems in the humid lowland tropics of Mexico. In Furtado, J. I. (ed.) *Tropical Ecology and Development* (pp. 601–8). Int. Soc. Trop. Ecol.: Kuala Lumpur.

Golley, F. B., McGinnis, J. T., Clements, R. G., Child, G. I. and Duever, M. J. (1975) *Mineral Cycling in a Tropical Forest Ecosystem* University of Georgia: Athens.

Golley, F. B. and Medina, E. (eds.) (1975) *Tropical Ecological Ecosystems*. Springer: New York.

Gomes, M. P. (1982) *A problemática indígena no Maranhão, especificamente nas áreas de influência imediata da ferrovia Carajás: Reserva Turiaçu, Reserva Caru e Reserva Pindaré*. Campinas, S. P., Univ. Estadual de Campinas, Dept. Ciências Sociais (3 Set.).

Gómez-Pompa, A., Vásquez-Yanes, C. and Gueriara, S. (1972) The tropical rain forest: a non-renewable resource. *Science* **177**: 762–5.

Gonçalves, A. R, L. (1979) *Determinação do tempo de residência da água de chuva em algumas bacias hidrográficas através de valores de isótopos estáveis*. M.S. Thesis, Univ. of São Paulo, Piracicaba, Brasil.

Goodland, Robert (1975) *The Cerrado Ecosystem of Brazil*. UNESCO: Paris.

—— (1977) *Environmental Assessment of the Tucuruí Hydroelectric Project, Rio Tocantins, Amazonia*. Eletronorte: Brasília.

—— *(1979) Environmental optimization in hydrodevelopment of tropical forest regions. In Panday, R. S. (ed.) Man-made Lakes and Human Health* (pp. 10–20) Univ. Suriname, Fac. Medicine: Parimaribo.

—— (1980) Environmental ranking of Amazonian development projects in Brazil. *Environmental Conservation* **7**(1): 9–26; (World Bank Reprint 198).

—— (1982) *Environmental Requirements of the World Bank*. Washington DC, World Bank, Office of Environmental Affairs (AIBS/ATB August Conf.) ms.

Goodland, Robert and Bookman, J. (1977) Can Amazonia survive its highways? *Ecologist* **7**: 376–80.

Goodland, R. J. A. and Irwin, H. S. (1975A). *Amazon Jungle: Green Hell to Red Desert? An Ecological Discussion of the Environmental Impact of the Highway Construction Program in the Amazon Basin*. Elsevier: New York.

—— (1975b) *A Selva Amazônica: do Inferno Verde ao Deserto Vermelho?* Translated from (1975a) by Regina R. Junqueira. Editora Itatiaia/Editora da Universidade de São Paulo.

—— (1977a) Amazon forest and cerrado: development and environmental conservation. In Prance, G. T. (ed.) *Extinction is Forever* (pp. 214–33) New York Botanic Garden.

—— (1977b) O cerrado e a floresta amazónica: desenvolvimento ecológico racional e conservação do meio ambiente. In *Seminario Regional de Desenvolvimento Rural Integrado* (Vol. II pp. 8–37). SUDAM; Belém.

Goodland, R., Irwin, H. S. and Tillman, R. E. (1978) Ecological development for Amazonia. São Paulo, *Ciência e Cultura* 30(3): 275–89.

Gordon, B. L. (1969) *Anthropogeography and Rainforest Ecology in Bocas del Toro Province, Panama.* Office of Naval Research Report, Department of Geography, University of California; Berkeley.

Goreau, T. J. (1981) *Biogeochemisty of Nitrous Oxide.* Ph.D. dissertation in geological sciences, Harvard University, Cambridge, Mass.

Goreau, T. J., Kaplan, W. A. Wofsy, S. C., McElroy, M. B., Valois, F. W. and Watson, S. W. (1980) Production of NO_2 and N_2O by nitrifying bacteria at reduced concentrations of oxygen. *Applied Environmental Microbiology* 40: 526–32.

Gornitz, V., Lebedeff, S. and Hansen, J. (1982) Global sea level trend in the past century. *Science* 215: 1611–14.

Gottleib, Otto R. (1981) New and underutilized plants in the Americas: solution to problems of inventory through systematics. *Interciencia* 6(1): 22–9.

Goulding, M. (1980) *The Fishes and the Forest, Explorations in Amazonian Natural History.* University of California Press, Berkeley.

Governo do Estado do Pará (1981) *Próvárzeas Pará (Programa de Aproveitamento Racional de Várzeas),* Secretaria de Estado de Agricultura, Comissão Estadual de Planejamento Agricola do Pará, Belém.

Greis, E. W. (1979) Trombetas and other deposits of Amazon basin bauxites (Brazil). *Trans. Amer. Inst. Min. Metal. Pet. Eng., Soc. Min. Eng.*

Grobecker, A. J., Coroniti, S. C. and Cannon, R. H. Jr. (1974) *The Effects of Stratospheric Pollution by Aircraft. Report of Findings. Executive Summary.* National Technical Information Service; Springfield, Virginia.

Gross, D. R. (1975) Protein capture and cultural development in the Amazon Basin. *American Anthropologist* 77(3): 526–49.

—— (1979) Getting to the frontier. *Journal of Development Studies.* 16(1): 99–112.

Guimarães, G. (1976) *Introdução da cultura de arroz irrigado no Maranhão,* Secretário da Agricultura, São Luis.

Guyot, M. (1971) Recherches ethnographiques dans les bassins des rios Caquetá et Putumayo, Amazonie colombienne: les Bora (Compte rendu de mission). *Journal de la Société des Américanistes* 58: 275–83.

—— (1974) La maison des indiens Bora et Miraña (Études sur la territoire et l'habitat dans l'ouest amazonien). *Journal de la Société des Américanistes* 61: 141–76.

—— (1975a) Le système culturel Bora-Miraña. In Centlivres, P. (ed.), *Culture sur brulis et évolution de milieu forestier en Amazonie de nord-ouest* (pp. 93–109). Geneva, Musée d'Ethnographie.

—— (1975b) Mission chez les Indiens Bora et Miraña (Amazonie colombienne, 1969–70). In *Amazonie Nord-Ouest* (pp. 17–28). Musée d'Ethnographie, Neuchatel, Switzerland.

Haines, Bruce L. (1983) Forest ecosystem SO_4-S input-output discrepancies and acid rain: are they related? *Oikos* 41(1): 139–43.

Haines, Bruce L. *et al.* (1983) Acid rain in an Amazon rainforest. *Tellus* **35**B(1): 77–80.

Hallsworth, E. G. (ed.) (1982) *Socio-economic Effects and Constraints on Tropical Forest Management.* Wiley: New York.

Hames, R. B. (1979) Game depletion and hunting zone rotation among the Ye'kuana and Yanomamo of Amazonas, Venezuela. Paper presented at the XLIII International Congress of Americanists, Vancouver, B.C., 25 pp.

—— (1980) Monoculture, polyculture, and polyvariety in tropical forest swidden cultivation. Paper read at the 79th Annual Meeting of the American Anthropological Association, Washington, D.C., 7 December 1980.

Hampicke, U. (1977) Net transfer of carbon between the land biota and the atmosphere, induced by man. In Bolin, B., Degens, E. T., Kempe, S. and Ketner, P. (eds.) *The Global Carbon Cycle.* Scientific Committee on Problems of the Environment (SCOPE) No. 13 (pp. 219–36) Wiley: New York.

—— (1980) The role of the biosphere. In Bach, W., Pankrath, J. and Williams, J. (eds.) *Interactions of Energy and Climate* (pp. 149–69) Dordrecht, Reidel, F. R. Germany.

Hanbury-Tenison, R. (1973) *A Question of Survival for the Indians of Brazil.* Angus and Robertson: London.

Harris, D. R. (1971) The ecology of swidden cultivation in the Upper Orinoco rain forest, Venezuela. *The Geographical Review* **61**: 475–95.

Harris, David R. (1972) Swidden systems and settlement. In Ucko, P. J. *et al.* (eds.) *Man, Settlement, and Urbanism* (pp. 245–62). Gerald Duckworth: London.

Hart, R. D. (1980) A natural ecosystem analog approach to the design of a successional crop system for tropical forest environments. *Biotropica* **12** (Supplement, Tropical Succession).

Hartshorn, G. S. (1982) (?) Ecological implications of tropical plantation forestry. In Sedjo, R. A. and Radcliffe, S. J. (eds.) *Comparative Economics of Plantation Forests.* Resources for the Future: Washington. (In press).

Harwood, J. H. (1980) Pesquisas para produção de biogas na Amazônia. *Acta Amazônica* **10**(2) 402–9.

Harwood, R. R. (1979) *Small Farm Development: Understanding and Improving Farming Systems in the Humid Tropics*, Western Press: Boulder, Colorado.

Hébette, J. and Acevedo, R. (1979) Colonização para Quém? *Série Pesquisa* **1**(1): 1–173. Universidade Federal do Pará, Núcleo de Altos Estudos Amazônicos (NAEA), Belém.

Hecht, S. B. (1979) Spontaneous legumes in developed pastures of the Amazon and their forage potential. In Sánchez, P. A. and Tergas, L. E. (eds.) *Pasture Production in Acid Soils of the Tropics* (pp. 65–78) Centro Internacional de Agricultura Tropical: Cali, Colombia.

—— (1980a) Some Environmental Consequences of Conversion of Forest to Pasture in Eastern Amazônia. Berkeley: University of California, Department of Forestry, Ph.D. Dissertation.

——(1982a) Cattle ranching in the Amazon: analysis of a development strategy. Berkeley, Ca. Univ. California Geography Dept. (Dissertation).

—— (1982b) Deforestation in the Amazon Basin: magnitude, dynamics and soil resource effects. In Sutlive, V. H. *et al.* (eds.) *Deforestation in the Third World* (pp. 61–100). College of William and Mary, Studies in Third World Socs. 13: Williamsburg, Virginia.

—— (1982c) Agroforestry in the Amazon basin. In Hecht, S. B. (ed.) *Amazonia: Agriculture*

196 · Man's impact on forests and rivers

and Land Use Research (pp. 331–72). (CIAT 1980 Conf.): University of Missouri Press; Columbia.
—— (ed.) (1982d) Amazonia: Agriculture and Land use Research. (CIAT 1980 Conf.). University of Missouri Press: Columbia.
—— (1983a) Ecology and agroforestry. International Tree Crops Journal (in press).
—— (1983b) Soil nutrient changes after converting forest to pasture. Biotropica (in press).
—— (1983c) The Environmental effect of cattle development in the Amazon basin. In Schmink, M. and Wood, C. H. H. (eds.) Frontier Expansion in Amazonia Gainsville, Fla. (ms).
—— (1983d) Pasture development in the Amazon. In Moran, E. F. (ed.) The Dilemma of Amazon Development. Westview Press: Boulder, Colorado.
Henderson-Sellers, A. (1981) The effect of land clearance and agricultural practices upon climate. Studies in Third World Societies 14: 443–85.
Herrera, R., Jordan, C. F., Klinge, H. and Medina, E. (1978) Amazon ecosystems: their structure and functioning with particular emphasis on nutrients. Interciencia 3(4): 223–32.
Herrera, R., Jordan, C. F., Medina, E. and Klinge, H. (1981) How human activities disturb the nutrient cycles of a tropical rainforest in Amazonia. Ambio 10(2–3): 109–14.
Herrera, R., Merida, T., Stark, N. and Jordan, C. F. (1978) Direct phosphorus transfer from leaf litter to roots through mycorrhizal connections. Naturwissenschaften 65: 208–9.
Humboldt, F. W. H. A. von et al. (1822). Nova genera et species plantarum 5, 117–18. Paris.
Hunter, R. J. (1969) The lack of acceptance of the pejibaye palm and a relative comparison of its productivity to that of maize. Economic Botany 23: 237–45.
Hyndman, D. C. (1982) Biotope gradient in a diversified New Guinea subsistence system. Human Ecology 10: 219–59.
IBASE (1983). Carajás: O Brasil Hipoteca seu Futuro. Achiame: Rio de Janeiro.
IBDF (1977) Polo Carajás: inventário florestal de reconhecimento. IBDF: Belém, I.
—— (1980) Programa de monitoramento da cobertura florestal do Brasil: Relatório do projeto desmatamento (Amazônia Brasileira). IBDF: Brasília. INPE/1649/RPE/103.
—— (1977) Geografia do Brasil (Vol. 1: Região Norte), Fundação Instituto Brasileiro de Geografia e Estatística (IBGE).
IBGE (1981) Programa Grande Carajás (Atlas). Rio de Janeiro, IBGE/CNRD/INCRA.
IDESP (1966) Pará e a cultura do arroz, Instituto de Desenvolvimento Económico – Social do Pará (IDESP), Belém.
—— (1972) Análise florestal de ucuúba numa área de várzea em Ponta de Pedras (Estudos Paraenses No. 37) Belém.
Idso, S. B. (1980a) The climatological significance of a doubling of earth's atmospheric carbon dioxide concentration. Science 207: 1462–3.
—— (1980b) Carbon dioxide and climate. Science 210: 6.
IPEAN (1972) Zoneamento agrícola da Amazônia. Belém, Boletim Técnico do IPEAN, 54.
Irion, G. (1976) Mineralogisch-geochemische Untersuchungen an der pelitischen Fraktion amazonischer Oberböden und Sedimente. Biogeographica 7: 7–25.
—— (1978) Soil Infertility in the Amazonian Rain Forest. Naturwissenschaften 65: 515–19.
Isto é (1982) Carajás: o avanço das obras, os debates, os investimentos e a vida no fantástico projeto amazonico. Isto é (April 4): 26–37.

IUCN (1975) *The Use of Ecological Guidelines for Development in the Amazon Humid Tropics*, Proceedings of the International Meeting, 20–22 Feb. 1974, Caracas, Venezuela. International Union for the Conservation of Nature and Natural Resources, New Series (No. 31): Morges, Switzerland.

Jacobs, M. (1980) Significance of the tropical rain forests on 12 points. *BioIndonesia* **7**: 75–94.

Janos, D. (1975) *Vesicular-Arbuscular Mycorrhizal Fungi and Plant Growth in a Costa Rican Lowland Rainforest*. (Ph.D. dissertation in biological sciences, University of Michigan, Ann Arbor, Michigan) University Microfilms International, Ann Arbor, Michigan.

Janzen, D. H. (1972) The uncertain future of the tropics. *Natural History* **81**: 80–90.

—— (1973) Tropical agroecoystems. *Science* **182**: 1212–19.

—— (1974a) Tropical blackwater rivers and mast fruiting by Dipterocarpaceae. *Biotropica* **6**: 69–73.

—— (1974b) The deflowering of Central America. *Natural History* **83**: 48–53.

—— (1976) Why bamboos wait so long to flower. *Annual Review of Ecology and Systematics* **7**: 347–91.

Jiménez Seminario, A. (1933) Breve estudio sobre la tribu Bora. *Revista Universitaria* (Cuzco) **22**: 173–91.

Johannessen, C. L. (1966) Pejibayes in commercial production. *Turrialba* **16**: 181–7.

Johnson, P. (1978) Land settlement: Amazonia – fighting the frontier fever, *Ceres*, **11**(4), 22–30.

Jordan, C. F. (1978) The environmental consequences of intensive forestry and the removal of whole trees from forests: the situation in Latin America. In Boyce, S. G. (ed.) *Biological and Sociological Basis for a Rational Use of Forest Resources for Energy and Organics* (pp. 141–8) USDA SE Forest Exper. Station, Asheville, North Carolina.

—— (1979) Stem flow and nutrient transfer in a tropical rain forest. *Oikos* **31**: 255–68.

—— (1980) Nutrient leaching from agro-ecosystems in the Amazon basin, and implications for recovery of the forest. In Furtado, J. I. (ed.) *Tropical Ecology and Development* (pp. 533–59) Int. Soc. Trop. Ecol.: Kuala Lumpur.

—— (1982a) Amazon rain forests. *American Scientist* **70**: 394–401.

—— (1982b) The nutrient balance of an Amazonian rain forest. *Ecology* **63**: 647–54.

—— (1982c) Nutrient cycling index of an Amazonian rain forest. *Acta Oecologica* **3**(3): 393–400.

Jordan, C. F. and Escalante, E. (1980) Root productivity in an Amazonian rain forest. *Ecology* **61**: 14–18.

Jordan, C. F., Golley, F. B., Hall, J. D. and Hall, J. (1980) Nutrient scavenging of rainfall by the canopy of an Amazonian rain forest. *Biotropica* **12**: 61–6.

Jordan, C. F. and Herrera, R. (1981) Tropical rain forests: are nutrients really critical? *Amer. Nat.* **117**(2): 167–80.

—— (1983) Biogeochemical cycles of tropical rainforests. In Knox, G. A. (ed.) *Ecoystem Theory and Application*. Wiley: London. (In press).

Jordan, C. F. and Heuveldop, J. (1981) The water budget of an Amazonian rain forest. *Acta Amazonica* **11**: 87–92.

Jordan, C. F. and Stark, N. (1978) Retención de nutrientes en la estera de raices de un bosque pluvial Amazónico. *Acta Científica Venezolano* **29**: 263–7.

Jordan, C. F. and Todd, R. L. and Escalante, G. (1979) Nitrogen conservation in a tropical rain forest. *Oecologia* **39**: 123–8.

Jordan, C. F. and Uhl, C. (1978) Biomass of a 'terra firme' forest of the Amazon basin. *Oecologia Plantarum* **13**: 387–400.

—— (1981) *Nutrient Dynamics of Slash and Burn Agriculture in the Amazon Basin.* Inst. of Ecology, Athens, Georgia. (In press) ms.

Jorge Padua, M. T. (1981) Situação atual do sistema de parques nacionais e reservas biológicas. Rio de Janeiro, *Bull. Fed. Bras. Conserv. Nat.* **16**: 35–41.

Junk, W. J. (1970) Investigations on the ecology and production-biology of the 'floating meadows' (*paspaloechinochloellum*) on the middle Amazon. I. The floating vegetation and its ecology, *Amazoniana*, **2**(4), 449–94.

—— (1975) Aquatic wildlife and fisheries. In IUCN *The Use of Ecological Guidelines for Development in the Amazonian Humid Tropics*, (Proc. International Meeting, Caracas, Venezuela, 20–22 Feb. 1974) (pp. 109–25). IUCN New Series, No. 31, Morges, Switzerland.

—— (1979) *Macrófitas aquáticas nas várzeas da Amazônia e possibilidades do seu uso na agropecuária*, INPA, Manaus.

—— (1980) Aquatic macrophytes: Ecology and use in Amazonian Agriculture. In Furtado, J. I. (ed.) *Tropical Ecology and Development*, Proceedings of Vth International Symposium of Tropical Ecology, 16–21 April 1979, Kuala Lumpur, Malaysia (pp. 763–70). The International Society of Tropical Ecology: Kuala Lumpur.

Junk, W. J. and Furch, K. (1980) Water chemistry and macrophytes of creeks and rivers in Southern Amazonia and the Central Brazilian Shield: *Proc. Vth Int. Symp. Tropical Ecology* (pp. 771–96). Kuala Lumpur.

Junqueira, M. R. de A. (1972) *Desarollo y perspectivas de la estura económica de juta em Amazonas*, IICA-CIRA, Bogotá, (M.A. Thesis).

Kaoru Tanaka (1957) Japanese immigrants in Amazonia and their future, *Kobe University Economic Review*, **3**: 1–23 (in English).

Katzer, Fr. (1903) *Grundzüge der Geologie des unteren Amazonasgebietes (des Staates Pará in Brasilien).* Max Weg: Leipzig.

Katzman, M. T. (1976) Paradoxes of Amazonian development in a 'resources starved' world, *The Journal of Developing Areas*, **10**: 445–60.

Keller, M. (1982) *Nitrous oxide biogeochemistry: a study in northern hardwood forests.* B.A. honours thesis in geological sciences, Harvard University, Cambridge, Mass.

Kempton, Willett, (1978) Category grading and taxonomic relations: a mug is a sort of a cup. *American Ethnologist* **5**: 44–65.

Kerr, R. A. (1982) CO_2 – climate models defended. *Science* **217**: 620.

Kerr, W. E. and Clement, C. R. (1980) Práticas agrícolas de conseqüências genéticas que possibilitaram aos índios de Amazônia uma melhor adaptação às condições ecológicas da região. *Acta Amazônica* **10**(2): 251–61.

Kerr, W. E., Posey, D. A. and Wolter Filho, W. (1978) Cupa, ou cipó babâo, alimento de alguns índios amazónicas. *Acta Amazônica* **8**(4): 702–5.

King, K. F. S. and Chandler, M. T. (1978) *The Wasted Lands: The Program of Work of the ICRAF.* International Council for Research in Agroforestry, Nairobi.

Klee, G. (ed.) (1980) *World Systems of Traditional Resource Management.* Halstead Press: New York.

Klein, O., Cordeiro, M., Madeira, L. C. L., da Rocha, M. A. and Dantas, M. (1983) *Salvar Carajás*. L & PM Editores: Pôrto Alegre.

Kleinpenning, J. M. G. (1973) *Brazilië*. Roermond. Panorama van de Wereld.

—— (1977) An evaluation of the Brazilian policy for the integration of the Amazon Region (1964–1974). In *Tijdschrift voor Economische en Sociale Geografie*, LXVIII, 5, pp. 297–311.

—— (1978) A further evaluation of the policy for the integration of the Amazon Region (1974–1976). In *Tijdschrift voor Economicsche en Sociale Geografie*, LXIX, 1–2, pp. 78–86.

Kleinschmidt, O. (1930) *Naturwissenschaft und Glaubenserkenntnis*. Martin Warneck: Berlin.

Klinge, H. (1973a) Root mass estimation in lowland tropical rain forests of Central Amazonia, Brazil. I. Fine root masses of a pale yellow latosol and a giant humus podsol. *Trop. Ecol.* **14**: 29–38.

—— (1973b) Struktur und Artenreichtum des zentralamazonischen Regenwaldes. *Amazoniana* **4**: 283–92.

—— (1976) Bilanzierung von Hauptnährstoffen im Ökosystem tropischer Regenwald (Manaus). Vorläufige Daten. *Biogeographica* **7**: 59–77.

Klinge, H. and Fittkau, E. J. (1972) Filterfunktionen im Ökosystem des zentralamazonischen Regenwaldes. *Mitt. Dtsch. Bodenkundl. Ges.* **16**: 130–5.

Kohlepp, G. (1980) Analysis of state and private regional development projects in the Brazilian Amazon basin. *Applied Geography and Development* **16**: 53–79.

Krahe, P. R. (1977) A Amazônia em face da crise energética. *Acta Amazônica* **7**(4): 443–8.

—— (1978) *Aripuanã: an Experiment in Energy Self-sufficiency in the Tropical Jungle*. INPA: Manaus, (ms).

Kramer, F. (1933) De natuurlijke verjonging in het Goenoeng-Gedehcomplex. *Tectona* **26**: 156–85.

Krugman, H. (1981) The German–Brazilian nuclear deal. *Bull. Atomic Sci.* (Feb): 32–6.

Kuhlmann, E. (1977) Vegetação. In *Geografia do Brasil: Região Norte*. Vol. I (pp. 59–94) IBGE: Rio de Janeiro.

Kukla, G. and Gavin, J. (1981) Summer ice and carbon dioxide. *Science* **214**: 497–503.

Lamb, R. (1980) Save the rainforests. *IUCN Bulletin* **11**(5): 17–32 (whole issue).

Landau, G. D. (1980) The treaty for Amazonian cooperation: a bold new instrument for development. *Georgia Journal of International and Comparative Law*, **10**(3): 463–89.

Lanly, J. P. and Clement, J. (1979) *Present and Future Forest and Plantation Areas in the Tropics*. FAO: Rome. Misc/79/1.

Lathrap, Donald (1968) Aboriginal occupation and changes in river channel on the central Ucayali, Peru. *American Antiquity* **33**: 62–79.

—— (1970) *The Upper Amazon*. Thames and Hudson: London.

Ledec, G. (1983) The political economy of tropical deforestation. In Leonard, J. (ed.) *The Politics of Environment and Development*. (In press).

Leopoldo, P. R., Franken, W., Matsui, E. and Salati, E. (1982a) Estimativa de evapotranspiração de floresta amazônica de terra firme. *Acta Amazônica* **12**(3) suplemento: 23–8.

Leopoldo, P. R., Franken, W. and Salati, E. (1982b) Balanço hídrico de pequena bacia hidrográfica em floresta amazônica de terra firme. *Acta Amazônica* **12**(3) suplemento: 7–13.

Leovy, C. W. (1980) Carbon dioxide and climate. *Science* **210**: 7.

Leslie, A. J. (1980) Logging concessions: how to stop losing money. *Unasylva* **32**(129): 2–7.

Lettau, H., Lettau, K. and Molion, L. C. B. (1979) Amazonia's hydrologic cycle and the role of atmospheric recycling in assessing deforestation effects. *Monthly Weather Review* **107**(3): 227–38.

Lian, M. S. and Cess, R. D. (1977) Energy balance climatic models: a reappraisal of ice-albedo feedback. *Journal of the Atmospheric Sciences* **34**: 1058–62.

Libonati, V. F. (1958) A juta na Amazônia, *Bol. Técnico do Instituto Agronômico do Norte, Belém.* (No. 34).

Lima, R. R. (1956) *A Agricultura nas Várzeas do Etuario do Amazonas*, Bol. Tec. do Instituto Agronômico do Norte, Belém. (No. 33).

Linares, O. F. (1976) Garden hunting in the American tropics. *Human Ecology* **4**(4): 331–50.

List, R. J. (1958) *Smithsonian Meteorological Tables.* Smithsonian Institution: Washington DC.

Lopes, A. de M., Cruz, E. de S., and Kass, D. L. (1973) Respostas do Arroz 'Adura' a adulação NPK, sob regime de irrigação natural (várzea do Rio Caeté – Municipio de Bragança – Pará), *INPEAN – Belém Communicado Técnico (No. 14)*, Belém.

Loucks, O. L. (1980) In Schmitt, L. E. (ed.) *Proceedings of the Carbon Dioxide and Climate Research Program Conference* April 24–25, 1980. The Institute for Energy Analysis/Oak Ridge Associated Universities: Washington DC.

Lovejoy, T. E. (1973) The Transamazonica: highway to extinction? *Frontiers* 1973 (Spring): 25–30.

——(1982a) Biological Diversity and Society. In *Proceedings of the U.S. Strategy Conference on Biological Diversity* (pp. 48–52) publication 9262 (Washington D.C., U.S. Department of State).

——(1982b) Designing refugia for tomorrow. In Prance, G. L. (ed.) *The Biological Model* (pp 673–80). Columbia University Press: New York.

Lovejoy, T. E. and Schubart, H. O. R. (1980) The ecology of Amazonian development. In *Land, People and Planning in Contemporary Amazônia.* Barbira-Scazzocchio, F. (ed.). Centre for Latin American Studies: Cambridge University.

Lowie, Robert (1948) The tropical forests: an introduction. In Stewart, J. H. (ed.) *Handbook of South American Indians* Bureau of American Ethnology Bulletin No. 143, Vol. 3: Washington D.C.

Lugo, A. E. and Brown, S. (1980) Tropical forests: sources or sinks of atmospheric carbon? *Unasylva* **32**(129): 8–13.

—— (1980–1) Tropical ecosystems and the human factor. *Unasylva* **33**(133): 45–52.

—— (1981) Tropical lands: popular misconceptions. *Mazingira* (UNEP) 5/2: 10–26.

—— (1982) Conversion of tropical moist forests: a critique. *Interciencia* **7**(2): 89–93.

Lyon, Patricia J. (1981) An imaginary frontier: prehistoric highland–lowland interchange in the southern Peruvian Andes. In *Networks of the Past: Regional Interaction in Archaeology.* Chacmool: Calgary, Alberta.

McDonald, D. R. (1977) Food Taboos: A Primitive Environmental Protection Agency (South America). *Antropolos* **2**: 734–47.

McElroy, M. B., Elkins, J. W., Wofsy, S. C. and Yung, Y. L. (1976) Sources and sinks for atmospheric N₂O. *Review of Geophysics and Space Research* **14**: 143.

McGregor, D. F. M. (1980) An investigation of soil erosion in the Colombian rainforest zone. *Catena* **7**: 265–73.

McNeil, M. (1964) Lateritic soils. *Scientific American* **211**(5): 86–102.

Magalhães Filho, J. C. (1960) Algumas considerações geográficas sobre o formador principal do rio Amazonas. *Revista Brasileira de Geografia* IBGE: Rio de Janeiro. **22**(1): 99–114.

Mahar, Dennis J. (1978) *Desenvolvimento Econômico da Amazônia: uma Análise das Políticas Governamentais.* IPEA/INPES, No. 30, Rio de Janeiro.

—— (1979) *Frontier Development Policy in Brazil: A Study of Amazonia,* Praeger: New York.

—— (1982) Development of the Brazilian Amazon: prospects for the eighties (ms: 9p). In Moran, E. F. (ed.) *The Dilemma of Amazonian Development.* Westview Press: Boulder, Colorado. (In press).

—— (1983) Public international lending institutions and the development of the Brazilian Amazon: the experience of the World Bank. In Schmink, M. and Wood, C. M. (eds.). *Frontier Expansion in Amazonia* Gainesville, Florida. (ms).

Malafaia, M. A., Rosas, E. de A., and Silva, J. L. (1969) *Destaque sobre a cultura do arroz no Estado Amazonas,* Ministério da Agricultura, Directoria Estadual do Amazonas, Grupo Executivo de Estatística, Análise e Estudos Económicas, Manaus, (*mimeo.*).

Manabe, S. and Stouffer, R. J. (1979) A CO₂-climate sensitivity study with a mathematical model of global climate. *Nature* **282**: 491–3.

Manabe, S. and Wetherald, R. T. (1967) Thermal equilibrium of the atmosphere with a given distribution of relative humidity. *Journal of the Atmospheric Sciences* **24**: 241–59.

—— (1975) The effects of doubling the CO₂ concentration on the climate of a general circulation model. *Journal of the Atmospheric Sciences* **32**: 3–15.

Manners, H. I. (1981) Ecological succession in new and old swiddens of montane Papua New Guinea. *Human Ecology* **9**: 359–77.

Marlier, G. (1973) Limnology of the Congo and Amazon Rivers. In Meggers, B. J. *et al. Tropical Forest Ecosystems in Africa and South America: A Comparative Review* (pp 223–38) Smithsonian Institution Press: Washington DC.

Marques, J., Salati, E. and Santos, J. M. dos (1980a) A divergência do campo do fluxo de vapor d'água e as chuvas na Região Amazônica. *Acta Amazonica* **101**: 133–40.

—— (1980b) Cálculos da evapotranspiração real na Bacia Amazônica através do método aerológico. *Acta Amazonica* **10**(2): 357–61.

Marques, J., Santos, J. M. dos and Salati, E. (1979a) O campo do fluxo de vapor d'água atmosférico sobre a região Amazônica. *Acta Amazonica* **9**(4): 701–13.

—— (1979b) O armazenamento atmosférico de vapor d'água sobre a região Amazônica. *Acta Amazônica* **9**(4): 715–21.

Marques, J., Santos, J. M. dos, Villa Nova, N. A. and Salati, E. (1977) Precipitable water and water vapour flux between Belém and Manaus. *Acta Amazonica* **7**(3): 355–62.

Marshall, E. (1981) By flood, if not by fire, CEQ says. *Science* **211**: 463.

Martine, G. (1980) Recent colonization experiences in Brazil: expectations versus reality. In Barbira-Scazzocchio, F. (ed.) *Land, People and Planning in Contemporary Amazonia* (pp. 80–94). Centre for Latin American Studies: Cambridge University.

—— (1982) Expansão e retração do emprêgo na fronteira agrícola. In Mueller, G. and Gligo,

N. (eds.) *Expansão da fronteira agropecuária* (Vol. II. p. 50) Univ. Brasília, Dept. Econ. 2 vols.

Martino, O. (1980) The mineral industry of Brazil. U.S. Bureau of Mines, *Mineral Yearbook* III: 163–81.

Maugh II, T. H. (1982) New link between ozone and cancer. *Science* **216**: 396–7.

Maybury-Lewis, David (1974) *Akwè-Shavante Society*. Oxford University Press: New York.

Medina, E. (1978) O futuro da bacia Amazônica. *Interciência* **3**(4): 196–9.

—— (1980) The Amazonian Pact: a general analysis. (58–71). In Barbira-Schazzochio, F. (ed.). *Land, People and Planning in Contemporary Amazonia* (pp. 58–71). Centre for Latin American Studies: Cambridge University.

Medina, E., Herrera, R., Jordan, C. F. and Klinge, H. (1977) The Amazon project of the Venezuelan Institute for Scientific Research. *Nature and Resources* **23**(4): 4–6.

Meggers, B. J. (1971) *Amazonia: Man and Culture in a Counterfeit Paradise*. Aldine: Chicago.

—— (1977) *Amazonia a Ilusão de um Paraíso*. Giv. Brasiliera: Rio de Janeiro.

Mergen, F. (ed.) (1981) *Tropical Forests: Utilization and Conservation*. Yale University Press: New Haven, Connecticut.

Mermel, T. W. (1982) *Major dams of the world. Water Power and Dam Constr.* (May): 93–104.

Minter (1982) Dez anos de consciência ecológica. Brasília, *Rev. Bimestral Minter* **8**(44): 58.

Miyazaki, N. E. and Morio, O. O. (1958) O aviamento na Amazonia (Estudio sócio-economico sobre a produçao de juta), *Sociologia*, xx(3): 366–96; (4): 530–63.

Molion, L. C. B. (1975) *A climatonomic study of the energy and moisture fluxes of the Amazonas Basin with considerations of deforestation effects*. Ph.D. dissertation in climatology, University of Wisconsin, Madison, Wisc.

Möller, F. (1963) On the influence of changes in the CO_2 concentration in air on the radiation balance of the earth's surface and on the climate. *Journal of Geophysical Research* **68**: 3877–86.

Mongi, H. O. and Huxley, P. A. (eds.) (1979) *Soils Research in Agroforestry*. Int. Cent. Res. Agroforestry: Nairobi.

Montague, Jerome J. (1981) His 'crop' in crocodiles. *International Wildlife* **11**(2): 21–8.

Monteiro, S. T. (1979) Migrações no Médio Amazonas (um pequeno ensaio sobre suas causas) *Perspectiva*, Ano. IV(11), 60–87 & appendices.

—— (nd) Anotações para uma história rural do médio Amazonas, *mimeograph*, EMATER-Amazonas, Manaus.

Moore, B., Boone, R. D., Hobbie, J. E., Houghton, R. A., Melillo, J. M. Peterson, B. J., Shaver, G. R. Vörösmarty, C. J. and Woodwell, G. M. (1981) A simple model for analysis of the role of terrestrial ecosystems in the global carbon budget. In Bolin, B. (ed.) *Carbon Cycle Modeling* (pp 356–85). Scientific Committee on Problems of the Environment (SCOPE) No. 16. Wiley: New York.

Moran, Emilio F. (1974) The adaptive system of the Amazonia caboclo. In *Man in the Amazon*. Wagley, Charles (ed.) University of Florida Press: Gainesville.

—— (1975) *Pioneer farmers of the Transamazon Highway: adaptation and agricultural production in the lowland tropics*, Ph.D. Thesis, University of Florida, Gainesville.

—— (1981a) *Developing the Amazon*. Indiana University Press: Bloomington.

—— (1981b) Mobility and resource use in Amazônia. In *Land, People and Planning in Contemporary Amazônia*. Barbira-Scazzocchio, F. (ed.) Centre for Latin American Studies: Cambridge University.

—— (1983a) Colonization in the Transamazon and Rondonia. In Schmink, M. and Wood, C. M. (eds.) *Frontier Expansion in Amazonia* Gainesville, Fla. (ms).

—— (ed.) (1983b) *The Dilemma of Amazonian Development*. Westview Press: Boulder, Colorado. (In press).

Mueller, C. (1980) Frontier based agricultural expansion: the case of Rondônia. In Barbira-Schazzochio, F. (ed.) *Land, People and Planning in Contemporary Amazonia* (pp. 141–53). Centre for Latin American Studies: Cambridge University.

Mueller, C. and Gligo, N. (eds.) (1982) *Expansão da fronteira agropecuaria e meio ambiente na América Latina*. Univ. Brasília, Dept. Economia: 2 vols.

Myers, N. (1976) An expanded approach to the problem of disappearing species. *Science* **193**: 198–202.

—— (1979) *The Sinking Ark: a New Look at the Problem of Disappearing Species*. Pergamon: New York.

—— (1980) *Conversion of Tropical Moist Forests*. National Academy of Sciences: Washington DC.

—— (1982) Deforestation in the Tropics: Who Wins, Who Loses. In Sutlive, Vinson, H., *et al.* (eds.). *Where Have All the Flowers Gone? Deforestation in the Third World* (pp. 1–24). Studies in Third World Societies No. 13, College of William and Mary: Williamsburg, Virginia.

—— (1981a) Aboriginal trade networks in Amazônia. In Francis, P. D., Kense, F. J. and Duke, P. G. (eds.) *Networks of the Past: Regional Interaction in Archaeology*. Chacmool: Calgary.

—— (1981b) Ethnic composition and settlement patterns on the Amazon at the time of contact. A paper given at the Annual Meeting, American Society for Ethnohistory, Colorado Springs, Colorado.

—— (1983) *A Wealth of Wild Species: Storehouse for Human Welfare*. Westview Press: Boulder, Colorado.

Myers, Thomas (1973) Toward reconstruction of prehistoric community patterns in the Amazonian Basin. In Lathrop, D. and Douglas J. (eds.) *Variations in Anthropology*. Illinois Archaeological Survey: Urbana.

—— (1974) Spanish contacts and social change on the Ucayali River, Perú. *Ethnohistory* **21**(2): 135–57.

National Academy of Sciences (1975) *Underexploited Tropical Plants with Promising Economic Value*. Washington DC.

—— (1982a) *Ecological Aspects of Development in the Humid Tropics*. Washington DC.

—— (1982b) *Carbon Dioxide and Climate: a Second Assessment*. Washington DC.

Nations, J. D. and Nigh, R. B. (1978) Cattle, cash, food and forest: the destruction of the American tropics and the Lacandon Maya alternative. *Culture and Agriculture* (Davis, Cal.) **6**:1–5.

Newell, R. E. and Dopplick, T. G. (1979) Questions concerning the possible influence of anthropogenic CO_2 on atmospheric temperature. *Journal of Applied Meteorology* **18**: 822–5.

Nicholaides III, J. J., Bandy, D. E., Sánchez, P. A. and Valvede, S. C., (1982) Continuous cropping potential in the Amazon. Paper presented at the Conference on *'Frontier Expansion in Amazonia'*, Center for Latin American Studies, University of Florida, Gainesville, Florida, February 8–11, 1982. (ms).

Nigh, R. B. and Nations, J. D. (1980) Tropical rainforests. *The Bulletin of the Atomic Scientists* **36**(3): 12–19.

Nimer, E. (1977) Clima. In *Geografia do Brasil: Região Norte* (Vol. I pp. 39–58). IBGE, Rio de Janeiro.

Noda, H., Junk, W. J. and Pahlen, A. (1978) Emprêgo de macrofitas aquaticas ('Matupa') como fonte de materia orgánica na cultura de feijão-de-asa (*Psophocarpus tetragonolobus*) em Manaus. *Acta Amazônica* **8**(1): 107–9.

Nordin, C. F. and Meade, R. H. (1982) Deforestation and increased flooding of the Upper Amazon. *Science* **215**: 426–7.

Norgaard, R. B. (1981) Sociosystem and ecosystem coevolution in the Amazon. *Journ. Environmental Economics and Management* **8**(3): 238–54.

North Carolina State University, Soil Science Department (1974–8) *Agronomic-Economic Research on Tropical Soils*. Annual Reports for 1974–8. North Carolina State University, Raleigh, 4 vols.

Nye, P. H. and Greenland, D. J. (1960) *The Soil under Shifting Cultivation* Commonwealth Agricultural Bureaux of Soils, Technical Communication No. 51 Harpenden, U.K.

Odum, H. T. (1968) *Hydrogen budget and compartments in the rain forest at El Verde, Puerto Rico, pertinent to consideration of tritium metabolism*. IOCS memorandum BMI-2.

Ojasti, J. (1980) Ecology of capybara raising on inundated savannas of Venezuela. In Furtado, J. I. (ed.), *Tropical Ecology and Development*, (pp. 287–93). The International Society of Tropical Ecology, Kuala Lumpur.

Oldfield, M. L. (1981) Tropical deforestation and genetic resources conservation. *Studies in Third World Societies* **14**: 277–345.

Oltman, R. E., Sternberg, H. O'R., Ames, F. C. and Davis, Jr, L. C. (1964) *Amazon River Investigations Reconnaissance Measurements of July*. U.S. Geol. Surv. Circ. 486.

OMM (1967) *Guia de práticas hidrometeorológicas*. Publicação OMM no. 168. TP. 82. Geneva.

ONERN (1976) *Inventario, evaluación e integración do los recursos naturales de la zona Iquitos, Nauta, Requena y Colonia Angamos*. Oficina Nacional de Evaluación de Recursos Naturales, Lima.

Oración, T. (1963) Kaingin agriculture among the Bukidnond of south eastern Negros, Philippines. *Tropical Geography* **17**: 213–24.

Paiva, G. de (1979) *Mineral Resources of Amazonia*. Rio de Janeiro, Assoc. Nacional Program. Econ. Social.

—— (1980a) Declarada a guerra ecológica na Amazônia. *Natureza* **16**: 152–65.

—— (1980b) *The Economic Significance of the Amazonian Forest* (March 3) Rio de Janeiro (ms).

Palmer, J. R. (1977) Forestry in Brazil – Amazonia. *Commonwealth For. Rev.* **56**(2): 115–31.

Pandolfo, Clara (1978) *A Floresta Amazônica Brasileira – Enfoque Económico-Ecológico*. Superintendência do Desenvolvimento da Amazônia (SUDAM): Belém.

—— (1979a) *A Amazônia Brasileira e suas Potencialidades*, Ministério do Interior,

Superintendência do Desenvolvimento da Amazônia (SUDAM), Departamento de Recursos Naturais, Belém, Pará.

—— (1979b) Bauxite, kaolin and clays in the Amazon region. São Paulo, *Ceramica* 25(109): 1–14.

Parker, Eugene (1981) Cultural ecology and change: A caboclo várzea community in the Brazilian Amazon. Ph.D. Dissertation, Department of Geography, University of Colorado, Boulder.

Parsons, J. J. (1976) Forest to pasture: development or destruction? *Rev. Biologia Tropical* 24(1): 121–38.

Peck, R. (1979) *Informe sobre o desenvolvimento de sistemas agrosilvo-pastoris na Amazônia.* EMBRAPA/IICA: Belém.

—— (1982) Forest research activities and the importance of multistrata production systems in the Amazon basin. In Hecht, S. B. (ed.) *Amazonia: Agriculture and Land Use Research* (pp. 373–86). University of Missouri, Columbia. (CIAT 1980 Conf.).

Pelzer, K. J. (1978) Swidden cultivation in Southeast Asia: historical, ecological, and economic perspectives. In Kunstadter, P., Chapman, E. C. and Sabhasri, S. (eds.), *Farmers in the Forest* (pp. 271–86). University Press of Hawaii: Honolulu.

Pendleton, R. A. (1956) The place of tropical soils in feeding the world. In *Smithsonian Report for 1955* (pp. 441–58). Smithsonian Institution: Washington DC

Penteado, A. R. (1967) *Problemas de colonização e de Uso da Terra na Região Bragantina do Estado do Pará.* Universidade Federal do Pará, Belém.

Pereira, H. C. (1962) The water balance of both treated and control valleys. *East African. Agric. and For. Jour. Special Issue* 27: 36–41.

—— (1967) Effects of land use on the water and energy budgets of tropical watersheds. In Sopper, W. E. and Lubl, H. W. (eds.) *Forest Hydrology* (pp. 435–50). Pergamon Press: Oxford.

Peterson, Norman E., Roberts, Donald E., Llewellyn, Craig H. and Pinheiro, Francisco P. (1981) Programa multidisciplinário de vigilencia de las enfermedades infecciosas en zonas colindantes con la carretera transamazónica en Brazil. *Bol. Oficina Sanitaria Panamericana* 91(2): 137–48.

Petrick, C. (1978) The complementary function of floodlands for agricultural utilization: the *várzeas* of the Brazilian Amazon region. *Applied Sciences and Development* 12: 24–46.

Pimentel, David (1979) *Increased CO$_2$ Effects on the Environment and in Turn on Agriculture and Forestry.* AAAS-DOE Workshop on Environmental and Societal Consequences of a Possible CO$_2$-Induced Climate Change. (Annapolis, Maryland).

Pimentel, David and Goodman, N. (1978) Ecological basis for the management of insect populations. *Oikos* 30: 422–37.

Pimentel, D., Levin, S. A. and Olson, D. (1978) Coevolution and the stability of exploiter–victim. *The American Naturalist* 112(983): 119–25.

Pinto, L. F. (1982) *Carajás: o ataque ao coração da Amazônia.* Editora Marco Zero: Rio de Janeiro.

Pirages, D. C. (ed.) (1977) *The Sustainable Society* Praeger: New York.

Pires, J. M. and Kourym, H. M. (1959) Estudio de um trecho de mata de várzea proximo de Belém. *Bol. Téc. Inst. Agron Norte*, Belém, 23: 1–63.

Pires, J. M. and Prance, G. T. (1977) The Amazon forest: a natural heritage to be preserved. In *Extinction is Forever* (pp. 158–94). New York Botanical Garden.

Plotkin, S. E. (1980) Energy from biomass *Environment* **22**(9): 6–40.

Plumwood, V. and Routley, R. (1982) World rainforest destruction: the social factors. *The Ecologist*: 4–22.

de Ponte, N. T., Moraes, V. H. F., Kass, D. L. and Anderson, S. D. (1977) *Cultura de Arroz em Várzea: I Trabalhos Experimentais em Igarapé-Miri, (Pará)*, DSP/SUDAM, Convênio SUDAM/FCAP – Belém.

Poore, M. E. D. (1976) The value of tropical moist forest ecosystems and the environmental consequences of their removal. *Unasylva* **28**(112/113): 127–43.

—— (1978) *Tropical Rain Forests and Moist Deciduous Forests: Sourcebook for a World Conservation Strategy*. Gland, IUCN GA. 78/10.

Popenoe, H. (1960) *Effects of shifting cultivation on natural soil constituents in Central America*. Ph.D. dissertation in agronomy, University of Florida, Gainesville, Florida.

Posey, Darrell A. (1976) Entomological considerations in southeastern aboriginal demography. *Ethnohistory* **23**(2): 147–60.

—— (1978) Ethnoentomological survey of Amerind groups in lowland Latin America. *Florida Entomologist* **61**(4): 225–9.

—— (1979a) Kayapó Controla Inseto com Uso Adequado do Ambiente. *Revista de Atualidade Indígena* **3**(14): 47–58.

—— (1979b) Kayapó Mostra Aldeia de Origem. *Revista de Atualidade Indígena* **3**(15): 50–7.

—— (1979c) Cisão dos Kayapó. *Revista de Atualidade Indígena* **3** (16): 52–8.

—— (1979d) Ethnoentomology of the Gorotire Kayapó of Central Brazil. Ph.D. dissertation, University of Georgia.

—— (1980) Algunas Observaciones Etnoentomológicas sobre Grupos Amerindos en la América Latina. *América Indígena* **15**(1): 105–20.

—— (1981a) Apicultura Popular dos Kayapó, *Revista de Atualidade Indígena* **20**(1): 36–41.

—— (1981b) Wasps, warriors and fearless men: ethnoentomology of the Kayapó Indians of Central Brazil. *Journal of Ethnobiology* **1**(1): 165–74.

—— (1981c) A typology of contact in the Amazon Basin. A paper given at the Annual Meeting, American Society of Ethnohistory, Colorado Springs, Colorado.

—— (1982a) The Keepers of the Forest. *Garden Magazine* (New York Botanical Garden): **6**(1): 18–24.

—— (1982b) The importance of bees to an Indian tribe of Amazonia. *Florida Entomologist* **5**(4): in press.

—— (1982c) O Conhecimento Entomológico Kayapó: Etnometodologia e Sistema Cultural. *Anuário Antropológico* **81**, in press.

—— (1982d) Indigenous ecological knowledge and development of the Amazon. In Moran, Emilio (ed.) *The Dilemma of Amazonian Development*. Westview Press: Boulder, Colorado.

—— (1982e) Time and space in divergent cultures: The Kayapó Indians face the future. *Revista Brasileira de Antropologia*, in press.

—— (1983a) Folk apiculture of the Kayapó Indians of Brazil. *Biotropica*. In press.

—— (1983b) Keeping of stingless Apidae by the Kayapó Indians of Brazil. *Journal of Ethnobiology*. In press.

—— (in press) Contact before contact. Typology of Post-Columbian Interaction with the Northern Kayapó of the Amazon Basin.

Posey, D. A., Frechione, J., Eddins, J., and Francelino da Silva, L. (in press a) Nuevas estrategias de raíces indígenas: Desarrollo en la Cuenca Amazónica.

Posey, D. A., Frechione, J., Eddins, J. and Francelino da Silva, L. (in press b) Ethnoecology as Applied Anthropology in Amazonian Development.

Posey, D. A., Frechione, J. and Francelino da Silva, L. (in press c) Folk Perceptions of Ecological Zones and Natural Resources in the Brazilian Amazon: Ethnoecology of Lake Coari.

Posey, J. W. and Clapp, P. F. (1964) Global distribution of normal surface albedo. *Geophysics International* **4**: 53–8.

Potter, G. L. Ellsaesser, H. W., MacCracken, M. C. and Luther, F. M. (1975) Possible climatic impact of tropical deforestation. *Nature* **258**: 697–8.

Prance, G. T. (1972) an ethnobotanical comparison of four tribes of Indians. *Acta Amazonica* **2**(2): 7–27.

—— (1973) The ethnobotanical diet of the Yanomamo Indians. *Mycologia* **65**: 248–50.

—— (1975) Flora and vegetation. In Goodland, R. J. A. and Irwin, H. S. (eds.) *Amazon Jungle: Green Hell to Red Desert? an Ecological Discussion of the Environmental Impact of the Highway Construction Program in the Amazon Basin* (pp. 101–11) Elsevier: New York.

—— (1978) The origin – and evolution of the Amazon flora. *Revista Interciência* **3**(4): 207–22.

—— (ed.) (1982a) *The Biological Model of Diversification in the Tropics*. Columbia University Press: New York.

—— (1982b) Forest refuges: evidence from woody angiosperms. In Prance, G. L. (ed.) *The Biological Model of Diversification in the Tropics* (pp. 137–56) Columbia University Press, New York.

Prance, G. T., Rodrigues, W. A. and da Silva, M. F. (1976) Inventário florestal de uma hectare de mata de terra firme, km 30 Estrada Manaus-Itacoatiara. *Acta Amazonica* **6**(1): 9–35.

Pyle, R. M. (1981) Butterflies: now you see them. *Defenders* (Jan–Feb): 4–10.

Ramanathan, V. (1981) The role of the ocean–atmosphere interaction in the CO_2 climate problem. *Journal of the Atmospheric Sciences* **38**: 918–30.

Ramos, A. R. (1980) Development, integration and the ethnic integrity of Brazilian Indians. In Barbira-Scazzocchio, F. (ed.) *Land, People and Planning in Contemporary Amazonia* (pp. 222–9). Centre of Latin American Studies Occasional Paper No. 3, Cambridge University.

Rappaport, R. A. (1967) *Pigs for the Ancestors: Ritual in the Ecology of a New Guinea People*. Yale University Press: New Haven, Connecticut.

—— (1969) Sanctity and adaptation. Working Paper for Wenner-Gren-Symposium 44: *The Moral and Aesthetic Structure of Human Adaptation*. Reprinted in: Io 7 (Febr. 1970) and in *Co-Evolution Quart*. **1**: 54–68.

—— (1971) The flow of energy in an agricultural society. *Scientific American*, 225.

Raven, P. A. (ed.) (1980) *Research Priorities in Tropical Biology*. National Academy of Sciences: Washington DC.

Reichel-Dolmatoff, Gerardo. (1971) *Amazonian Cosmos*. University of Chicago Press.

—— (1976) Cosmology as ecological analysis: A view from the rain forest. *Man* **11**(3): 307–18.

—— (1978) Desana animal categories, food restrictions, and the concept of color energies. *Journal of Latin American Lore* 4(2): 243–91.

Reis, Arthur Cézar Ferreira (1960) *A Amazônia e a Cobiça Internacional*, Companhia Editôra Nacional: Sâo Paulo.

Ribeiro, Darcy (1970) *Os Índios e a Civilização*. Ed. Civilização Brasileira.

Ribeiro, M. N. G. and Villa Nova, N. A. (1979) Estudos climatológicos da Reserva Ducke, Manaus, AM. III. Evapotranspiração. *Acta Amazonica* 9(2): 305–9.

Richards, P. W. (1952) *The Tropical Rain Forest*. Cambridge University Press.

Riddell, R. (1981) *Ecodevelopment: Economics, Ecology, Development*. Farnborough, U.K., Gower Publ.

Rodrigues, W. A. (1972) Á ucuúba de várzea e suas aplicações, *Acta Amazonica*, III(2) 20–47.

Roosevelt, A. C. (1980) *Parmana: Prehistoric Maize and Manioc Subsistence along the Amazon and Orinoco*. Academic Press: New York.

Rosenblat, Angel (1954) *La Población Indígena y el Mestizaje en América*. Editorial Nova: Buenos Aires.

Ross, Eric B. (1978a) Food taboos, diet, and hunting strategy: The adaptation to animals in Amazon cultural ecology. *Current Anthropology* 19(1): 1–16.

—— (1978b) The evolution of the Amazon peasantry. *Journal of Latin American Studies* 10(2): 193–218.

Ruderman, M. A. Foley, H. M. and Chamberlain, J. W. (1976) Eleven-year variation in polar ozone and stratospheric-ion chemistry. *Science* 192: 555–7.

Russell, C. E. (1983) Nutrient cycling and productivity of native and plantation forests at Jari Forestal, Pará, Brazil. Ph.D. dissertation, University of Georgia, Athens.

Russell, C. E., Jordan, C. F. and North, R. M. (1982) *Jari: A Lesson in Tropical Forestry*. University of Georgia, Institute of Ecology, (ms).

Russell, E. W. (1973) *Soil Conditions and Plant Growth, 10th edn* Longmans: London.

Sá, P. C. R. O. de (1982) Grande Carajás: tema para reflexão. *Rev. Bras. Tecnol.* (Brasília) 13(1): 31–43.

Sagan, C. Toon, O. B. and Pollack, J. B. (1979) Anthropogenic albedo changes and the earth's climate. *Science* 206: 1363–8.

St. John, T. and Alvim, P. de T. (1982? nd) *Soil Enrichment Brought about by Gmelina arborea Roxb. in an Amazonian Oxisol*. INPA: Manaus, (ms).

Salas, G. de las (ed.) (1979) *Workshop: Agro-forestry Systems in Latin America*. Turrialba, CATIE.

Salati, E. (1979) Floresta Amazónica e a concentração de gaz carbônico na atmosfera. *Suplemento Cultural do Estado de São Paulo* No. 130.

—— (1981) Floresta e clima da Amazônia. Rio de Janeiro, *Bull. Fed. Bras. Conserv. Nat.* 16: 120–35.

Salati, E., Dall'Olio, A., Matsui, E. and Gat, J. R. (1979) Recycling of water in the Amazon Basin: An isotopic study. *Water Resources Research* 15(5): 1250–8.

Salati, E., Marques, J. and Molion, L. C. B. (1978) Origem e distribuição das chuvas na Amazônia. *Interciencia* 3(4): 200–6.

Salati, E. and Ribeiro, M. de N. G. (1979) Floresta e Clima. *Acta Amazônica* 9(4) suplemento: 15–22.

Samstag, T. (1981) *The Times*, London, February 23rd 1981, p. 6.

Sánchez, P. A. (1976) *Properties and Management of Soils in the Tropics*. Wiley: New York.

Sánchez, P. A., Bandy, D. E., Villachica, J. H. and Nicholaides, J. J. III (1982) Amazon Basin soils: management for continuous crop productioin. *Science* **216**: 821–7.

Sánchez, P. A. and Buol, S. W. (1975) Soils of the tropics and the world food crisis. *Science* **188**: 598–603.

Sánchez, P. A. and Tergas, L. E. (eds) (1979) *Pasture Production in Acid Soils of the Tropics*. Cali, Colombia, CIAT.

Santos, B. A. (1981) *A Amazônia: Potência Mineral e Perspectivas de Desenvolvimento*. São Paulo.

Saunders, J. (1974) The population of the Brazilian Amazon today. In Wagley, Ch. (ed.) *Man in the Amazon* (pp. 160–80) Gainesville, Florida.

Schmidt, G. (1972) Chemical Properties of some Waters in the Tropical rainforest region of Central Amazonia. *Amazoniana* **3**: 199–207.

Schmink, M. (1982) Land conflicts in Amazonia. *American Ethnologist* **9**(2): 341–57.

Schmink, M. and Wood, C. H. (eds.) (1983) *Frontier Expansion in Amazonia*. Univ. Fla., Cent. Lat. Amer. Studies: Gainesville.

Schneider, S. H. Kellog, W. W. and Ramanathan, V. (1980) Carbon dioxide and climate. *Science* **210**: 6.

Schubart, H. O. R. (1977) Critérios ecológicos para o desenvolvimento agrícola das terra-firmes da Amazônia. *Acta Amazonica* **7**: 559–67.

—— (1981 nd) *Ecologia e Desenvolvimento na Área de Influência do Programa Grande Carajás*. Manaus, INPA (ms).

Schubart, H. O. R., Junk, W. J. and Petrere Jr, M. (1976) Sumário de ecologia Amazônica. *Ciência e Cultura* **28**(5): 507–9.

Schubart, H. O. R. and Salati, E. (1982) Natural resources for land use in the Amazon region: the natural systems. In Hecht, S. B. (ed.) *Amazonia: Agriculture and Land Use Research* (pp. 211–40) (CIAT 1980 conf.) University of Missouri Press: Columbia.

Schultes, R. E. (1980) The Amazonia as a source of new economic plants. *Economic Botany* **33**(3): 259–66.

Scott, G. A. J. (1975) Soil profile changes resulting from the conversion of forest to grassland in the Montaña of Peru. *Great Plains–Rocky Mountain Geographical Journal* **4**: 124–30.

—— (1978) *Grassland Development in the Gran Pajonal of Eastern Peru: A Study of Soil–Vegetation Nutrient Systems*. Hawaii Monographs in Geography, No. 1. Department of Geography, University of Hawaii at Manoa, Honolulu.

Secco, R. de S. and Mesquita, A. L. (1982) *Notas Sobre a Vegetação de Canga da Serra Norte I*. Museu Goeldi: Belém.

Sedjo, R. A. (1980) Forest plantations in Brazil and their possible effects on world pulp markets. *Journ. Forestry* **78**(1): 702–5.

Seiler, W. and Crutzen, P. J. (1980) Estimates of gross and net fluxes of carbon between the biosphere and the atmosphere from biomass burning. *Climatic Change* **2**: 207–47.

SEMA (1980) *Comité Especial de Estudos Integrados de Bacias Hidrográficas: CEEIBH*. Brasília, Secretário do Meio Ambiente/Electrobras/DNAEE.

Senado Federal (1981) *Simpósio Alternativas para Carajás*. Minas e Energia Económica: Brasília.

210 · Man's impact on forests and rivers

Seubert, C. E., Sánchez, P. A. and Valverde, S. (1977) Effects of land clearing methods on soil properties of an ultisol and crop performance in the Amazon jungle of Peru. *Tropical Agriculture* (Trindidad) **54**(4): 307–21.

Singer, R. (in press) The role of fungi in Amazonian Forests and in Reforestation. In Sioli, H. (ed.) *The Amazon. Limnology and Landscape Ecology of a Mighty Tropical River and its Basin*. Monographiae Biologicae, Dr. W. Junk, The Hague.

Sioli, H. (1950) Das Wasser im Amazonasgebiet. *Forsch. u. Fortschr.* **26**: 274–80.

—— (1954) Beiträge zur regionalen Limnologie des Amazonasgebietes. II. Der Rio Arapiuns. *Arch. f. Hydrobiol.* **49**: 448–518.

—— (1955) Beiträge zur regionalen Limnologie des Amazonasgebietes. III. Über einige Gewässer des oberen Rio Negro Gebietes. *Arch. f. Hydrobiol.* **50**: 1–32.

—— (1963) Beiträge zur regionalen Limnologie des Amazonasgebietes. V. Die Gewässer der Karbonstreifen Unteramazoniens (sowie einige Angaben über Gewässer der anschließenden Devonstreifen). *Arch. f. Hydrobiol.* **59**: 311–50.

—— (1972) Ökologische Aspekte der technisch-kommerziellen Zivilisation und ihrer Lebensform. *Biogeographica* **1**: 1–13.

—— (1973) Recent human activities in the Brazilian Amazon region and their ecological effects. In *Tropical Forest Ecosystems in Africa and South America* Meggers, Betty L., Ayensu, Edward S. and Duckworth, W. Donald (eds.) Smithsonian Institution: Washington DC.

—— (1975a) Problemas do aproveitamento da Amazônia. *A Amazônia Brasileira Em Foco (10)* (pp. 21–47). julho/junho 1974, Commissão Nacional de Defesa e pelo Desenvolvimento da Amazônia (CNDDA), Rio de Janeiro.

—— (1975b) Amazon tributaries and drainage basins. In Hasler, A. D. (ed.) *Coupling of Land and Water Systems* (pp. 199–213) Ecological Studies: Analysis and Synthesis, Vol. 11, Springer Verlag: Berlin.

—— (1980) Prospective efforts of actual development schemes on the ecology of the Amazon basin. In Furtado, J. I. (ed.) *Tropical Ecology and Development* (pp. 711–16) Proceedings of the Vth International Symposium of Tropical Ecology, 16–21 April 1979, Kuala Lumpur, Malaysia. The International Society of Tropical Ecology, Kuala Lumpur.

—— (1981) Foreseeable consequences of actual development schemes and alternative ideas. In Barbira-Scazzocchio, F. (ed.) *Land, People and Planning in Contemporary Amazonia* (pp. 257–68) Centre of Latin American Studies, Occas. Publ. 3, Cambridge University.

Skillings, D. N. (1981) CVRD Carajás iron ore project in Amazon region. *Skillings Mining Review* **70**(24): 12–24.

Skillings, R. F. and Tcheyan, N. O. (1979) *Economic Development Prospects of the Amazon Region of Brazil*. Johns Hopkins Univ., School Adv. Internat. Studies., Washington DC.

Smith, N. J. H. (1974) Destructive exploitation of the South American river turtle. From Yearbook of the Association of Pacific Coast Gegoraphers Vol. 36(c). Oregon State University Press.

—— (1977) Human exploitation of terra firme fauna in Amazonia. *Ciencia and Cultura* **30**(1): 17–23.

—— (1978) Agricultural productivity along Brazil's Transamazon Highway.

Agroecosystems **4**: 415–32.
—— (1979) *A Pesca no Rio Amazonas*. Manaus, INPA.
—— (1980) Anthrosols and human carrying capacity in Amazônia. *Annals of the Association of American Geographers* **70**(4): 553–66.
—— (1981) *Man, Fishes and the Amazon*. Columbia University Press: New York.
—— (1981b) *Man, Fishes and the Amazon*. Columbia University Press: New York.
—— (1982) *Rainforest Corridors: The Transamazon Colonization Scheme*. University of California: Berkeley.
Smithsonian Institution (1980) Interdependence of fish and trees in the Amazon River basin in Brazil, *Environmental Conservation* **7**(3): 228.
Smole, W. J. (1976) *The Yanoama Indians: A Cultural Geography*. University of Texas Press: Austin.
Soares, L. de C. (1977) Hidrografia. In *Geografia do Brasil: Região Norte* (Vol. I pp. 95–166). IBGE, Rio de Janeiro.
Soemarwoto, O. (1976) Ecology and health in Indonesian villages. *Ekistics* **41**(245): 235–9.
Sombroek, W. G. (1966) *Amazon Soils*. Centre f. Agricult. Public. and Documentation: Wageningen.
Soukup, J. (1970) *Vocabulario de los Nombres Vulgares de la Flora Peruana*. Colegio Salesiano: Lima.
Spears, J. S. (1979) Can the wet tropical forest survive? *Commonw. For. Rev* **58**(3): 165–80.
—— (1980a) Can farming and forestry coexist in the tropics? *Unasylva* **32**(128): 2–12.
—— (1980b) *Small Farmers – Or the Tropical Forest Ecosystem?* Washington DC. World Bank (ms).
Spectrum (1982) O projeto Grande Carajás. *Spectrum, Jornal Brasileiro de Ciências* **2**(7): 43.
Spurgeon, O. (1974) Sea Cows eat their way to domestication. *New Scientist* **63**: 238–9.
—— (1980) Agroforestry: a promising system of improved land management for Latin America. *Interciencia* **5**: 176–8.
Stallard, R. F. and Edmond, J. M. (1981) Geochemistry of the Amazon 1. Precipitation chemistry and the marine contribution to the dissolved load at the time of peak discharge. *Journal of Geophysical Research* **86**: 9844–58.
Stark, N. M. (1969) Direct nutrient cycling in the Amazon Basin. In *II° Simpósio y Foro de Biologia Tropical Amazónica* (pp. 172–7).
—— (1971) Nutrient cycling. I. Nutrient distribution in some Amazonian soils. *Tropical Ecology* **12**: 24–50.
Stark, N. M. and Holley, C. (1975) Final report on studies of nutrient cycling on white and black water areas in Amazonia, *Acta Amazônica* **5**(1): 57–76.
Stark, N. M. and Jordan, C. F. (1978) Nutrient retention by the root mat of an Amazonian rain forest. *Ecology* **59**(3): 434–7.
Stark, N. M., Kinzey, W. and Pawlowski, P. (1980) Soil fertility and animal distribution (Amazonian Peru). In Furtado, J. I. (ed.) *Tropical Ecology and Development* (pp. 101–12). Int. Soc. Trop. Ecol.: Kuala Lumpur.
Stark, N. M. and Spratt, M. (1977) Root biomass and nutrient storage in rain forest oxisols near San Carlos de Río Negro. *Tropical Ecology* **18**: 1–9.
Sternberg, H. O'R. (1956) *A Água e o Homem na Várzea do Caseiro*, Ph.D. Thesis, Rio de Janeiro.

—— (1968) Man and environmental change in South America. In Fittkau, E. J., Elias, T. S., Klinge, H., Schwabe, G. H. and Sioli, H. (eds.) *Biogeography and Ecology in South America. Vol. I* (pp. 413–45). D. W. Junk: The Hague.

—— (1973) Development and conservation. *Erdkunde* 23: 253–65.

—— (1975) *The Amazon River of Brazil*, Franz Steiner Verlag: Wiesbaden.

—— (1980) Amazonien: Integration and Integrität. In *Integration in Lateinamerika* (pp. 293–322). Wilhelm Fink Verlag: Munich.

—— (nd) *O Pulmão Verde*. Regional Latin-American Conference of International Geographical Union, Rio de Janeiro, August 1982. (In press.).

Stocks, Anthony (1980) Candarhi and Cocamilla swiddens in Eastern Peru. Paper read at the 79th Annual Meeting of the American Anthropological Association, Washington DC, 7 December 1980.

Stout, Mickey and Thomson, Ruth (1974) Fonémica Txukahamei (Kayapó). *Série Lingüística* 3: 153–76.

Stuiver, M. (1978) Atmospheric carbon dioxide and carbon reservoir changes. *Science* 199: 253–8.

Surujbalhy, R. S. (1977) Game farming is a reality. *Unasylva* 29(116): 13–15.

Sutlive, Vinson, H., Altshuler, Nathan and Zamora, Mario D. (eds.) (1981a) Where have all the flowers gone? *Deforestation in the Third World*. College of William and Mary, Studies in Third World Socs. 13. Williamsburg, Virginia.

—— (1981b) Blowing in the wind: *Deforestation and Long-range Implications*. College of William and Mary, Studies in Third World Socs. 14. Williamsburg, Virginia.

Tardin, A. T., Lee, D. C. L., Santos, R. J. R., de Assis, O. R., dos Santos Barbosa, M. P., de Lourdes Moreira, M., Pereira, M. T., Silva, D. and dos Santo Filho, C. P. (1980) *Subprojeto Desmatamento, Convênio IBDF/CNPq-INPE 1979*. INPE Relatório No. INPE-1649-RPE/103, São José dos Campos, São Paulo.

—— (1980a) "Fabricação de queijo tipo 'Amazonas' a nivel de propreidades, *EMBRAPA-Manaus Communicado Técnico*, No. 6, September 1980.

Teixeira, L. B. (1980b) *Secudor Solar: Alternativa para Secagem de Alimentas*, EMBRAPA/Manaus Communicado Téchnico (No. 8).

Thomas, R. H., Sanderson, T. J. O. and Rose, K. E. (1979) Effect of climatic warming on the West Antarctic ice sheet. *Nature* 277: 355–8.

Toenniessen, G. H. (1981) *Profile of the Amazon Basin and its Agricultural Development Potential*. Rockefeller Foundation: New York (ms).

Toledo, J. M. and Serrão, E. E. S. (1982) Pasture and animal production in Amazonia. In Hecht, S. B. (ed.) *Amazonia: Agriculture and Land Use Research* (pp. 281–310). University of Missouri Press: Columbia.

Torres Espinoza, W. (1980) Prácticas agropecuarias en la Amazonia ecuatoriana. In *Consulta científica subregional sobre las actividates de corte y quema en el ecosistema del bosque tropical* (pp. 37–53). Man and the Biosphere Program: Iquitos, Peru.

Turner, Terrance, (1965) Social structure and political organization among the Northern Cayapó. Ph.D. Dissertation, Department of Social Relations, Harvard University.

Ucko, P. J. and Dimbleby, G. W. (1969) *The Domestication and Exploitation of Plants and Animals*. Aldine: Chicago.

Uhl, C. (1980) *Studies of forest, agricultural and successional environments in the upper Rio Negro region of the Amazon basin* Michigan State University: East Lansing.

(dissertation).

—— (1982) Recovery following disturbances of different intensities in the Amazon rain forest of Venezuela. *Interciencia* **7**(1): 19–24.

—— (1983) You can keep a good forest down. *Natural History* **92**(4): 69–79.

Uhl, C., Clark, K., Clark, H. C. and Murphy, P. (1981) Early plant succession after cutting and burning in the Upper Rio Negro region of the Amazon Basin. *Journal of Ecology* **69**: 631–49.

Uhl, C. and Jordan, C. F. (1982) Nutrients as a major constraint to sustained yield forest production in the upper Rio Negro region of the Amazon basin. In Hallsworth, E. G. (ed.) *Socio-economic Effects and Constraints on Tropical Forest Management* (pp. 143–57). Wiley: New York.

Uhl, C., Jordan, C. F. and Montagnini, F. 1982 Traditional and innovative approaches to agriculture on Amazon basin oxisols. In Todd, R. (ed.) *Nutrient Cycling in Agroecosystems*. Wiley: London, (In press).

Uhl, C. and Murphy, P. (1981) A comparison of energy values and productivities between successional vegetation and agricultural crops after cutting and burning a tierra firme rain forest in the Amazon basin. *Agroecosystems* **7**: 63–83.

United Nations Educational Scientific and Cultural Organization (UNESCO)/United Nations Environmental Programme (UNEP)/United Nations Food and Agriculture Organization (UN-FAO). (1978). *Tropical Forest Ecosystems: a State of Knowledge Report*. UNESCO, Paris.

UNICEF, 1981 (? nd) *The UNICEF Home Gardens Handbook*. UNICEF: New York.

United States, Council of Environmental Quality (1980) *Global Energy Futures and the Carbon Dioxide Problem* U.S. Government Printing Office: Washington DC.

USDS (1980) *The World's Tropical Forests: A Policy Strategy and Program for the United States*. Washington DC, U.S. Dept. of State, publ. 9117.

Valverde, O. and Freitas, T. L. R. de (1980) *O problema florestal da Amazônia brasileira*. Ed. Vozes: Petrópolis.

Valverde, S. C. and Bandy, D. E. (1982) Production of annual food crops in the Amazon. In Hecht, S. B. (ed.) *Amazonia: Agriculture and Land Use Research* (pp. 243–80). Centro Internacional de Agricultura Tropical (CIAT), Cali, Colombia. (CIAT series 03-3(82)).

Van der Weert, R. (1974) Influence of mechanical forest clearing on soil conditions and the resulting effects on root growth. *Tropical Agriculture* (Trinidad) **51**(2): 325–31.

Van Valen, L. (1971) The history and stability of atmospheric oxygen. *Science* **171**: 439–43.

van Wambeke, A. (1978) Properties and potentials of soils in the Amazon basin. *Interciencia* **3**(4): 233–41.

Vasey, D. E. (1979) Capybara ranching in Amazonia?, *Oryx* **15**(1): 47–9.

Vickers, William I. (1976) Cultural adaptation of Amazonian habitats: the Siona-Secoya of Eastern Ecuador. University Microfilms International, Ann Arbor, Michigan.

—— (1980) An analysis of Amazonian hunting yields as a function of settlement age. In Hames, R. (ed.) *Studies in Hunting and Fishing in the Neotropics*. Bennington College: Bennington, Vermont.

Vidal, L. (1982a) *Levantamento da situação atual dos Indios Xikrín do Posto Indigeno Kateté: Julho, 1982: Recommendações frente ao projeto Carajás*. Universidade de São Paulo.

—— (1982b) Aspectos contemporaneos da Questão Indígena no Brasil. Paper presented at Conference on 'Frontier Expansion in Amazonia', University of Florida, Gainesville. (mimeo).

Vieira Filho, J. P. B. (1982) *Retrospectiva e atualidade da saude dos Indios Xikrin e Gavião: Necessidades presentes e futuras frente ao projeto Carajás.* São Paulo, Escola Paulista de Medicina.

Villa Nova, N. A., Salati, E. and Matsui, E. (1976) Estimativa da evapotranspiração na bacia Amazônica. *Acta Amazonica* **6**(2): 215–28.

Volbeda, S. (1982a) *Bevolkingsontwikkelingen in Amazônia Legal. Een identificatie van frontiers.* Nijmegen. Publikatie 32, Vakgroep Sociale Geografie van de Ontwikkelingslanden.

—— (1982b) *Urbanisatie in Amazônia Legal. Een identificatie van pionierssteden, hun onstaan en hun rol in het integratieproces van Amazônia.* Nijmegen. Publikatie 33, Vakgroep Sociale Geografie van de Ontwikkelingslanden.

Voss, A. de (1977) Game as food. *Unasylva* **29**(116): 2–12.

Wade, N. (1979) CO_2 in climate: gloomsday predictions have no fault. *Science* **206**: 912–13.

Wadsworth, F. H. (1980) *Conversion of tropical moist forests.* Int. Soc. Trop. Foresters **1**(3): 2.

Wang, C. H. et al. (1976) *Sulfur Deficiency – A Limiting Factor to Rice Production, I: The Lower Amazon Basin. II: Sulfur Requirement for Rice Production* International Rice Research Institute: New York.

Watts, R. G. (1980a) Climate models and CO_2-induced climatic changes. *Climate Change* **2**: 387–408.

—— (1980b) Comments on 'a non-equilibrium model of hemispheric mean surface temperature'. *Journal of the Atmospheric Sciences* **37**: 471–2.

Weaver, P. (1979) Agri-silviculture in tropical America. *Unasylva* **31**(126): 2–12.

Weiss, R. F. (1981) The temporal and spatial distribution of tropospheric nitrous oxide. *Journal of Geophysical Research* **86**: 7185–95.

Weiss, R. F. and Craig, H. (1976) Production of atmospheric nitrous oxide from combustion. *Geophysical Research Letters* **3**: 751–3.

Welcomme, R. L. (1979) *Fisheries Ecology of Floodplain Rivers*, Longmans: London.

Wetterberg, G. B., Prance, G. T. and Lovejoy, T. E. (1981) Conservation progress in Amazonia: a structural review. *Parks* **6**(2): 5–10.

Whiffen, T. W. (1915) *The North-west Amazons.* Constable: London.

Whittaker, R. H. and Likens, G. E. (1973) Primary production: the biosphere and man. *Human Ecology* **1**(4): 357–69.

Wilhelmy, H. (1973) Amazonia as a living area and an economic area. *Applied Science and Development* **1**: 115–35.

Williams, Llewelyn (1960) Little-known wealth of tropical forests. Proceedings, Fifth World Forestry Congress. Seattle, Vol. **3**: 2003–7.

WMO: World Meteorological Organization (1967) *Guia de Práticas Hidrometeorológicas* WMO Publication No. 168, TP 82, Geneva.

Woessner, R. A. (1980) Forestry operations and wood utilization at Jari. Santiago, *World Woods Conf.* (December).

—— (1982) Plantation forest and natural forest utilization in the lower Amazon basin. Escanaba, Michigan (Mead Paper Co.) Soc. Amer. Forestry.

Wong, C. S. (1978) Atmospheric input of carbon dioxide from burning wood. *Science* **200**: 197–200.

Wood, C. H. and Schmink, Marianne (1979) Blaming the victim: small farmer production in an Amazon colonization project. *Studies in Third World Societies* **7**: 77–93.

Wood, C. H. and Wilson, J. (1982) The role of the Amazon frontier in the demography of rural Brazil. Paper presented at the Conference on *'Frontier Expansion in Amazonia'*, Center for Latin American Studies, University of Florida, Gainesville, Florida. February 8–11, 1982.

Woodwell, George M. (1978) The carbon dioxide question, *Scientific American* **238**(1): January.

Woodwell, G. M., Whittaker, R. H., Reiners, W. A., Likens, G. E., Delwiche, C. C. and Botkin, D. P. (1978) The biota and the world carbon budget. *Science* **199**: 141–6.

World Bank (1981) *Brazil: Integrated Development of the Northwest Frontier.* World Bank: Washington DC.

—— (1982a) *Tribal Peoples and Economic Development: Human Ecologic Considerations.* Washington DC.

—— (1982b) *The Environment, Public Health and Human Ecology: Considerations for Economic Development.* Washington DC.

Yen, D. E. (1974) Arboriculture in the subsistence of Santa Cruz, Solomon Islands. *Economic Botany* **28**: 247–87.

Index